Risk Management Solutions for Sarbanes-Oxley Section 404 IT Compliance

Risk Management Solutions for Sarbanes-Oxley Section 404 IT Compliance

John S. Quarterman

WILEY

Wiley Publishing, Inc.

Risk Management Solutions for Sarbanes-Oxley Section 404 IT Compliance

Published by
Wiley Publishing, Inc.
10475 Crosspoint Boulevard
Indianapolis, IN 46256
www.wiley.com

Copyright © 2006 by John S. Quarterman
Published by Wiley Publishing, Inc., Indianapolis, Indiana
Published simultaneously in Canada

ISBN-13: 978-0-7645-9839-5
ISBN-10: 0-7645-9839-2

Manufactured in the United States of America

10 9 8 7 6 5 4 3 2 1

1B/SQ/RS/QV/IN

No part of this publication may be reproduced, stored in a retrieval system or transmitted in any form or by any means, electronic, mechanical, photocopying, recording, scanning or otherwise, except as permitted under Sections 107 or 108 of the 1976 United States Copyright Act, without either the prior written permission of the Publisher, or authorization through payment of the appropriate per-copy fee to the Copyright Clearance Center, 222 Rosewood Drive, Danvers, MA 01923, (978) 750-8400, fax (978) 646-8600. Requests to the Publisher for permission should be addressed to the Legal Department, Wiley Publishing, Inc., 10475 Crosspoint Blvd., Indianapolis, IN 46256, (317) 572-3447, fax (317) 572-4355, or online at http://www.wiley.com/go/permissions.

Limit of Liability/Disclaimer of Warranty: The publisher and the author make no representations or warranties with respect to the accuracy or completeness of the contents of this work and specifically disclaim all warranties, including without limitation warranties of fitness for a particular purpose. No warranty may be created or extended by sales or promotional materials. The advice and strategies contained herein may not be suitable for every situation. This work is sold with the understanding that the publisher is not engaged in rendering legal, accounting, or other professional services. If professional assistance is required, the services of a competent professional person should be sought. Neither the publisher nor the author shall be liable for damages arising herefrom. The fact that an organization or Website is referred to in this work as a citation and/or a potential source of further information does not mean that the author or the publisher endorses the information the organization or Website may provide or recommendations it may make. Further, readers should be aware that Internet Websites listed in this work may have changed or disappeared between when this work was written and when it is read.

For general information on our other products and services or to obtain technical support, please contact our Customer Care Department within the U.S. at (800) 762-2974, outside the U.S. at (317) 572-3993 or fax (317) 572-4002.

Wiley also publishes its books in a variety of electronic formats. Some content that appears in print may not be available in electronic books.

Trademarks: Wiley and the Wiley logo are trademarks or registered trademarks of John Wiley & Sons, Inc. and/or its affiliates, in the United States and other countries, and may not be used without written permission. All other trademarks are the property of their respective owners. Wiley Publishing, Inc., is not associated with any product or vendor mentioned in this book.

Wiley also publishes its books in a variety of electronic formats. Some content that appears in print may not be available in electronic books.

To G.

About the Author

John S. Quarterman has previously coauthored *The 4.2BSD Berkeley Unix Operating System*[1] and its successor edition, as well as *The Matrix: Computer Networks and Conferencing Systems Worldwide*[2] and other books.

Mr. Quarterman is CEO of InternetPerils, Inc., an Internet business risk management company that is extending risk management strategies available to business into new areas such as insurance, catastrophe bonds, and performance bonds.

He has 26 years of experience in internetworking, beginning with work on ARPANET software at BBN. In 1990, he incorporated MIDS, which published the first maps of the whole Internet and conducted the first Internet Demographic Survey. In 1993, he started the first series of performance data about the entire Internet, visible on the web since 1995 as the Internet Weather Report, which together with the Internet Average and ISP Ratings, were some of the most cited analyses available.

Credits

Executive Editor
Carol Long

Senior Development Editor
Kevin Kent

Production Editor
Angela Smith

Copy Editor
Foxxe Editorial Services

Editorial Manager
Mary Beth Wakefield

Production Manager
Tim Tate

Vice President and Executive Group Publisher
Richard Swadley

Vice President and Publisher
Joseph B. Wikert

Project Coordinator
Michael Kruzil

Graphics and Production Specialists
Carrie Foster
Jennifer Heleine
Stephanie D. Jumper
Julie Trippetti

Quality Control Technician
Amanda Briggs

Proofreading and Indexing
TECHBOOKS Production Services

Contents

About the Author   vii

Preface   xxiii

Acknowledgments   xxvii

Chapter 1   **Introduction**   1

What Is It?   2

    Dependence and Defense   2

    Deceit and Compliance   3

How and Why Did It Get So Bad?   4

    Different Communications Cause Different Growth   4

    Option Value, Not Traffic Volume   6

    Power Laws Breed Scale-Free Networks   7

    Scale-Free Networks Breed Option Value   8

    Options, Not Discounts   8

    Different Networks Value Different Content   9

    Internet Mutation Grows Groups   10

    Online Wealth Breeds Cyber-Crooks   11

    Don't Forget *Force Majeure*   11

Who Manages This Risk?   11

Who Needs This Risk Managed?   12

How Do They Need It Managed?   13

Notes   13

Chapter 2   **The Risk: Big and Growing Fast**   15

Traditional Risks Transfer   15

    Theft Isn't Just Physical Anymore   15

    Fraud Can Be Faster   16

Privacy Can Evaporate   16
Perils Can Affect Brand Reputation   16
Third-Party Claim Risk   16
First-Party Loss Risk   17
Traditional Internet Risk   17
Content Risks   17
Communication Method Risks   17
Internet Operational Risk   18
Internet Collapse Predicted, Again and Again   18
From Power Failures to Spam   18
It's Alive! Or Is It?   19
Decentralization Also Enables Storms and Pirates   21
Perils: Hazards That Can Cause Problems   21
Anomalies: Problems That Directly Affect Business   22
Deceptive Practices   22
Spam: Unsolicited Bulk Electronic Mail   22
Phishing: Conning Users Out of IDs   23
Spoofs: Faked Electronic Mail   25
Pharming: Fraudulent Misdirection   25
Spyware: Logging Keystrokes   25
Adware: Stealing Eyeballs   25
Botnets of Zombies   25
Mules Carrying Real Money   26
Blackmail: Simple Online Crime   26
Scob: Complexity and Consequences   27
Unfair Practices   27
Causes across the Board   28
The Root Causes Are Not Technical   28
Online Exploits Are Not a Hobby Anymore   28
Microwaved Wireless   29
Don't Forget Force Majeure   29
Effects on Business   29
A Worst-Case Worm   29
Reputation Damage   30
The Internet As Complicator   30
Sailing the Ocean Sea   30
Many Navies on That Ocean   31
Don't Try to Drain the Ocean   31
Magnifiers That Make Everything Worse   31
Monoculture Considered Harmful   32
The Boll Weevil   32
Monoculture Cotton, Fragile Economy   32
Prevention Needs History and Observation   33
Monoculture Communications Providers   33
All the World, All the Time   34
What Affects the Internet the Most?   34

Other Monocultures	35
Router Monoculture	35
Looking Ahead	36
Ecosystem and Market	36
Show Me	36
Health and Prosperity	37
Fame and Fortune	37
Denial and Damage	37
Inertia Increases Damage	38
Risk Causes Fear	39
Notes	40

Chapter 3	**Solutions and Providers**	**45**
	Resilience: Backups, Redundancy, and Diversity	45
	Backups: Copy It or Lose It	46
	Redundancy: Separate Power, Connectivity, and Geography	46
	Diversity: Differing Targets Are Harder to Hit	47
	Fortification: Security Solutions	49
	Encryption: Make It Useless to Steal	51
	I&AM: Identity and Access Management	51
	Firewalls: Perimeter Defense	51
	VPN: Virtual Private Network	52
	SSL-VPN: Secure Socket Layer VPN	52
	FIM: Federated Identity Management	52
	Managed Security Monitoring (MSM)	53
	Internet Hardware Vendors	54
	Security and Performance	54
	Security Summary	55
	Observation and Orientation: Performance Solutions	57
	Performance Measurement	57
	Route Optimization	57
	SLA: Service Level Agreements	57
	Internet Risk Assessment and Management	58
	Decentralized Collective Action As Internet Management	58
	Open Decentralization Is Strength, Not Weakness	58
	Internet Research	60
	DETER: Cyber Defense Technology Experimental Research	60
	CIED: Center for Internet Epidemiology and Defenses	60
	STIM: The Security through Interaction Modeling Center	61
	DNS-OARC: Domain Name System Operations, Analysis, and Research Center	61
	CAIDA: Cooperative Association for Internet Data Analysis	62
	Clearinghouses	62
	CERT: Computer Emergency Response Team	62
	US-CERT: United States Computer Emergency Response Team	62

SANS: SysAdmin, Audit, Network, Security   63
NCFTA: National Cyber-Forensics & Training Alliance   63
InfraGard: Guarding the Nation's Infrastructure   63
EFF: Electronic Frontier Foundation   63
Others   64
Anti-Exploit Groups   64
Phishing   64
Commercial Clearinghouses   64
Beyond Protocols   64
Hurricane History   65
Hurricane Ivan Disconnects the Cayman Islands   67
Risk Transfer: Internet Insurance   67
InsureTrust   67
AIG   68
SafeOnline   68
Electronic Crime   68
Spam as Felony   68
Phishing and Spyware   69
Theft and Blackmail   69
From Prevention to Management   69
Notes   70

Chapter 4   **Strategies for Affected Verticals**   **73**
Strategies   73
Financial Instruments   74
Reputation Systems   74
Contractual Risk Transfer   75
Other   75
Developing a Strategy   75
Prevention: Resilience and Fortification   75
Crisis Management: Contingency Plans   76
Risk Transfer: Compensation for Loss   76
Value Drivers: What Is at Risk?   77
Money   77
Reputation   77
Risk Assessment: Linking Risks to Value Drivers   78
Risk Management Assessment: Choosing Solutions   78
Industries and Solutions   78
Banks: Quantification for Capital Withholding   79
Financial Institutions: Favorite Targets   79
Large Enterprises: Beyond Compliance to Competitiveness 80
Small Enterprises: Risk As Opportunity   80
Internet Service Providers: Bonded and Insured   80
Government: Research before Guarantee   81
Insurers: A Range of New Products   81
Force Is Not Security   82

The Illicit Bazaar		82
Wealth Is Not the Solution		83
A Radical Solution		84
To Fix a Broken Network, Make It More Connected		85
Influence the Uncommitted		86
Hypocrisy: A Real and Present Danger		87
Motivation: Overcoming Inertia		87
Companies Can Collapse Like Societies		88
Denial Can Be Managed		90
Risk Produces Fear, Reason Can Manage Fear		91
Act before Damage		91
From Fear to Advantage		92
Notes		92
Chapter 5	**Banks and Basel II**	**95**
	What Is Basel II?	95
	Operational Risk Approaches	97
	Basic Indicator Approach	97
	Standardized Approach	97
	Advanced Measurement Approaches (AMA)	98
	Implementation of AMA	101
	Incident Reports	101
	Slow Links	101
	Nonredundant Routes	103
	Congestion	104
	A Path of Action	106
	Management Summaries	106
	Obligation Failure	107
	Physical Damage	108
	System Failure	108
	Process Failure	109
	A Path of Action	110
	Notes	110
Chapter 6	**Financial Institutions Beyond Quantification**	**113**
	Qualifying the Unquantifiable	113
	Physical Security May Not Be Secure	114
	The Something You Have Needs to Be Different	115
	Anomaly Profiling and Longer Codes	115
	FedLine: Advantage or Menace?	116
	Risk Transfer Instruments beyond Insurance Policies	117
	Insurance Policies	117
	Catastrophe Bonds	119
	Live Cats	119
	Stripped Cats	119
	Popular Cats	119
	Exceptional Conditions	120

Tsunami Insurance   120
2004, Record Year for Disasters   121
Global Warming Insurance   121
Cumbre Vieja Submerging Florida   122
Local Losses Covered by Global Investment   123
Performance Bonds beyond Outages   123
Reliability over Price in ISP Selection   123
Tsunami Smith: Mad Dog or Prophet?   124
How Did He Know?   124
Tsunami Early Warning System   125
Internet Analysis: Beyond Information Sharing   125
FS/ISAC: Financial Services Information Sharing and
Analysis Center   125
APWG: Anti-Phishing Working Group   126
Incidence of Risk beyond the Firewall   126
Extent of Risk: Local Causes, Effects a World Away   126
The Economic Consequences of Anomalies   127
Disaster Accounting   127
Costs of Breach of Confidentiality   128
Early Warning and Tracking   128
Traditional Security: The Arthashastra   128
Modern Risk Management?   129
No-Go Areas for Commerce?   130
Turning Externalities into Profits   131
Bandwidth Futures   132
Collateral Shredding   132
Smart Connections   133
Economic Derivatives   133
Financial Derivatives of Network Laws   134
Innovation Will Outmode Specifics   134
Hindsight Is 10/20   135
Notes   136

Chapter 7   **Large Enterprises: Big Risks, Big Solutions**   **141**
Risk Management As Corporate Management   141
EWRM: Enterprise-Wide Risk Management Systems   141
Profits Up the Stovepipe   142
Agility for New Connections   143
Personal Empowerment and Group Connections   143
Focus, Emergence, and Research   144
The Pattern That Connects   144
Deeper Than Mission   145
Risk Management As Agility   145
New Responses to Risk   145
$100 Billion Cyberhurricane Risk   146
Incident Reports   146

Management Summaries   146
Risk Aggregations   147
Basic Security   147
Backups and Encryption   148
Shipping and Encryption   148
Outsourcers Also Need Security   149
Passwords and Humint   149
Even a Little Diversity Is Good   149
Layers of Security   150
Security or Loss of Confidence?   150
Don't Try to Secure Alone   151
Financial Risk Transfer Solutions   151
Self-Insurance   151
Insurance   151
Bonds   152
Vulnerability Disclosure Hurts Share Price   152
Vulnerability Bounties   152
Vulnerability Restraints?   153
Balancing Property and Propriety   153
Restraining the Wind   154
A Draft, Not Yet a Hurricane   155
Protection or Harassment?   156
Fear Can Cause Alarm   156
PR Disaster or Public Service?   157
Kowtowing Is Not Security   157
If It's Broke, Don't Sue It   157
P2P: Piracy or Market Demand?   158
Hollywood's Origins in Piracy   158
Pirates or Innovators?   159
Risk Also Means Opportunity   159
Notes   161

Chapter 8   Small Enterprises: Surviving Risks   167
Small Company, Big Risk   167
Risk Management As Good Business Planning   168
Risk Management As a Competitive Advantage   169
Prevention before Cure   169
Slim but Flexible   169
Smaller Can Mean Younger   169
What's a Cybernative?   169
Cybernatives As a Competitive Advantage   170
Risk Means Opportunity   171
Privatization of Research   171
Exporting Internet Security to New Industries   172
Riding the Fifth Wave   172
Riding the Long Tail of Content   173
Reach Just Your Users   174

Cathedral or Bazaar?   175
The Fifth Wave: Everywhere, All the Time   177
In a Glass World, Obscurity Is Not Security   179
Open Software for Better Software   180
Open Your Software without Giving Away the Store   182
Early Release and Stock Price   182
Go Global   182
Small As Competitive   183
Notes   184

Chapter 9   Internet Service Providers: Bonded and Insured   187
Catastrophe Bonds for *Force Majeure* Events   187
Retrocessional SCOR   188
Cat Bonds As New Money   188
Performance Bonds As Risk Backbone   189
The Experience of Electric Utilities   189
ISP SLAs Inside and Out   190
Increasingly Specific Inside   191
Still, Most of the Internet Is Outside   191
Self-Verification Leads to Goodwill Payouts   191
ISP Performance Bonds   192
The Bonded Marketing Advantage   192
Better SLAs for Product Differentiation   193
Turning an Economic Externality into a Competitive
Advantage   193
Bond Issuers   194
Insurance Companies   194
Bond Markets   195
Government   195
Pricing   195
Beyond Performance   195
Notes   196

Chapter 10   Governments: Guarantors of Last Resort   197
Alerting Businesses   198
Preventive Advice for Enterprises and Insurers   198
Coercive and Ameliorative Action   199
Government Departments and Agencies As Large
Enterprises   200
Law Enforcement   200
Deceptive Practices   201
Spam   201
Phishing   202
Pharming   202
Spyware   202
Adware   203
Unfair Practices   203

Vendor Liability As a Driver for Insurance 203
Security Vulnerabilities: Unforeseen, Chronic, and Unfixed 204
The Biggest Offenders Have the Most Lobbyists 204
The Bigger They Are, the Harder They Fall 205
Let the Punishment Fit the Crime 206
Levels of Government Trying Different Legal Regimes 207
Are There Too Many Crimes? 207
SOX Considered Nitpicking 207
Not Every Citizen Is a Terrorist 209
Not Every Foreigner Is a Terrorist 209
Economy Is Security 210
Innovation Drives Productivity 210
Economic Policy and Business Judgment 211
Funding Research As Economic Policy 211
What Not to Fund: Specific Technical Requirements 212
Security Management Standards 213
Internet Broadband for Economic Security 214
Terrorism and Economics 215
Terrorism: A Means to Political Ends 215
Terrorism, Crime, and Sabotage 216
Attacking Systems Provides Leverage 216
From Phishing to SCADA Attacks 216
What Is Critical Infrastructure, Anyway? 217
Effects, Not Damage 217
Leveraging Opinion Is More Effective Than Leveraging Violence 217
Keeping Terrorists from Using the Internet 218
Military Networks Aren't Immune 219
Self-Healing Networks 220
How Can the Military Protect Itself? 221
Watch the Watchers 221
Encourage the Economy 221
The Modern Military Eats from the Internet 222
The Ancient Anasazi: An Archaeological Cautionary Tale 223
Cliff Forts versus Coordinated Mesas 223
Fear Is Not Security 224
Alert to All Risks 225
Notes 227

Chapter 11　Insurers and Reinsurers 231
Policies: How to Make It Easy 232
Assessments: Sprinkler Systems 232
Adjustments: Internet Forensics 232
The Risks: First and Third Party 232
First-Party Loss: Your Company Is Harmed 232
Third-Party Loss: Someone Else Is Harmed 233
Brief History: Claims Drive New Insurance 233
What Is Physical Damage? 233
Ingram Micro: Maybe It Is 233

AOL v. St. Paul: Maybe It Isn't   234
Moral: Don't Depend on Property and Liability Insurance   234
Early Cyber-Insurance Programs   234
Awareness and Observation   235
Quantification and Aggregation   236
Policy Language: Still in Process   237
Shortcomings of Traditional Products   237
Collective Action through Financial Instruments   238
Financial Liability Can Help Drive Insurance   238
Legal Liability Can Help Drive Insurance   239
Insurance Can Help Drive Security   239
Bonds for Financial Depth and Stability   240
Catastrophe Bonds: Financial Capacity   240
Performance Bonds: Beyond Outages   240
Capital Withholding: Banks as Self-Insurers   241
Options for Internet Business Risk   241
Insurance Strategies   241
Technology Risk by Technology Companies   241
Media Risk from Content Distribution   242
EBusiness Risk by Users of Networks   243
First-Party Loss   244
Pricing: Internet Insurance As a Profitable Business   245
Value of Outages to Insurance Customers   245
Disaster Accounting   246
Let the Customer Choose   246
Skewed Populations   246
Adverse Selection   246
Moral Hazard   247
Perception and Price   247
Quality of Service Can Determine Price   247
Price Can Determine Quality of Service   247
Underwriting, Assessments, and Tailoring   247
Underwriting and Premium Rates   248
Tailored Policies   248
Case Studies   248
BJ's Warehouse: The Poster Child for Network Liability
Insurance   249
System Administration As a Criminal Activity   250
Targeting the C-Class   250
Leveraging Technology with Financial Risk-Transfer
Instruments   252
Notes   252

Chapter 12   Summary: Managing Internet Risk in a Scale-Free World   255
The Pain: Storms, Pirates, and Outages   255
The Problem: We're All Neighbors on the Internet Sea   256

Can't Ignore It; Can't Fix It; Need to Manage It   256
Not Just Another Infrastructure   257
A Different Kind of Connectivity   257
A Different Scale Can Be a Different State   257
The Solution: Something Old, Something Borrowed,
    Something New   258
Old: Deploy Traditional Best Practices   258
Borrowed: Import Tools from Other Industries   258
New: Feedback through Insurance and Reputation   259
Newer: Turn Externalities into Affordances   260
Notes   261

Index   **263**

Preface

This book is about expanding Internet business risk management strategies into resilience such as software diversity; into financial risk transfer instruments such as insurance policies, catastrophe bonds, performance bonds, and self-insurance as in Basel II; and into reputation systems.

Traditional Internet performance and security solutions are no longer adequate to manage Internet business risks that have increased rapidly starting in 2000. As recently as 2003, many chief-level officers (CEOs, CFOs, CTOs, and so forth) and boards considered business interruption due to worms, viruses, cable cuts, routing flaps, and attacks to be off their radar; they thought the Internet "just worked." By the first quarter of 2004, after the northeast power outage, the myDoom and SoBig worms clogging the Internet infrastructure, and the leak of Microsoft's NT and Windows 2000 source code, placing still more opportunities in the hands of crackers, some S&P 500 CEOs changed their minds and now think they are facing a potential $100 billion global cyber-catastrophe risk. The SoBig worm alone caused $30 billion in damages.[3] Such cyberhurricanes blur the line between security and performance; degraded performance can cause a customer to abandon a transaction or even seek another vendor.

Many Internet risks outside the firewall cannot be eliminated by any single enterprise. Encryption is good, but what if the packets don't arrive? Intrusion prevention can stop worms at the firewall, but congestion can still make customer accesses too slow. Dynamic rerouting can find uncongested routes, but what if there are none? Such risks have grown too large and frequent to be accepted. They have grown beyond gale force into cyberhurricanes that are *force majeure* events affecting entire industries or the whole Internet.

Insurance has been the traditional solution to *force majeure* risks since Lloyd's was formed in a coffee shop in London in the seventeenth century. Newer risk management instruments include catastrophe bonds, such as those used to protect against earthquakes and flood. Electric utilities use performance bonds to protect themselves against brownouts as well as blackouts. Such instruments can extend the Internet financial risk management strategies from accept or eliminate into hedge, insure, or self-insure. Just as ship owners in the age of mercantilism had to use new innovations such as joint stock companies and insurance to enable global trade by sea, companies that use the Internet need to add risk management strategies new to the Internet, such as insurance, catastrophe bonds, and performance bonds.

This book summarizes the problem, details the types of risks and their effects, and describes current and extended solutions and providers, and then the bulk of the book discusses specific industries: their particular risk and what they can do about it.

Who This Book Is For

The reader is assumed to be a competent user of the Internet. Technical or business experience will be helpful, yet since the book combines several fields, no reader can be expected to have extensive prior experience in all of them. This book is for you if you are:

- Corporate executives with strategic responsibility for Internet risk, for example, CEOs, CFOs, CTOs, CIOs, attorneys, and boards of directors. You really are the primary audience for the book.

- IT professionals who wish to learn more about nontechnical risk management strategies, their application to Internet risks, and how they drive further application of technical strategies. Security, network, software, and hardware engineers will be asked by executives for technical opinions about risk management solutions; such opinions will be more relevant in the context of broader risk management strategies.

- Insurance executives, actuaries, and brokers who produce and sell insurance and bonds on behalf of insurers and reinsurers.

- Financial services company personnel who advise their clients on risk management solutions and who may sell some instruments such as cat bonds and performance bonds.

- Employees of Internet security and performance companies, because insurers will want to see security and performance solutions in place before selling insurance, just as they want to see sprinkler systems before they will sell fire insurance.

- A business school offering risk management courses, because you need to prepare your students to manage Internet risk, and you can use this book as a textbook. Internet security companies giving tutorials could use this book.

And just because Sarbanes-Oxley is referenced in the title doesn't mean this book has application only to the United States. Other countries have similar laws, such as the Personal Information Protection and Electronic Documents Act (PIPEDA) in Canada and the Data Protection Directive (DPD) in Europe. The risk management solutions discussed in this book reach beyond the borders of any one country, just as the Internet reaches beyond them. Accordingly, readers of this book can be worldwide.

Distinctive Features

This book has several distinguishing features compared to books on related topics:

- This book will help convince those who are most at risk from the recent and continued rise of cyberhurricanes that they should do something; it will let those who are convinced see inside those risks and indicate strategies for risk management.

- Other books usually treat only one of performance, security, or insurance; this book combines all three in its discussion of risk management strategies.

- Unlike the few previous high-priced books and reports on Internet risk management, this one is affordable and easy to read.

Notes

1. Samuel J. Leffler, Marshall Kirk McKusick, Michael J. Karels, and John S. Quarterman, *The Design and Implementation of the 4.3BSD UNIX Operating System* (Reading, MA: Addison-Wesley, 1989).

2. John S. Quarterman, *The Matrix: Computer Networks and Conferencing Systems Worldwide* (Digital Press, 1990).

3. mi2g, "Silently preparing for the $100 billion cyber-catastrophe risk," *News Alert* (mi2g, February 16, 2004).

Acknowledgments

This book is about expanding Internet business risk management strategies into resilience such as software diversity; into financial risk transfer instruments such as insurance policies, catastrophe bonds, performance bonds, and self-insurance as in Basel II; and into reputation systems.

Traditional Internet performance and security solutions are no longer adequate to manage Internet business risks that have increased rapidly starting in 2000. As recently as 2003, many chief-level officers (CEOs, CFOs, CTOs, and so forth) and boards considered business interruption due to worms, viruses, cable cuts, routing flaps, and attacks to be off their radar; they thought the Internet "just worked." By the first quarter of 2004, after the northeast power outage, the myDoom and SoBig worms clogging the Internet infrastructure, and the leak of Microsoft's NT and Windows 2000 source code, placing still more opportunities in the hands of crackers, some S&P 500 CEOs changed their minds and now think they are facing a potential $100 billion global cyber-catastrophe risk. The SoBig worm alone caused $30 billion in damages.[3] Such cyberhurricanes blur the line between security and performance; degraded performance can cause a customer to abandon a transaction or even seek another vendor.

Many Internet risks outside the firewall cannot be eliminated by any single enterprise. Encryption is good, but what if the packets don't arrive? Intrusion prevention can stop worms at the firewall, but congestion can still make customer accesses too slow. Dynamic rerouting can find uncongested routes, but what if there are none? Such risks have grown too large and frequent to be accepted. They have grown beyond gale force into cyberhurricanes that are *force majeure* events affecting entire industries or the whole Internet.

CHAPTER 1

Introduction

The value of the Internet lies in its connections,
but some connections are more valuable than others.
—David P. Reed

Internet risks beyond the firewall have grown rapidly since 2000 into cyber-hurricanes that are *force majeure* risks that threaten every enterprise that uses the Internet, yet they are beyond the control of any enterprise. Some big company CEOs are now convinced they face $100 billion cyberhurricane risk per large company. Fortune 500 boards and shareholders won't like multiday business interruptions of their companies. Small companies face the same risks, except with fewer resources to meet them. Meanwhile, government has passed laws such as Sarbanes-Oxley (SOX) in the United States, the Personal Information Protection and Electronic Documents Act (PIPEDA) in Canada, and the Data Protection Directive (DPD) in Europe that add layers of compliance to an already difficult task. Small private companies may avoid SOX compliance, but no one is immune to the general problem: every organization that uses the Internet for commerce or communications gets, along with the great benefits of reach and convenience, many aggregate risks that can only be met completely through collective action.

This book is about the big picture of Internet security, including some pieces people don't usually think of together, and some pieces most people have not yet thought about at all. In particular, traditional solutions to Internet risk are inadequate, even together, and only suffice in conjunction with financial risk transfer instruments such as insurance.

This book examines the problem and existing partial solutions, proposes some new solutions, discusses who needs them, and which ones apply to which affected parties. It will help readers understand this new and rapidly growing problem of cyberhurricane risk and how to control it. Bring risk management from the fringes of the company to the center. Coordinate your company around a new core competence: risk management.

What Is It?

The need to manage Internet business risk arises from several sources. Businesses have become much more dependent on the Internet since 2000, and their susceptibility to natural disasters, misdeployment, mischief, and criminal attack has increased accordingly. Meanwhile, since 1990 an assortment of rogue traders and other charismatic but unscrupulous individuals have caused many billions of dollars of losses to companies and shareholders ranging from BCCI to Enron, and a legislative and supervisory reaction has ensued, resulting in new laws and accords ranging from SOX to Basel II.

Dependence and Defense

Web pages have become a global broadcast medium cheaper and more flexible than TV, and more used than trade shows or trade magazines. Enterprises follow up web leads with customer contacts via electronic mail, instant messenger, and voice over IP, which are cheaper and more convenient than the telephone. Customers submit bug reports via mailing lists; sales people use protected web tools to manage sales pipelines; suppliers use groupware to manage just-in-time delivery, as illustrated by the ellipses in Figure 1-1. Global reach with selective focus!

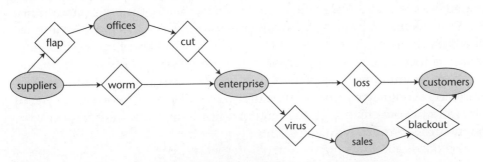

Figure 1-1:   Some perils of Internet group communications

People who expect information and communication in seconds are disappointed when they don't get it, and global reach permits global risks, not just beyond the firewall but beyond any one country. Problems can come from anywhere on the globe and at anytime, involving counterparties in multiple countries. Cable cuts caused by backhoes or fishing trawlers, worms, routing flaps, Internet Service Provider (ISP) routing misconfigurations, hardware failure, failing routers, floods, tunnel fires, meteorological hurricanes, and terrorist attacks can all occur outside the enterprise's perimeter yet can affect the enterprise's Internet communications with its customers, suppliers, outsourcers, distributed offices, and the sales force; see the diamonds in Figure 1-1. Unlike traditional computer or intranet problems, there is nothing an enterprise Information Technology (IT) department can do directly to fix problems outside the firewall.

Firewalls and encryption are good and useful, but they alone can't deal with problems outside the firewall that interrupt business transactions. Other means can help, such as redeployment of Internet connections and servers to avoid single points of failure, and ongoing measurement of problems as they occur. Beat your competition by providing more accessible and reliable services to your customers.

Some of the big risks such as worms exploit vulnerabilities in specific operating systems or software. One way to reduce an enterprise's vulnerability to such monoculture exploits is to diversify; if the company uses three operating systems or three web browsers or three database servers, it is hard for a single exploit to affect all of them the same way at the same time. Using the same software across the enterprise is easy and convenient; that's why enterprises do it. But it also introduces many perils that can be avoided by diversity. Don't let your company be held hostage or made a target by monoculture software.

It is easier to pay attention to the more numerous small Internet risks that happen more frequently and that may be partially controlled by traditional security measures. Yet Internet risk has a long-tailed distribution, extending to a few very large incidents that cannot be so controlled and that can individually cause more economic damage than all the small ones. Ignoring the important longer-term, larger-scale risk in order to focus on the more numerous short-term risks may not be a good path to corporate competitiveness or even survival. It is better to control your Internet business risk before your board or your shareholders ask why you didn't.

Deceit and Compliance

In the past 5 to 10 years laws have been passed to require increasing operational accountability of corporations, including for Internet risk, such as the Sarbanes-Oxley Public Company Accounting Reform and Investor Protection

Act (SOX), the Gramm-Leach-Bliley Financial Services Modernization Act (GLBA), the Health Insurance Portability and Accountability Act (HIPAA), and the Family Educational Rights and Privacy Act (FERPA), which are all U.S. Federal government laws. U.S. states have also gotten into the act, for example, with the State of California Information Practices Act requiring notice (SB 1386). Other countries have passed related laws, such as Canada's Personal Information Protection and Electronic Documents Act (PIPEDA) and the European Union's Data Protection Directive (DPD) of 1998.

Some important agreements are not laws at all yet may have as much effect as similar laws, especially the Basel II New Capital Accord among big international banks.

Meanwhile, customers increasingly expect not only protection of their information but also continuous access to it; a stock trade next Tuesday isn't as good as one today. Yet no matter how good your technical solutions, eventually they will fail. Financial risk transfer instruments can take over for problems that can't be handled technically. Insurers are waking up to the need to address this market, which they think is a multi-billion-dollar market for them. Diligence only raises so high; after that insurance is cheaper.

How and Why Did It Get So Bad?

As Eric Schmidt, CEO of Google noted in the summer of 2003:

> The rate of the adoption of the Internet in all its forms is increasing, not decreasing. . . . The fact that many [Internet companies] are in a terrible state does not correlate with users not using their products.[1]

Security problems in the Internet have gotten bad fast in the past few years, and will continue to do so.

Different Communications Cause Different Growth

This is due to the differing effects of Sarnoff's Law, Metcalfe's Law, and Reed's Law, each of which has attracted different uses and users of the Internet, followed by criminals, crackers, and terrorists who prey on them.

These three growth laws are illustrated in Figure 1-2, which shows the value of a broadcast network derived from Sarnoff's law increasing slowly, the value of a two-way network such as the telephone or the Internet using electronic mail or instant messaging (IM) increasing faster according to Metcalfe's Law, and the value of a group-forming network such as the Internet with group communications growing increasingly faster due to Reed's Law.

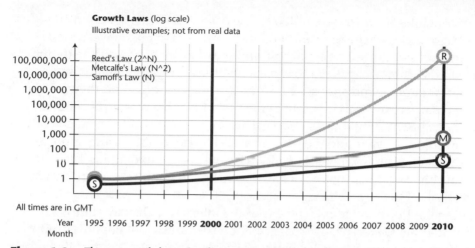

Growth Laws (log scale)
Illustrative examples; not from real data

Reed's Law (2^N)
Metcalfe's Law (N^2)
Sarnoff's Law (N)

All times are in GMT

Year   1995 1996 1997 1998 1999 **2000** 2001 2002 2003 2004 2005 2006 2007 2008 2009 **2010**
Month

Figure 1-2:   Three growth laws for three types of communications

- **Sarnoff's Law** applies to traditional broadcast networks such as newspapers, radio, and television, where the value of the network is directly proportional to the number of readers, listeners, or viewers. It is named after David Sarnoff (1891–1971), radio and TV pioneer, president and chairman of RCA, and founder of NBC. Such broadcast media are often supported either by advertising or by subscription fees, both of which produce income indirectly or directly, according to the number of participants. Of course, different advertisers are interested in different subsets of TV viewers, resulting in various forms of more detailed measurement or estimation of subgroups, such as Nielsen ratings. Sarnoff's Law is, thus, just an approximation, a rule of thumb, which can be used to very roughly characterize the nature of the value of a broadcast network.

- **Metcalfe's Law** applies to networks in which participants can engage in two-way communication with each other, such as the telephone or electronic mail or IM. It is named after Bob Metcalfe, inventor of Ethernet, founder of 3COM, and longtime columnist for *InfoWorld*. The value of a two-way communication network increases according to how many pairs of users can talk to each other, that is, according to N*N or N squared (N^2), rather than just N, where N is the number of users.

- **Reed's Law** applies to networks where groups of users can communicate in a many-to-many manner with each other[2]; these are sometimes called group-forming networks. Reed's Law is named after David Reed, designer of the User Datagram Protocol (UDP) that is used for name lookups and other purposes on the Internet, and coauthor of an influential paper about the end-to-end principle, which is one of the fundamental principles of the Internet.[3] Telephone conference calls have some of these group-forming characteristics, yet they don't scale well (they work best with very few people and they hardly work at all with hundreds), they are difficult to coordinate (they typically require pre-arrangement and special calling numbers and codes), and they require all participants to be present at the same time. Ham radio is another example. The Internet is where many-to-many group-forming communications have found their most natural home to date, using applications ranging from the old USENET newsgroups to mailing lists to multiparty IM to Internet Relay Chat (IRC) to Point to Point (P2P) file sharing. Even telephone conference calls can take on new group-forming life in combination with use of the Internet to display slides, files, and other materials to all participants. The number of possible groups that could form on such a network is proportional to 2 to the Nth power (2^N), and thus grows much faster than the number of pairs ($N*N$) or the number of users (N).

Remember, all these laws are approximations or rules of thumb used to characterize certain types of value derivable from certain types of networks. They are not laws in the sense of physical laws like gravity. Insofar as they attempt to quantify value, they quantify potential value, only some of which will ever be actual.

Option Value, Not Traffic Volume

A recent paper has gone to great lengths to debunk Metcalfe's Law and Reed's Law and to substantiate a compromise growth rate for the Internet and similar networks. The substitute rate is faster than Sarnoff's Law yet slower than the other two.[4] While such an analysis is useful for investigating issues such as why more ISPs don't merge to get greater value from being larger, it misses the point that these three laws characterize different kinds of networks that value different kinds of content.

By value, Reed's Law (and the others) are not referring to traffic volume, nor even directly to revenue generation. Instead, they are referring to something much more like Black-Merton-Scholes option value.[5] Buying a network link is partly buying options you may never exercise—options to connect to people you may never actually reach but whom you can, because of the network, or to connect to some people only rarely. Many people buy cell phones just so they can call 911 if their car breaks down. I correspond with Eric Raymond only a few times a year over the Internet, but every time I do, it's worthwhile. Such options are not reflected in Internet traffic measurements.

Nonetheless, people do pay to have such options. If such options didn't matter, there would be no Internet, because everyone would simply buy a few fast links to the few people they talked to all the time. I remember when, in the late 1980s and early 1990s, some companies seriously considered that as an alternative to the Internet. Even to mention such a thing sounds strange now. There used to be multiple closed commercial networks such as CompuServe, Prodigy, Minitel, and others that didn't really talk to each other, much less the Internet. Almost all of them are gone as separate entities, and the few that survive, most notably AOL and MSN, are far more closely connected to the Internet than they or their predecessors were 10 years ago. Traffic is only part of the story; reach is also important, even when most users seldom use it.

Power Laws Breed Scale-Free Networks

It is often some of the least frequently used connections that lead to sales, because they lead into new companies or to receptive people. Seldom-contacted acquaintances are more likely to lead to new jobs than one's close friends. These are two examples of what are called scale-free networks, because they consist of many small clusters connected loosely into larger clusters, which are in turn connected, and so on, yet they have no typical size of cluster.

Scale-free networks don't fit the familiar Bell curves that describe typical heights of people. If you pick any group of a thousand adults in the United States or Europe, you can predict pretty accurately what the average height of those people will be, and how many will be taller or shorter. If you graph the numbers of people at any given height, you'll get a Bell curve, with a peak in the middle, tapering off to short, thin edges; it looks like a bell.

Graph instead the wealth of individuals in the United States, and you don't get a Bell curve. Instead, the curve starts with a few individuals with very high wealth, tapering off quickly at first and then gradually to a very long tail of people with less money. Most of the money is owned by a small percentage of the people, and many more people have much less.

There is no typical scale of wealth, and there is no limit to the amount of wealth an individual can accrue. This is because wealth distribution in the United States is a power law. This doesn't mean that those who have more money have more power (although that is probably also true). It means that the distribution of wealth is described by an equation involving a power, such as N to the power of 2 (N squared or N^2) as in Metcalfe's Law or 2 to the power of N (2^N) as in Reed's Law.

The number of distributed copies of movies follows another power law. Most movie distribution on cinema screens or store shelves is occupied by a thousand or so titles, and then there are many more titles that don't get much distribution, trailing off into a long tail of distribution. This long tail of distribution is quite important to Internet economics and opportunities, and we will discuss it in more detail in Chapter 8.

A network whose size measurements follow a power law is called a scale-free network because there is no typical size or scale for its various pieces, such as clusters of nodes.

Scale-Free Networks Breed Option Value

Scale-free networks occur everywhere from the internal structure of cells to power grids to groupings of galaxies, as described by Watts and Strogatz in 1998[6] and as elaborated by Barabasi.[7] Two more examples are the Internet and the World Wide Web, with some implications explained by Weinberger.[8]

People tend to communicate the most with those who they know, but that doesn't mean less frequent connections outside of one's own clique aren't valuable. A good sales or job lead can be worth a lot more than daily idle chatter. Even if your close connections are all mavens who are very knowledgeable in their particular areas, nonetheless for some purposes a connector to another group of people can be more useful, to use Malcolm Gladwell's terminology.[9] As Reed's original paper about Reed's Law noted: "The value of the Internet lies in its connections, but some connections are more valuable than others."[10]

The Internet and cell phone text messages permit many people to communicate who might not otherwise, forming new groups on scales from tiny to worldwide. This phenomenon goes back at least as far as protests related to the Tiananmen Square demonstrations in Beijing in 1998, which saw reports faxed out from China, distributed on USENET, and used as the basis of sympathetic demonstrations at Stanford and elsewhere. Such phenomena, called smartmobs by Howard Rheingold,[11] have become much more common recently, ranging from pointless but amusing pranks in which groups of people who never met before appear and sing a song, to protests against the World Trade Organization (WTO), to rapid reaction to humanitarian problems. Basically, people talk to each other more, and in more different groups, now that they have group-forming communication networks.

One of the things they talk about is your company and your products, which means that reputation is even more important these days than it used to be. We will come back to reputation systems later. For now, it is enough to say that the ability to see and make reputation is part of the option value of group-forming networks.

Options, Not Discounts

To people not familiar with scale-free networks and their associated group-forming option value, it may seem intuitive to some people to discount option value because it is not present value. Option value may not seem valuable because the user isn't using it right now.

But you don't want to discount it if:

- You're an investor looking for the next hot startup.
- You're a corporate executive trying to write a risk management plan.
- You're a security professional trying to deal proactively with an otherwise inexplicable increase in exploits.
- You're a miscreant discovering ways to exploit those loose connections, spammers being the most obvious and phishers some of the most recent.
- You're an insurance company trying to determine whether selling insurance for an aggregated risk that might get simultaneous claims from all customers is going to be too expensive, or a reinsurer trying to decide whether that risk is big enough to float a bond.

Note that some of these cases are very similar to options and financial derivatives. Investors' discount value on future returns varies with their risk tolerance. An investor in a hot startup has a high risk tolerance and, thus, does not discount the potential future return very much; an ordinary investor with a low risk tolerance would steeply discount future returns and decide not to make so risky an investment. For that matter, people don't really disregard option value in their own lives, as the sales of automobile club memberships and life insurance attest.

The Internet provides options of doing things that go well beyond simply protecting other activities. It is an interesting question how closely economists' Merton-Scholes theorem of option value applies to Internet communications and how well Black-Merton-Scholes quantification of such value can be used. Already it is clear that the Internet has drawn us all to a higher risk tolerance. Global reach with selective focus is an option many people want, and once they have it they don't want to give it up.

Different Networks Value Different Content

So, what is it about the Internet that makes it so addictive? Different technical means of networking enable different types of communication, which enable different content.

With a broadcast network, Sarnoff's Law indicates that content itself is king. The content provider with the best articles, programs, or visuals draws the most users and wins. Before the Internet, the ARPANET research facility with the fastest CPU or biggest disk might draw the most remote users. Newspapers of record, Top 40 radio stations, and TV news anchors thrive in such a network. That is the world of media moguls, huge media companies, and passive consumers. That world is ending. Don't risk your company by betting on traditional broadcast media.

With an interactive pairwise network and Metcalfe's Law, fast and reliable pairwise connections are the main thing because they get more people communicating with each other. Yahoo! groups are a good example of this. Telemarketing and unfortunately spam also thrive in such a network. This is a world of users talking to users, often about content provided by others, such as your products. They'll do this with or without your help. Don't risk being viewed as unresponsive; help them do it.

With a group-forming network and Reed's Law, facilitation of group formation and interaction is the main thing. Chat rooms do this, and eBay makes a big business out of it. Multiplayer games do this, especially where users have fast broadband access. Web logs (blogs), where anyone can mount a soapbox but nobody has to listen and many people no longer listen to the formerly authoritative television news anchors, thrive in such a network. Unfortunately, so does phishing, in which miscreants try to trick users out of personal identification so they can steal money. This is a world of users producing content and distributing it to each other without need for monopoly media. Customers and bloggers will find out about security flaws in your software. Don't risk vulnerability disclosure before you have a patch ready; help customers and others help you, so the new world of connectivity works for you by working for them.

Internet Mutation Grows Groups

As the Internet has grown in reach, users, speed, and applications, it has passed through these three phases of characteristic utility. Sometime in these first years of the twenty-first century it reached the level of group-forming for many of its corporate users. We don't see the old paper manila folder with a handwritten distribution list circulating among offices so much anymore; instead, when the boss wants an article read by his or her officers, having the assistant send them all electronic mail is so much easier; after all, the article itself is usually online, anyway. Sales contacts are not always as interested in the personal visit by the sales guy or even a telephone call when they can instead get online access to the product and to a discussion group with the professional services group or even with other customers. Banks don't even want to send paper statements anymore, now that their customers can pick them up online and banks can contact all their customers through the net.

It is the group-forming ability that has made people and corporations so dependent on the Internet. A favorite television show or book can be hard to turn off or put down, but there's always another, even with nostalgia for the last. Telephone calls home still have their appeal, but it's often more convenient to send several mail messages to the family or the customers than to try to round them up for the telephone. And only the Internet enables us to do so many things with and about a company's products and with as many appropriate groups of people related to them.

Unfortunately, where there is opportunity, there are also crooks.

Online Wealth Breeds Cyber-Crooks

All this reach and power of the Internet has not been lost on those who would rather turn a quick buck at many other people's expense than to go to the work of building a legitimate company. Real companies dependent on the Internet can be attacked, defrauded, denied service, held up by protection rackets, have their customers fooled into giving sensitive information to the wrong people, and so on. The types of miscreants indulging in such questionable behavior have changed from bored teenagers to professional criminals as the amount of money to be had has grown rapidly in the past few years. Spam reached a point where a few bad guys could make hundreds of thousands of dollars each per month (while costing thousands of other people, ISPs, and enterprises many times that in lost time, overloaded facilities, and mail missed because it was mislabeled as spam). Now that law enforcement is finally putting some of the bigger spammers behind bars, the miscreants are increasingly moving into other lines of crime. Botnet herders compromise hundreds and thousands of computers across the Internet and sell use of them to spammers and phishers and others. Phishers send out mail enticements pretending to be Internet vendors, banks, or ISPs so that they can con users into sending in passwords or Social Security numbers or other information that can be used to steal the users' identities and, thus, their money.

Don't Forget *Force Majeure*

Even if all this criminal activity could be stopped, there are still the risks of natural disasters, system misconfigurations, cable cut accidents, and the like that will still interfere from time to time with enterprises' ongoing dependence on the Internet. For that matter, the line between deliberate and inadvertent is blurry on the Internet. Phishing, for example, appears to the average target to be as hard to track back to a human perpetrator as a tornado. It is possible to make the tracks of such scams more visible, just as the tracks of tornados are recorded by meteorological stations. Still, just as there is tornado insurance even with tornado tracking, there needs to be phishing insurance even with phishing tracking.

Who Manages This Risk?

Currently, much of this risk is not managed. It is true that many companies spend increasing amounts on traditional Internet security, such as firewalls, patches, and policies, but many risks, especially those beyond the firewall, cannot be eliminated by such measures. The traditional solution to the unmanaged risks has been simply to accept them, assume the Internet "just works," and get on with business. This approach is failing, now that enterprises are increasingly dependent on the Internet and the risks of using it are increasing dramatically, especially the less frequent yet now much bigger risks such as a worst-case worm.

Who Needs This Risk Managed?

Every individual or enterprise that uses the Internet needs this risk managed, as do the ISPs that provide the Internet.

Inside each enterprise (above a certain size) there tend to be several executives and departments who need to collaborate on Internet business risk management. This may not be easy, because usually those parties are not used to cooperating to the degree that is needed.

- Information Technology (IT, in the person of the chief information officer ([CIO], VP engineering, or chief technology officer [CTO]) wants to just fix the problem, but sometimes that's just not possible. Maybe there is no existing patch, or the problem is outside the firewall in somebody else's ISP, or it's a counterparty problem with an outsourcer or vendor. Nevertheless, IT needs to be involved in determining the risks actually and potentially encountered and in evaluating the technical feasibility and appropriateness of any assessment, adjustment, or amelioration measures.

- Finance (in the person of the chief financial officer [CFO] or treasurer) may recognize the risk, yet have no financial tools that can determine the probability of losing money. If an ISP or service provider is a few seconds too slow and customers give up for today, or a few days too long and customers go to another vendor, how slow is it and how long does that take, for how many customers, for how much value of trade, and how likely is all that? For that matter, why did we spend all this IT money and it still fails like this?

- Strategy (CEO and board of directors) needs to coordinate business and technical perspectives, and often to get outside help: these things are not usually core competence. Self-insurance is a possibility, but buying insurance or other risk transfer instruments is often better. External validation is useful both in dealing with the problems and also for compliance with external regulations such as SOX or Basel II.

Other departments may also get involved. Marketing can make a competitive advantage out of doing risk management right, and sales can make hay with that.

How Do They Need It Managed?

It is time to extend Internet risk management strategies, beyond the traditional accept ("the Internet just works") or eliminate (technical performance and security solutions), into new territory involving securitizing risk, such as hedge, insure, or self-insure (such as the banking world's Basel II formula to compute capital withholding according to credit and operational risk). Certain types of insurance are applicable to the Internet, especially catastrophe bonds to expand available capital to cover mass outages and performance bonds to manage ISP Service Level Agreement (SLA) risk. Such instruments have been used for many years in managing risks such as earthquakes and electricity blackouts and brownouts. Forward-thinking Internet security experts such as Hal Varian,[12] Dan Geer,[13] and Bruce Schneier[14] have been saying for years that technology alone isn't enough; the future of Internet security is insurance. The speed, convenience, and capabilities of the Internet come with hazards of cyberspace just like ocean navigation came with hazards of current and hurricanes. It is time to apply insurance solutions to managing these new classes of *force majeure* Internet risks.

Notes

1. Thomas L. Friedman, "Is Google God?," *New York Times* (June 29, 2003). www.cnn.com/2003/US/06/29/nyt.friedman

2. David P. Reed, "The Law of the Pack," *Harvard Business Review,* pp. 23–4 (February 2001).
   http://doi.contentdirections.com/mr/hbsp.jsp?doi=10.1225/F0102C

3. J. H. Saltzer, D. P. Reed, and D. D. Clark, "End-to-End Arguments in System Design," *Second International Conference on Distributed Computing Systems,* pp. 509–512 (April 1981). http://web.mit.edu/Saltzer/www/publications/endtoend/endtoend.txt

4. Andrew Odlyzko and Benjamin Tilly, *A refutation of Metcalfe's Law and a better estimate for the value of networks and network interconnections* (Digital Technology Center, University of Minnesota, Minneapolis, MN, March 2, 2005). www.dtc.umn.edu/~odlyzko/doc/metcalfe.pdf

5. strategy+business, "Network theory's new math," News.com, CNET (January 1, 2003). http://news.com.com/2009-1069-978596.html

6. D. J. Watts and S. H. Strogatz, "Collective Dynamics of Small-World Networks," *Nature,* Volume 393, pp. 440–442 (1998).

7. Albert-Laszlo Barabasi, *Linked: How Everything Is Connected to Everything Else and What It Means* (Plume, April 29, 2003).

8. David Weinberger, *Small Pieces Loosely Joined: A Unified Theory of the Web* (Perseus Books Group, May 2003). `www.smallpieces.com`

9. Malcolm Gladwell, *Tipping Point: How Little Things Can Make a Big Difference* (Little, Brown and Company, February 2000).

10. Op. cit. Reed, "The Law of the Pack."

11. Howard Rheingold, *Smart Mobs: The Next Social Revolution* (Perseus Publishing, 2002). `www.smartmobs.com/book`

12. Hal R. Varian, "Managing Online Security Risks," *New York Times* (June 1, 2000). `http://www.sims.berkeley.edu/~hal/people/hal/NYTimes/2000-06-01.html`

13. Daniel E. Geer, Jr., "Risk Management Is Where the Money Is," *Digital Commerce Society of Boston* (November 3, 1998). `http://catless.ncl.ac.uk/Risks/20.06.html`

14. Bruce Schneier, "Schneier on Security: The Insurance Takeover," *Information Security* (February 2001).

CHAPTER 2

The Risk: Big and Growing Fast

When people see damage, is when they start acting.
—Darin Figurskey

The previous chapter alluded to many Internet business risks; the present chapter defines those and other risks in more detail, along with some of their causes and effects, so that later chapters can refer back here.

Traditional Risks Transfer

Most traditional risks transfer into the Internet world, where many of them are magnified by the ease and convenience of the Internet. For that matter, many risks represent interactions between traditional problems such as physical theft and online problems such as fraudulently obtaining identifying information.

Theft Isn't Just Physical Anymore

Old-fashioned bank robberies are hard to pull off through the Internet, but even more money can be stolen more easily, and with no risk of loss of life. Similarly, most things that require physical force are relatively difficult to accomplish through the Internet, but other things that may be even more lucrative and less personally risky to the perpetrators may become possible. Yet stealing physical objects may be the key to online fraud, as in stealing tapes with personal identifying information while the tapes are in transit or at repositories, as discussed in Chapter 7.

Fraud Can Be Faster

I bought a camera once in Singapore, and when I returned stateside I got a call from American Express asking how I'd liked my trip to Taipei.

When I informed them I had never been to Taipei, they asked if I had my card.

I said I did, in my hand.

They said they'd be sending me a new one, because somebody had copied the card number and other information and made up a physical copy that they'd been using on a shopping spree in Taipei, about $2,000 in each store.

With the Internet, the crooks don't even have to make up a physical card; if they can steal the appropriate names and numbers, they can steal money. And if they can steal many names and numbers, they can go on many shopping sprees at the same time.

Conversely, if they can steal some personal information by conning people into revealing it over the Internet, and combine it with other information stolen perhaps by lifting tapes, they can make up usable ATM or debit or perhaps credit cards, as discussed in Chapter 6.

Privacy Can Evaporate

Privacy is increasingly an issue as more commerce moves online, and as more laws take effect such as HIPAA, which requires certain standards for handling confidential information. Many companies are not yet taking online or even offline privacy seriously enough, as evidenced by the rash of thefts of confidential personal information discussed in Chapter 7.

Perils Can Affect Brand Reputation

Much ink has been spilled over so-called domain name squatters and how big companies supposedly have some sort of natural right not to have their brand names diluted by, for example, people with domains that match their own surnames. Many lawyers still derive income from this sort of foofaraw even in the present age of search engines in which few people ever actually type a domain name anymore. However, some real risks to brand and company reputations are bigger and elsewhere. A company that does not manage risk and fails to serve its customers through an Internet outage or slowdown loses reputation (see Chapter 6) and risks legal liability (see Chapter 11). A company that fails to secure personal information that is then stolen loses reputation and risks government prosecution, regulatory intervention, and loss of business (see Chapter 7).

Third-Party Claim Risk

Failure to supply service to customers or failing to keep private other people's information can lead to third-party claims. As you will see in Chapter 11, failure to provide access that customers are paying for can even lead to civil and criminal liability, not only for the company but even for corporate officers or other employees.

First-Party Loss Risk

Losing customers can lead to first-party claims on insurance, but most traditional insurance policies no longer cover many Internet risks, if they ever did. As you will also see in Chapter 11, legal precedents are mixed as to whether insurance can be required to cover such things, but fortunately newer kinds of insurance more adapted to the Internet are becoming available.

Traditional Internet Risk

Internet security seems stuck in a rut of traditional risks and traditional solutions. Here are a few of the traditional risks.

Content Risks

The traditional solution to Internet content theft is encryption. That can work well, provided that the encryption method is sufficiently strong and no one knows the keys who shouldn't. Much encryption in common use probably isn't strong enough to stop government intelligence agencies, but at least it will slow down small-time crooks and corporate espionage. Governments have on many occasions attempted to legislate *key escrow*, that is, legal requirements for organizations to tell government agencies their keys. Fortunately, key escrow has never yet been implemented. Yet people do know encryption keys—people inside the encrypting organization, and maybe some who have left or who were told. Even if information is encrypted by an automatic system, somebody programmed that system, and somebody has a password to modify it in case of problems. People make mistakes, carry grudges, sell out to higher bidders, and so on. Encryption can be subverted by people.[1, 2, 3, 4, 5] Nonetheless, encryption is generally better than no encryption.

Communication Method Risks

The biggest communication method risk in the news in 2005 is not even theft of massive numbers of Social Security numbers from universities through the Internet and on research computers, losing information about 3,500 students and alumni of the University of California at San Diego,[6] 55,200 affiliates of the University of Texas at Austin,[7] 98,369 graduate students or graduate-school applicants of the University of California at Berkeley,[8, 9] and 178,000 students, alumni, and employees of San Diego State University.[10] More newsworthy is theft of financial and other information on unencrypted physical media from couriers carrying them between business locations. Banks are long accustomed to sending currency between locations in guarded trucks, or even sending small amounts in the pockets of bank officials. They can't encrypt paper bills, certificates, or bonds, and apparently the habit of sending clear-text financial instruments has carried over to the electronic world. This is a communication risk that can be greatly reduced by encryption. See Chapter 7 for more on this.

Internet Operational Risk

As long as relatively few companies did business on the Internet, traditional Internet security was mostly adequate for traditional risks. Now that more ships of Internet commerce are carrying more cargo across that sea, more is at risk from storms and pirates who have appeared to threaten such ventures.

Internet Collapse Predicted, Again and Again

Back in 1996, Bob Metcalfe, inventor of Ethernet, founder of 3COM, after whom Metcalfe's Law is named, predicted,

> *The Internet is collapsing; the question is who's going to be caught in the fall. The Internet might possibly escape a "gigalapse" this year. If so, I'll be eating columns at the World Wide Web Conference in April. Even so, Scott Bradner should still be concerned about the Internet's coming catastrophic collapses.*[11]

Bob got a lot of press and ongoing discussion out of that prediction.

As it happened, he didn't have any long-term data when he made it. He came to me, and I supplied him some. Partly because of that data, he changed his prediction from a gigalapse to lots of little catastrophes, and ate his prediction.

Once again Internet collapse was predicted in 2004, at the People for Internet Responsibility (PFIR) conference on Preventing the Internet Meltdown,[12] organized by Lauren Weinstein, Peter G. Neumann, and Dave Farber. The conference had an interesting lineup, with many of the usual suspects who have been active in organizations from the Internet Engineering Task Force (IETF), which specifies and standardizes Internet protocols, to the Electronic Frontier Foundation (EFF), which defends civil liberties on the Internet, to the U.S. Department of Homeland Security (DHS). The first speaker listed is the same person Bob Metcalfe named: Scott Bradner of Harvard, long influential in IETF.

From Power Failures to Spam

How was 2004's prediction any different from 1996's? The concerns were different. Metcalfe said:

Let's be concerned that large portions of the Internet might be brought down not by nuclear war but by power failures, telephone outages, overloaded domain name servers, bugs in stressed router software, human errors in maintaining routing tables, and sabotage, to name a few weak spots.[13]

In other words, he indicated mostly failures in the basic routing fabric of the Internet, or in its underlying physical infrastructure.

In announcing the PFIR conference, Weinstein said:

A continuing and rapidly escalating series of alarming events suggest that immediate cooperative, specific planning is necessary if we are to have any chance of avoiding the meltdown. "Red flag" warning signs are many. A merely partial list includes attempts to manipulate key network infrastructures such as the domain name system; lawsuits over Internet regulatory issues (e.g., VeriSign and domain registrars vs. ICANN); serious issues of privacy and security; and ever-increasing spam, virus, and related problems, along with largely ad hoc or non-coordinated "anti-spam" systems that may do more harm than good and may cause serious collateral damage.[14]

In other words, he indicated mostly problems external to the technical infrastructure of the Internet, most of them either attacks on parts of the Internet or reactions to such attacks. A lot has changed in 8 years. Basically, use of the Internet has skyrocketed since 2000, making it an attractive target for all sorts of nuisances and attacks. It's not that any of Metcalfe's concerns of Internet storms have gone away. Rather, to them have been added numerous new problems of piracy, legal and political manipulation, and privacy.

It's Alive! Or Is It?

Back in 1996, Metcalfe described the problem:

Because the Internet's builders believed that it defies management—it's alive, they say—they punted, leaving no organized process for managing Internet operations. Where are circuits inventoried, traffic forecasts consolidated, outages reported, upgrades analyzed and coordinated? As my programming friends would say, the Internet Engineering and Planning Group and the North American Network Operators' Group are by most accounts no-ops—they exist, but they don't do anything.

But the Internet is not alive. It's actually a network of computers. And somebody, hopefully cooperating ISPs, should be managing its operations.[15]

In 2004, Weinstein's description of the root cause is essentially the same:

Most of these problems are either directly or indirectly the result of the Internet's lack of responsible and fair planning related to Internet operations and oversight.

A perceived historical desire for a "hands off" attitude regarding Internet "governance" has now resulted not only in commercial abuses, and the specter of lawsuits and courts dictating key technical issues relating to the Net, but has also invited unilateral actions by organizations such as the United Nations (UN) and International Telecommunications Union (ITU) that could profoundly affect the Internet and its users in unpredictable ways.[16]

Metcalfe's specter haunting the Internet back in 1996 was telephone companies taking over from traditional ISPs. That one happened, but it didn't really have much effect on the management problem Metcalfe was concerned about. Telcos don't seem to report Internet problems even to the FCC any more consistently than non-telco ISPs did, nor do telco ISPs seem to be any better coordinated about handling outages and slowdowns. Meanwhile, telephone companies are shifting all their communications, including voice, to be carried over the Internet or over Internet protocols. So even though telephone companies now are the biggest ISPs, the operational result is more that the Internet took over the telephone companies. Weinstein's 2004 specter of the UN and ITU is currently in progress. It may happen, too.

However, the telcos didn't solve the problem. Will the UN or the ITU? I have my doubts. Having once spent years dealing with properly constituted standards committees, including some of the European or UN model of national delegations constituting the committees, I see plenty of opportunities for committees as impediments and patronage. This happened with the International Organization for Standardization's Open System Interconnection (ISO-OSI) protocols, which were Europe's answer to TCP/IP; as you will see in Chapter 10, the properly constituted OSI committees delegated separate pieces of the problem to separate countries, and the result was very slow development and adoption, while the TCP/IP protocols coordinated loosely by IETF and the Internet was implemented by those who wanted to use it spread quickly until OSI was left behind.

The main reason that many people are interested in shifting anything about the Internet to the UN or ITU is frustration at the current role of the Internet Corporation for Assigned Names and Numbers (ICANN). ICANN was appointed by the U.S. Department of Commerce (DoC) to take over a role formerly handled essentially by one person (Jon Postel), a role that was almost solely technical. ICANN has increasingly taken on governance roles, which is frustrating both to people who would like technical decisions made for technical reasons and for people who don't think the U.S. should de facto control the Internet. However, ICANN is a long and convoluted story that is somewhat beside the point here.

The main point is that centralization in any organization may not be an effective solution to Internet organization.

Decentralization Also Enables Storms and Pirates

The decentralized Internet model has won over the centralized telephone
model, but that doesn't mean decentralization doesn't have its own problems.
As Scott Bradner wrote back in 1996:

> . . . with the global trend towards telecommunications deregulation the structure
> of the global telephone network is getting to look more like the fragmented
> Internet does.[17]

The Internet's decentralized model has won, and that's a good thing.

> Is a systemic collapse of such a system possible? Some pundits try to claim that it
> is—they come up with nightmare scenarios where all the ISPs get routing
> updates that their routers see as some form of death pill, or all of the ISP routers
> get simultaneously sabotaged by some evil force. Some even point to the melt-
> down of the inter-telephone switch signaling protocols a few years back. Is sys-
> temic collapse probable? No. The Internet is far too diverse these days.[18]

However, Bradner was not trying to say there can't be problems:

> I do have to agree with Bob [Metcalfe] that there will continue to be vendor and
> facility specific outages. As some of the vendors continue to expand their cus-
> tomer bases the effect of outages will grow (megalapses if you will). But how do
> these outages compare with the outages experienced by other service providers? A
> few months ago a major failure of the power grid left most of the western U.S. try-
> ing to communicate by candlelight, and on an average day, more than 30,000
> people in the U.S. are without telephone service for an average of 5 hours each.
> (See http://www.atis.org/atis/nrsc/whatsne2.htm) These are
> quite real problems and the problems on the Net are no less real.[19]

Add to such traditional *force majeure* events newer ones caused by worms,
viruses, Trojans, botnet herders, plus spamming, phishing, pharming, and all
the other current security problems of the Internet, and indeed problems in
cyberspace are as real as those in meatspace (which is what IETF people call
the offline world). But that's no reason to go back to centralized solutions, even
if we could. We need to find decentralized solutions to the Internet's security
problems; the next chapter discusses such solutions.

Perils: Hazards That Can Cause Problems

In this book, we often distinguish between perils and anomalies. *Perils* are situations, practices, bugs, or other vulnerabilities or hazards that can cause
problems. A stack of old newspapers is a fire hazard, or peril, which may either
spontaneously combust and start a fire, or, if lit by some other means may

magnify a fire. Internet perils abound, ranging from unpatched bugs to mono-culture software to unplugged firewall holes to nonredundant links and over-loaded routers outside the firewall. In Internet security, such things are usually called *vulnerabilities*. However, the word *vulnerability* often has the connotation of being about software. In this book, we use the insurance jargon word *peril* to include hazards that are not software bugs.

Anomalies: Problems That Directly Affect Business

In this book, we use the word *anomaly* for a problem actually resulting from a peril. In Internet security, such things are usually called *exploits*. However, the word exploit often has the connotation of being caused by a human and requiring a software bug to exploit. In this book, we use the use word *anomaly* to include problems that are not instigated by humans or that are not exploiting software bugs. Some anomalies may not affect business directly, but it is useful to keep track of even those that don't, to see patterns that can help predict or ameliorate the ones that do when they happen. Categorizing anomalies of all types can help in building financial risk transfer instruments and reputation systems and in deciding when to apply them.

Deceptive Practices

Commerce continues to embrace the Internet and to become dependent upon it. In banking in particular, deposits, withdrawals, balances, statements, lines of credit, and other financial transactions and instruments are increasingly available via and used over the Internet. Financial institutions that are based on the Internet are even more dependent on it. Any enterprise that does commerce through the Internet is at risk of financial or identity theft involving the Internet.

Spam: Unsolicited Bulk Electronic Mail

Spam is unsolicited bulk electronic mail. More than half of all the mail passing through most ISPs is spam. Most people on the Internet today cannot remember a time without spam. The earliest spam goes back before the Internet to the 1970s on the ARPANET, and spam was a problem on USENET newsgroups in the 1980s. But the big explosion in spam started about 1994, as the web brought the Internet to the masses and a few sociopathic con artists decided to Make Money Fast! by sending mail to many people so a few suckers would buy. The Internet provides leverage to expand such cons far past what old-time snake-oil salesmen could manage on their horses and buggies, and far past what is possible with telephone cons, because a spammer can send millions of messages to millions of people in a day. The huge majority of those people do not want anything to do with spam, nor do the huge majority of the ISPs whose resources the spammers steal. Big spammers literally make millions of dollars, while costing other people in aggregate hundreds of millions. Spamming is a different category of crime from a one-on-one con, and the amount of collateral damage to the 99 percent of people and organizations that don't want spam in order to get profit from the tiny percent who are foolish enough to buy makes spam truly sociopathic.

For many years, many Internet users would try to dismiss spam as merely a nuisance that users could handle by deleting unwanted messages. In recent years, as the costs have mounted, such apologies for spam have become more rare. The obvious costs include the time it takes to sort through one's mailbox, trying to find legitimate messages among the junk mail selling nostrums to augment body parts and begging money for random charities. Somewhat less obvious costs include the reluctance many individuals now have to depend on mail or even to read it. Younger Internet users often prefer instant messages (IM) because IM has not yet fallen prey to spam.

People sometimes still have a hard time seeing that the bigger costs are aggregate. Service providers waste huge proportions of their budgets for hardware, CPU cycle, and Internet bandwidth carrying mail messages that turn out to be spam. They waste even more money paying people to deal with the problem. They lose the respect of their users if they don't try to filter spam, yet they can lose even more reputation if they try too hard and filter legitimate mail.

Some providers try to turn this scourge of spam into a business opportunity by building walled gardens that their users can hide behind, protected from spam and other wild fauna of the Internet. But this strategy has never worked long term on the Internet. Earlier walled gardens such as CompuServe and Prodigy eventually merged with more communicative providers, or at least ones with better user experiences. And as users become more sophisticated, they want more direct access to the Internet at large, not just to the parts of it displayed on the inside walls of a garden.

Most people do not buy from spammers, but it only takes a very small percentage of responses to millions of messages to make spammers a lot of money. Money they make by stealing far greater amounts of resources from everyone else. Spam is not business; spammers are sociopathic criminals.

Phishing: Conning Users Out of IDs

One reason that spam may not be increasing as fast as previously is that apparently some spammers have moved on to other ways of making ill-gotten gains, including phishing. *Phishing* involves stealing a user's identity for purposes of financial gain, usually either by social engineering or technical subterfuge.

Social Engineering

Social engineering is tricking people into behaving in a particular way by playing on their fears. Most Internet users are familiar with the annoying electronic mail messages they get claiming to be from a financial institution that needs the user to connect to a web page and supply a missing password or Social Security number, saying things like these:

- You can't use your ATM card without supplying the following information to this web site.

- Your account with us will be deactivated if you don't . . .

- Download and install *URL* to protect your computer, where *URL* is disguised spyware or bot.

Phishing messages have the logos and appearance of the financial institution, but lead to a web page that is not associated with that financial institution. Most people are wary of such messages and do not fall for the trap. But it only takes a few percent to make phishing lucrative for the phisher.

In that way phishing is like spam, except phishing is more targeted, and thus uses fewer messages to reach its marks. Unfortunately, that makes phishing harder to detect. However, users in general have caught on very quickly that phishing is bad; there has been no long-drawn-out apology for phishing such as there was for spam. Perhaps it is easier for users to see that phishers are criminals who don't care how many people they inconvenience or cost resources.

Technical Subterfuge

In addition to the social-engineering approach, phishers also use technical subterfuge that may involve planting spyware on the user's computer via bugs in a web browser, bugs in the user's electronic mail reading program, or software bugs in the user's operating system or elsewhere—spyware that watches for the user's passwords or other identifying information and reports it back to the phisher.

Losses beyond Money

Individuals do not usually end up paying for losses from phishing. Credit cards have long covered losses to fraud above minimal amounts, usually by making merchants pay. While the amount of actual financial loss from phishing is still low as a proportion of any enterprise's online revenue, any loss from such scams is worrisome.

Reputation is a bigger worry for the targeted enterprises. Reputation damage can extend beyond the Internet. A user who has seen too many phishing messages claiming to be from Bank X may not want to bank at Bank X even through an ATM or teller window.

There is even a worse reputation, to the Internet itself. Already many Internet mail users are wary of believing any mail from financial institutions. This is a problem for those institutions, because they see significant economies of scale in increasing use of the electronic mail and the web for financial transactions. It is a problem for all Internet users and for Internet commerce.

Spoofs: Faked Electronic Mail

Phishing mail messages are one kind of spoof. A *spoof* is more generally any electronic mail message or other online communication that is faked to resemble a real message from a corporation or other source.[20]

Pharming: Fraudulent Misdirection

To quote the Anti-Phishing Working Group (APWG), `www.antiphishing.org`, "Pharming crimeware misdirects users to fraudulent sites or proxy servers, typically through DNS hijacking or poisoning."

If this definition seems jargon-filled, that's part of the point. Miscreants who do pharming use technical means that the average user knows little about, so that the user won't notice.

- **DNS hijacking** involves changing a domain name registration so that it is owned by someone else.
- **DNS poisoning** involves supplying falsified responses for some DNS queries for a domain.

It is not clear that new laws are needed, since fraud is already illegal. Pharming is sometimes facilitated by spyware, for which there are already laws and bills in progress.[21]

Spyware: Logging Keystrokes

Spyware is software that surreptitiously collects information from a computer and sends it elsewhere. Some spyware reads files, other spyware looks inside communications, and some spyware bypasses all encryption by logging keystrokes as the user types on the keyboard.

Adware: Stealing Eyeballs

Adware, like spyware, is software the user didn't ask for that somehow gets on the computer. Adware displays advertisements to the user. A piece of adware may also incorporate spyware, for example, to see which ads the user pays attention to.

Botnets of Zombies

Miscreants called *bot herders* collect herds of *zombies* or *bots*. Bot is short for robot. A bot is a computer that has been compromised so that someone unauthorized can control it. Bots are often called zombies because their controllers can let them sleep for as long as they like and then have them do their bidding. The rightful owner of the computer is usually oblivious to such compromise.

Herds of bots are usually called *botnets*. Bot herders collect hundreds or thousands of bots and then sell control of them to other people who use them. Buyers include spammers, phishers, and attackers.

Mules Carrying Real Money

Botnets, spamming, phishing, and other illicit activities constitute an international illegal online market. At some point, money has to change hands or goods have to be shipped. Reshippers of such goods or funds are called mules;[22] this is a traditional term for carriers of drugs or money or other illegal goods. Mules are especially susceptible to being caught by law enforcement because they carry ill-gotten goods or funds, often in different countries than the original phishers or other scammers, and often in the offline world.

Blackmail: Simple Online Crime

Old-style mob protection rackets may also be moving online, or maybe just simple blackmail. In one reported case, an individual demanded $17 million:

> In a pair of missives fired off Feb. 3, 2004, the stalker said that he had thousands of proprietary MicroPatent documents, confidential customer data, computer passwords, and e-mail addresses. He warned that if Videtto ignored his demands, the information would "end up in e-mail boxes worldwide."[23]

Companies that face such demands have few alternatives. Tracking down this perpetrator took a long time, but did eventually yield success:

> The basement of the home was stocked with parts for makeshift hand grenades and ingredients for ricin, one of the most potent and lethal of biological toxins.[24]

The perpetrator was apparently smart enough not to send messages from his house:

> Last March, on the same day that they raided his home, the authorities arrested the stalker as he sat in his car composing e-mail messages that he planned to send wirelessly to Videtto. The stalker has since pleaded guilty to charges of extortion and possession of toxic materials.[25]

Such a perpetrator can drive around and use various wireless networks, becoming even harder to track.

A study by a student at Carnegie Mellon University (CMU) indicates that this case was not an isolated problem.[26] Exactly how big the problem is is hard to say, which is another problem in itself. Ignoring it won't make it go away.

Actually paying such blackmail would only accelerate turning it into a real protection racket.

Scob: Complexity and Consequences

Scob was the attack that exploited a bug in Internet Explorer to exploit an option in the IIS database server to cause the web server to append a JavaScript Trojan horse loader to image files to retrieve a keystroke monitor that mailed its results to the cracker. (A Trojan horse, or Trojan, is a program that sits undetected on a computer waiting for some event, such as remote activation by an attacker, before doing anything.)

There have been reams of reports from security companies about how scob worked, and more about who was behind it, how connections to the addresses it used to report were blocked, and so on. It's good to see so many people and companies on the ball, busily producing forensics.

But what does scob mean in a larger sense?

For one thing, even image files are no longer safe from exploits. I suppose it's good that people realize that anything can be broken.

For another, because there was no patch for IE at the time, a few more people will take software diversity seriously and use other browsers. This could even lead to competition among browsers on security; for example, it seems that Mozilla is offering a $500 bounty per critical bug.[27] Both diversity and any resulting security competition would be good.

However, even patching bugs in individual facilities won't solve the class of attacks that scob represents, because scob exploited a combination of bugs or features in several different facilities. Some of them weren't even bugs for that facility, it was only when they were used in combination that they turned into bugs. Checking for such combinations is far more complex than debugging a single facility. Software diversity will help somewhat with this, because for example a browser and a database server from different vendors are less likely to have the same types of design flaws and coding styles. But diversity, like traditional security solutions such as patches, firewalls, intrusion detection, and so on, none of which stopped scob, has its limits.

And attacks like scob will happen again. Phishing in general is on the rise, and scob is a kind of phishing that doesn't even require the user to consciously interact. So, such an attack can be an automated money-making machine.

Unfair Practices

Spyware and adware often involve software being inadvertently picked up over the Internet. But what about similar software that is installed by a hardware or software manufacturer or vendor? Such software is just as annoying or detrimental to the user, even though it wasn't picked up over the Internet. It should be enough that the customer has bought the vendor or OEM's equipment without ads for related products being planted on it or unauthorized reports on the user's activities being sent back.

Causes across the Board

The causes of specific perils and anomalies range from accident to ill-understood complexity to forces of nature to political espionage, industrial sabotage, to disgruntled present or former employees. Increasingly popular is plain old greed.

The Root Causes Are Not Technical

In other words, the root causes aren't technical—they're usually either acts of God, ignorance, or normal human motives. It is easy to become fixated on a particular type of technique such as social engineering or software bug exploits. Yet those are merely means to an end, and the end is increasingly money.

Online Exploits Are Not a Hobby Anymore

Time was that many exploits were let loose by smart college students learning about the Internet, such as the Morris Worm of November 2, 1988.[28] Many of these people called themselves hackers, in emulation of real computer hackers.

Real *hackers* are people who create software or debug things (often software or hardware) out of creativity or to show it can be done. Many of them are heroes of the computing revolution,[29] such as Ken Thompson and Dennis Ritchie, who invented Unix in an attic, or Ray Tomlinson, who invented networked electronic mail because he wanted to use it, or Richard Stallman, who invented GNU Emacs and founded the Free Software Foundation (FSF), or Steve Wozniak, who invented the Apple computer, or Richard Garriott, who invented some of the earliest commercial computer games, or Roberta Williams, who wrote a popular computer game, or Linus Torvalds, who invented Linux, or even, in his early days of writing an implementation of BASIC, Bill Gates, to name just a few of the best known.

People who break into computers or networks are *crackers*. It is not impossible for a hacker to be a cracker, but most crackers are not hackers; they aren't doing it out of creativity; they're doing it to break things. For more about this difference, see Chapter 8.

Then there was a time when many exploits came from bored teenagers trying to prove they were smart, such as much of the 1990s. Many of these people didn't even write their own exploits; they merely ran scripts written by someone else. Thus came the name for this kind of cracker: *script kiddies*.

Nowadays an increasing number of exploits are perpetrated by criminals in it for the money, from individual underground entrepreneurs paying for their mortgages to organized gangs. The press often calls these people hackers, but they're not: they're crackers, miscreants, and often just plain criminals.

Confusing criminals with creative people leads to the suppression of creativity, which is detrimental to the economy and increases difficulties in catching criminals. Mislabeling people is a risk in itself.

Microwaved Wireless

Not every risk is intentional. At the DefCon security conference in 2005 the attendees tried attacking test networks to see how quickly they could break them. However, according to attendee Bruce Hubbert,

> The wireless attacks we saw—jamming, de-authentication, denial-of-service, MAC spoofing, fake and soft APs—were to be expected . . . We were more surprised to find that an abundance of Bluetooth devices, microwave ovens, 802.11 frequency-hopping devices, and Web cameras were more effective at knocking out the conference's wireless network.[30]

It's best not to jump to conclusions or accusations.

Don't Forget Force Majeure

Hurricanes, earthquakes, floods, and other natural disasters may have limited effects on the Internet, yet Hurricane Ivan disconnected a whole country, the Cayman Islands. The line between *force majeure* and malicious is often blurred; somebody wrote and released every worm that has attacked the Internet, but the effects of many of them are more like networkwide storms than like a burglar.

Effects on Business

Internet risks can go beyond direct loss of business during periods of lost connectivity, beyond costs to clean up exploits, beyond lost customers that went to competitors in the near term. Such risks can cause reputational damage with long-lasting effects.

A Worst-Case Worm

What is the most aggregation we can expect to see for damages on the Internet? At a conference in May 2004, two researchers attempted to answer that question with a paper:

> *Worms represent a substantial economic threat to the U.S. computing infrastructure. An important question is how much damage might be caused, as this figure can serve as a guide to evaluating how much to spend on defenses. We construct a parameterized worst-case analysis based on a simple damage model, combined with our understanding of what an attack could accomplish. Although our estimates are at best approximations, we speculate that a plausible worst-case worm could cause $50 billion or more in direct economic damage by attacking widely-used services in Microsoft Windows and carrying a highly destructive payload.*[31]

This $50 billion dollar estimate is actually conservative. The paper was supposed to have three authors, not two; the third author thought a higher estimate should be included.

Also, the estimate given is only for the United States. About half of the Internet is outside the United States, so it is probably safe to assume that total worldwide damages would be even higher. A simple linear multiple of 2 may not be accurate, since the rest of the world isn't as closely connected topologically as the United States is. On the other hand, most of the Internet in the rest of the world is in Europe, Japan, East Asia, Canada, Australia, and New Zealand, all of which are tightly connected within themselves and closely connected to the United States. The Slammer worm, for example, did not respect national boundaries.

So, there is good research to indicate that some Fortune 500 CEOs' fears of a $100 billion dollar risk are very well founded.[32]

Reputation Damage

As I discuss in Chapter 7, failing to secure information can lead to investigation by law enforcement and regulatory bodies, uncomplimentary press reports, and significant reputational damage.

The Internet As Complicator

The Internet itself as a group of communications media such as IM, mailing lists, blogs, and traditional news delivered online is a magnifier of anything that is newsworthy. Such communications are used by the miscreants before there is news, and they can spread the word about problems and produce copycat attacks.

Sailing the Ocean Sea

When Columbus ventured beyond the coasts of the Old World into what he called the Ocean Sea that surrounded the whole world, he encountered storms, currents, and winds; when Magellan sailed around the world he didn't make it all the way because he encountered hostile natives. In those days it took 3 years to circumnavigate the globe; on the Internet it takes less than 3 seconds.

Internet attacks can originate anywhere in the world and attack anywhere in the world. You don't have to sail halfway around the world to encounter hostile natives; the Russian Mafia or Chinese gangs or U.S. spammers can attack anywhere in the world. Even *force majeure* events that are not directly caused by humans can spread worldwide via the Internet. Even the biggest natural disasters, such as hurricanes and tsunamis, are usually limited to a continent or an ocean. Internet disasters are limited only by the entire Internet Ocean Sea.

Many Navies on That Ocean

Competition can also originate anywhere in the world. As Thomas L. Friedman points out, a few decades ago if an ambitious young person were given a choice of growing up in Utica, New York, or Bangalore, India, the obvious choice would have been Utica, because it is in the United States, a developed country. Nowadays, Bangalore might be preferable, because while India still has millions of people living in Third World conditions, Bangalore has First World communications media, universities, and an employment pool, which, along with much lower wages, adds up to a competitive advantage. Internet commerce very often turns into global competition. Companies that want to compete need to manage global risks, and risk management can be a competitive advantage.

Don't Try to Drain the Ocean

A popular reaction to all this danger of commerce on the Internet is to try to regulate and control the Internet until it becomes safe. That would be throwing the baby out with the bathwater, or, considering the difficulty of it, more like trying to drain the ocean. Such efforts, if they succeeded, would harm the commerce they were trying to protect; better would be to spend similar effort improving commerce. I've already discussed this previously, but it's worth reemphasizing.

Magnifiers That Make Everything Worse

Once an exploit is discovered, it is particularly easy for a miscreant to cause damage if the software vendor has not published a patch, or if users have not applied the patch. If a company has no redundancy, a miscreant can cause significant denial-of-service or compromise of information by attacking a single computer. Or if a company has redundancy in multiple servers, but they are all running the same software and secured the same way, a miscreant may be able to compromise them all at once.

Monoculture Considered Harmful

Monoculture cotton crops and the economy they supported proved suscepti-ble to a small insect in the early twentieth century.[33] There are parallels in the Internet in the early twenty-first century.[34] Portions of this section appeared on the Internet in the online peer-reviewed journal *First Monday* and are used here with permission.

The Boll Weevil

In the early part of the twentieth century, a quarter-inch reddish-brown insect, *Anthonomous grandis grandis,* spread across most of the southern United States. Its path included:

Texas, 1890–1904

Oklahoma, 1904

Alabama, 1915

Georgia, 1920

The boll weevil eats the cotton plant. It wiped out much of the cotton crop in the affected states. Severe economic consequences ensued, because cotton was the main crop, and only one strain of cotton was grown. Farmers faced bank-ruptcy. Towns failed.

Monoculture Cotton, Fragile Economy

Monoculture cotton was bad anyway, because cotton exhausted the soil. Together with bad weather, it resulted in the Dust Bowl. Depression.

Farmers had grown particular strains of cotton, such as long-staple cotton or Sea Island cotton, because even though it was hard to pick, it had a depend-able market. Sea Island cotton is supposed to be the best for making clothes; in Ian Fleming's novels James Bond would only wear shirts made from Sea Island cotton. Bankers liked it because they had predictable farmers (usually going deeper into debt to the bank). It was a predictable economy.

It was also an economy with problems. Many of the farmers were share-croppers who did not own their own land and who had to pay much of their crop as rent. Their diet was heavy on sugar and starch and low on various other necessary nutrients. The lack of B vitamins led to widespread incidence of pellagra. Suffice it to say that there were human costs associated with the cotton economy. However, because it was predictable, people put up with it.[35]

But it was a fragile economy because it was based on one crop. Any disease or parasite or predator or weather anomaly that could destroy that crop could destroy the economy it supported. It was going to happen sooner or later. As it happened, the damage was done by the boll weevil.

The boll weevil led to diversification: corn, soybeans, peanuts. A stronger national and world economy eventually resulted. Farmers, vendors, and bankers were wealthier.

Prevention Needs History and Observation

Texas wasn't the first place the boll weevil took its toll. In 1848 it had "practically caused cotton cultivation to be abandoned in the state of Coahulia [sic], Mexico."[36]

Apparently nobody remembered that when the bug reached Texas.

And when the weevil crossed the Red River into Indian Territory in 1904, the Oklahoma Experiment Station was not prepared to deal with it. No preparations were made. Data about the weevil had to be obtained by Oklahoma after the fact from U.S. Bureau of Entomology stations in Victoria and College Station, Texas.

There was apparently no organization tasked with looking at current and potential effects of the weevil on cotton crops throughout the United States. If there had been, much economic damage could have been averted.

Monoculture Communications Providers

On September 11, 2001, which worked better, the telephone system or the Internet? There was one main telephone company in New York City. Many people had great difficulty getting telephone calls through for many hours. There were multiple Internet providers. Many people exchanged electronic mail and instant messages with no difficulties. There were problems with some specific Web servers, and there were some routing problems that persisted in some cases for about 90 minutes, but the Internet in general survived quite well.

A single provider Internet:

- Wouldn't have survived September 11
- Wouldn't have carried full spectrum news about it
- Wouldn't have had access to primary sources, such as the full text of Tony Blair's speech to his party (almost all traditional news sources carried truncated versions)

The city of New York even requested Metronet to bring back their Richochet wireless Internet service for use by disaster recovery personnel. The telephone system was not dependable in this emergency. The Internet was.

All the World, All the Time

Numerous useful things can be seen by looking at topology and performance of ISPs and their customers worldwide, such as which ISPs have differing performance into which cities, and which are affected where by specific events ranging from hurricanes to phishing. Such information has uses from capacity planning to criminal forensics.

Such information can also take into account financial stability: a bankrupt ISP is an ISP with fewer competent technical people, which will probably be reflected in its performance sooner or later. Knowing how soon this is likely to happen requires looking at many ISPs over time.

Capacity planning has aspects of contingency planning. Which combination of ISPs will produce best redundancy for an enterprise in the face of physical, financial, routing, or other failure? It is necessary to collect and collate such information for it to be available for analysis and interpretation. Similarly, past performance can provide evidence of performance instability.

Some ISPs are more related than it might appear from their service offerings. Many ISPs buy transport from other ISPs; similar performance of those ISPs can result. Not necessarily identical, however. Sometimes a small ISP buying transport from a big one can actually show better performance than the big one, because the small one covers a smaller geographical area and, thus, has less speed of light delay to contend with.

Such observations can help enterprises determine what combination of nonredundant routes, high connectivity, and good performance to select for best survivability. Nodes along paths from an enterprise to its customers can be anywhere in the world, such as on the island of Mauritius, off Madagascar in the Indian Ocean. High-net-worth individuals can live where they please. That means we need to look at the entire Internet all the time: balanced worldwide coverage.

If you want to know if the boll weevil is likely to attack your cotton, you'd best be looking at past, current, and potential paths of the weevil worldwide. If we want to be able to recommend better crop rotation, we'd better have the past history, current alternatives, and stability factors lined up as evidence.

What Affects the Internet the Most?

Which kinds of events had the most effect on the Internet?

    Code Red worm (IIS)

    September 11 attacks

    Nimda worm (Outlook)

    September 26 cable cuts

Few people know which of those events had the most effect on the Internet, nor on what part of the Internet—which applications, providers, cities, links. The answer depends on how you measure it, but physical attacks, even the worst terrorist attacks, generally do not affect Internet use by businesses as much as do worms. Physical damage, even undersea cable cuts, tends to get fixed quickly, while monoculture software breeds vulnerabilities that breed ongoing exploits. Nonredundant network routes constitute a similar kind of problem, one that most businesses are not aware exists.

If people don't know that growing only one kind of cotton is bad for their economic health, they won't grow anything else. If they don't know what other crops will help, they won't grow them. If they don't know about crop rotation and interleaved rows, they probably won't use those techniques. If they don't have observations of how such techniques actually work in practice, they won't be able to adjust as better ones are found.

Other Monocultures

Cotton wasn't the only monoculture crop that led to economic disaster. In the late nineteenth century an aphid-like insect, *Phylloxera vastatrix*, destroyed most of the world's vineyards, leading to the little-known fact that most French wines today are actually grown from Texas grapevine stock. The company that knows where to get disease-resistant vine stock will be in demand.

Many recent attacks on the Internet have been disproportionately attacks on monoculture applications, namely Internet Explorer, Outlook, and IIS, all provided by a single vendor, Microsoft. We can make that visible. Such visibility promotes diversity. Diversity will enhance corporate, national, and world security. Diversity should also be valuable to other providers.

Router Monoculture

Monoculture is not limited to operating systems or application software, nor even to application servers. Monoculture can exist in network routers, as well. And if an exploit becomes widely known for a widely used router, big problems could result. As Michael Lynn remarked shortly after he gave a conference presentation about a method to use vulnerabilities in Cisco routers (he didn't describe any specific vulnerabilities), "What politicians are talking about when they talk about the Digital Pearl Harbor is a network worm," he said. "That's what we could see in the future, if this isn't fixed."[37]

Even a network router worm wouldn't take down the whole Internet. But if it takes down your ISP, the result could look the same to you and your customers. See Chapter 7 for more on this particular case.

Looking Ahead

We need to look ahead. We can look at potential protocols, such as Multipurpose Label Switching (MPLS), Internet Protocol version 6 (IPv6), streaming video, and so on. We need to do that, but we also need to avoid getting buried in minutiae. Being tied to specific protocols such as Simple Network Management Protocol (SNMP) can radically limit the scope of the viewing instrument. That would be a platform-centric approach. A more network-centric approach can work better: Look at the big picture, and zoom in on customer-relevant details.

We can also look at deeper philosophical questions.

Still end-to-end?[38]

Still decentralized?

Still no settlements among big ISPs?

All VPN?

Cryptography used, required, or prohibited?

W3 consortium and web patents?

Government control?

Given the state of the financial market, and especially the failures of so many ISPs and Internet content providers, everything about the Internet is now open to question. Given overbuilding of fiber optics, reallocation of spectrum, and legal manipulations of media companies, everything about communications in general is also open to question. We can and should examine all these and other issues. Many companies do. Someone needs to look at the big picture.

Some questions do seem to have clear answers, however. A centralized Internet would be a monoculture Internet, with little room for diversity, not to mention for survivability.

Ecosystem and Market

The Internet is an ecosystem. It is composed of many interacting parts, ISPs, datacenters, enterprises, and end users, each of them drawing sustenance from the others and from raw materials. Each of them needs to make informed decisions. This is an ecology, and this ecology, whose life forms are corporations and people, is also a market.

A market needs price differentiation. Perhaps via some form of service ratings?

Show Me

An ecology evolves by natural selection. Internet evolution has been hampered by difficulty of selection.

Many people find it difficult to understand how an ISP between their company and their customers can be of interest to their company, since neither they nor their customers are directly connected to it or paying it. Talking about it seldom convinces anyone. Drawing it often does. Animating such drawings to indicate the problem and how it would improve if the company changed ISPs can be very convincing. ISPs and bandwidth traders and their customers need Internet performance made visible so that they can differentiate their services. That way buyers can choose and suppliers can compete.

Visibility enables differentiation, and thus selection. Visibility can enable evolution of the Internet ecology. Visibility can make this market.

Health and Prosperity

An Internet with visible performance will be an Internet in which providers continue to leapfrog one another. It will be an Internet in which buyers can select suppliers rationally. It will be an Internet of stronger providers. It should also be an Internet of continuing diversity, diversity that will manifest itself as robustness in the face of disasters and attacks.

That direction leads to a healthy and prosperous Internet, a healthy and prosperous country, and a healthy and prosperous world.

Fame and Fortune

A monoculture Internet would be like the old pre-1995 telephone system, in which there were only a few suppliers (AT&T and GTE) and performance was not an issue.

The boll weevil never went away, you know. It is merely kept at bay through crop diversity, more resistant cotton varieties, different planting methods, pesticides, and constant monitoring. A visible and rapidly evolving Internet will be an Internet in which continually more sophisticated performance analysis is needed.

That's a market in which fortunes can be made.

Denial and Damage

Denial can cause damage.

In the summer of 1953 tornados had damaged several states, but everyone knew Massachusetts didn't have tornados.

The official forecast for Central Massachusetts called for a continuation of hot, humid weather with the likelihood of afternoon thunderstorms, some possibly severe. U.S. Weather Bureau storm forecasters believed there was the potential for

tornadoes in New York and New England that afternoon and evening. The Buf-
falo, New York office warned western New York residents of the possibility for a
tornado, but the official forecast released from the Boston office did not mention
the threat, based in part on the rarity of Massachusetts tornadoes, and perhaps
partly on the potential psychological impact on those residing in the area.[39]

Even after the funnel touched down in Worcester County, Massachusetts, on
June 9, 1953, forecasters at the Boston Weather Bureau office at Boston's Logan
Airport discounted telephone calls from the affected area, dismissing them as
crank calls. After all, everyone knew Massachusetts didn't have tornados.

Meanwhile, debris started falling 35 miles east of the funnel, some onto Harvard's Blue Hill Meteorological Observatory. Not just small pieces, either: 6-
foot planks and 10-foot square pieces of wall and roof. The Harvard observers
managed to convince Logan to put out a new advisory. I don't know if they
waved a plank at the telephone.

But the damage had been done. It was too late to evacuate, tape windows,
or take cover.

The damage was estimated at $52 million ($349 million in 2002 dollars) and
included 4,000 buildings and hundreds of cars.[40]

The *Worcester Telegram and Gazette* ran a picture of freshman Senator John F.
Kennedy touring the disaster area.

It was an F4 (some say F5) tornado, with winds up to 250 miles per hour. Yet
denial was so great that trained meteorologists refused to believe the funnel
existed while it was flinging cars into the air, demolishing houses, and throwing debris as far as 50 miles away; a mattress was found in Boston Harbor.

As Darin Figurskey, meteorologist, said, "When people see damage, is when
they start acting."[41]

Affected parties moved quickly to start a statewide storm-spotting network
to watch for future storms. They even did some historical research. It turns out
Massachusetts actually has about three tornados per year, and the earliest one
on record was reported in June 1643 by Governor Winthrop. It's amazing what
you can see when you stop denying that you can see it, and even more when
you have multiple eyes watching.

Several people affected by the Worcester tornado went on to pioneer tornado chasing, tornado cataloguing, and Doppler radar.[42]

It seems the best time to make risk management plans is before the disaster
happens.

Inertia Increases Damage

Even after we've heard about the Worcester Tornado and seen the Blaster
Worm in action, why don't we make risk management plans? Bruce Sterling

caught another reason: "We prefer almost any humiliation to the severe mental challenge of building a new and original order all our own."[43]

Inertia: We'd rather say it can't happen here or shake our heads at people who live on hurricane-prone beaches than do something about our own house in central Massachusetts before it blows into Boston Harbor. Those companies that indulge in inertia and head-shaking may get left behind, or dispersed like refugees from an island nation submerged by a rising sea, "without any false hope of a return to their drowned Jerusalem."[44]

Sterling's poetic description may seem overdone, yet companies that are held down by their local brick-and-mortar past will have difficulty floating on the rising global Internet scale-free sea.

Risk Causes Fear

What happens when an unexpected tornado strikes? People run away in fear.

What happens when terrorists use airplanes to destroy the tallest buildings in Manhattan? People also reacted in fear, which produced some irrational behavior. According to David Ropeik, director of risk communication at the Harvard Center for Risk Analysis, "Driving went up, and flying went down."[45]

This was even though flying was still much safer than driving. And even though the likelihood of terrorists succeeding in that particular tactic again was very small, given that it only worked because passengers and crew thought they were dealing with hijackers, not suicidal terrorists.

As a result, approximately 1,018 more people died in highway accidents in the fourth quarter of 2001 than in the same quarter of 2000, according to the University of Michigan Transportation Research Institute.[46] Ropeik recommends pre-empting fear-based reactions with more information about what is actually risky and what can be done about it.[47]

Referring to cancer, Ropeik remarked: "The nastier a way to die it is—the more painful, awful, and horrible—the more fear it evokes."[48]

Apparently the same is true for terrorism. After all, that's the point of terrorism: to evoke terror! And the purpose of evoking terror is to provoke a disproportionate reaction from the terrorists' opponents, thus damaging their image in the eyes of the people the terrorists want to support them and gaining new converts to the terrorists' cause. The terrorists' avowed political purposes, such as getting occupying troops out of certain territories, are seldom actually accomplished. For example, after decades of armed struggle, the Irish Revolutionary Army (IRA) finally disarmed in 2005, with the British government still in Northern Ireland. Nonetheless, terrorists are pretty good at producing terror and in provoking irrational reactions to it.

Corporations can produce the same kinds of problems for themselves. Their reaction to an unexpected risk can be to fire the employee involved or to sue the outsider who seems opposed. Such tactics can backfire, producing legal, financial, or reputational problems out of proportion to the perceived risk.

Maybe FDR was right when he said in his first inaugural address in 1933 during the Great Depression: "The only thing we have to fear is fear itself."

If we can manage fear, we can manage risk.

Notes

1. Bruce Schneier, *Secrets and Lies*. (Wiley Publishing, Inc., 2000).

2. Tsutomu Shimomura and John Markoff, *Takedown: The Pursuit and Capture of Kevin Mitnick, America's Most Wanted Computer Outlaw—By the Man Who Did It*. (New York: Hyperion Books, January 1996).

3. Kevin D. Mitnick, William L. Simon, and Steve Wozniak, *The Art of Deception: Controlling the Human Element of Security*. (Wiley Publishing, Inc., October 2003).

4. Kevin D. Mitnick and William L. Simon, *The Art of Intrusion: The Real Stories Behind the Exploits of Hackers, Intruders & Deceivers*. (Wiley Publishing, Inc., February 2005).

5. Bruce Sterling, *The Hacker Crackdown: Law And Disorder On The Electronic Frontier*. (New York: Bantam, November, 1993).

6. Eleanor Yang, "UCSD breach leaves 3,500 exposed," *Union-Tribune Staff Writer*. (January 18, 2005). `http://attrition.org/errata/dataloss/ucsd01.html`

7. "Data Theft Incident Response," *Data Theft and Identity Protection*, University of Texas at Austin (June 13, 2005). `www.utexas.edu/datatheft`

8. Matt Hines, "Laptop theft puts data of 98,000 at risk," *News.com* (CNET, 29 March 2005). `http://news.com.com/Laptop+theft+puts+data+of+98,000+at+risk/2100-1029_3-5645362.html`

9. "UC Berkeley police investigating theft of laptop containing grad student ID data," *UC Berkeley News*, University of California at Berkeley (March 28, 2005). `www.berkeley.edu/news/media/releases/2005/03/28_security.shtml`

10. Karen Kucher, "SDSU says computer server was infiltrated: Personal data at risk, thousands are warned," *Union-Tribune*. (March 17, 2004). `www.signonsandiego.com/news/computing/20040317-9999-news_7m17hacker.html`

11. Bob Metcalfe, "From the Ether," *InfoWorld.* (November 18, 1996). `www.infoworld.com/cgi-bin/displayNew.pl?/metcalfe/bm111896.htm`

12. Lauren Weinstein, Peter G. Neumann, and Dave Farber, *Preventing the Internet Meltdown*, PFIR, Furama Hotel, Los Angeles, CA (July 26–28 2004). `www.pfir.org/meltdown`

13. Op. Cit. Metcalfe, "From the Ether."

14. Op. Cit. Weinstein, et al., *Preventing the Meltdown.*

15. Op. Cit. Metcalfe, "From the Ether."

16. Op. Cit. Weinstein, et al., Preventing the Meltdown.

17. Scott Bradner, "The Net through doom colored glasses," Network World. (1996). `http://www2.sobco.com/nww/1996/metcaffe-debate.html`

18. Ibid.

19. Ibid.

20. Timothy L. O'Brien, "New kind of criminal is prowling the Web," The International Herald Tribune. (August 8, 2005). `www.iht.com/bin/print_ipub.php?file=/articles/2005/08/07/business/thugs.php`

21. "A price worth paying?" Economist. (The Economist Newspaper Limited, London, May 19, 2005), pp. 71–73. `www.economist.com/printedition/displaystory.cfm?story_id-3984019`

22. Byron Acohido and Jon Swartz, "Cybercrooks lure citizens into international crime," USA TODAY. (July 10, 2005). `www.usatoday.com/money/industries/technology/2005-07-10-cyber-mules-cover_x.htm`

23. Op. Cit. Timothy L. O'Brien, "New kind of criminal is prowling the Web."

24. Ibid.

25. Ibid.

26. Gregory M. Bednarski, Enumerating and Reducing the Threat of Transnational Cyber Extortion against Small and Medium Size Organizations, National Cyber Forensics and Training Alliance (2004). `www.ncfta.net/Articles/InformationWeek-CMU_Cyber_Extortion_Study.pdf`

27. John Leyden, "Mozilla to pay bounty on bugs," The Register (August 3, 2004). `www.theregister.co.uk/2004/08/03/mozilla_bug_bounty/`

28. Eugene H. Spafford, "The Internet Worm Program: An Analysis," Computer Communications Review (November 29, 1988). `ftp://coast.cs.purdue.edu/pub/doc/morris_worm`

29. Op. Cit. Kevin D. Mitnick and William L. Simon, "The Art of Intrusion: The Real Stories Behind the Exploits of Hackers, Intruders & Deceivers."

30. Mobile Pipeline Staff, "When Networking Wirelessly, Beware The Microwave," InformationWeek. (August 2, 2005). `www.informationweek.com/story/showArticle.jhtml?articleID=167100068`

31. Nicholas Weaver and Vern Paxson, "A Worst-Case Worm," The Third Annual Workshop on Economics and Information Security (WEIS04). (Digital Technology Center, University of Minnesota, May 13–14, 2004).

32. mi2g, "Silently preparing for the $100 billion cyber-catastrophe risk," News Alert. (mi2g, February 16, 2004). `http://mi2g.com/cgi/mi2g/frameset.php?pageid=http%3A//mi2g.com/cgi/mi2g/press/160204.php`

33. John S. Quarterman, "Monoculture Considered Harmful," First Monday, Vol. 7, No. 2. (February 2002). `www.firstmonday.dk/issues/issue7_2/quarterman`

34. Dan Geer, Rebecca Bace, Peter Gutmann, Perry Metzger, Charles P. Pfleeger, John S. Quarterman, and Bruce Schneier, CyberInsecurity: The Cost of Monopoly. (September 2003). `www.ccianet.org/filings/cybersecurity/cyberinsecurity.pdf`

35. David S. Quarterman, Personal recollections (2001).

36. G. A. Bieberdorf, History of the Distribution of the Mexican Cotton Boll Weevil in Oklahoma. (1926). `www.obweo.org/histmexbw.html`

37. Robert Lemos, "Cisco, ISS file suit against rogue researcher," SecurityFocus. (July 27, 2005). `http://online.securityfocus.com/news/11259`

38. J. H. Saltzer, D. P. Reed, and D. D. Clark, "End-to-End Arguments in System Design," Second International Conference on Distributed Computing Systems (April 1981), pp. 509–512. `http://web.mit.edu/Saltzer/www/publications/endtoend/endtoend.txt`

39. Keith C. Heidorn, Ph.D., "Weather Almanac for June 2003: The Worcester Tornado Of 1953." (June 1, 2003). `www.islandnet.com/~see/weather/almanac/arc2003/alm03jun.htm`

40. Ibid.

41. Ibid.

42. Ibid.

43. Bruce Sterling, "The World Is Becoming Uninsurable, Part 2," Viridian Note, 00022. `www.viridiandesign.org/notes/1-25/Note%2000022.txt`

44. Ibid.

45. Craig Lambert, "Society's Casino," Harvard Magazine. (July–August 2005). `www.harvard-magazine.com/on-line/070578.html`

46. Ibid.

47. David Ropeik and George Gray, *Risk: A Practical Guide for Deciding What's Really Safe and What's Really Dangerous in the World Around You.* (Houghton Mifflin, October 2002).

48. Ibid.

CHAPTER 3

Solutions and Providers

*. . . the more diverse and accurate the base information used to
generate a storm track, the greater the level of confidence
that can be ascribed to that particular track.*
—Al Sandrik

While SOX and other laws and regulations include many useful practices, they
do not begin to touch on many worthwhile and even basic Internet business risk
management practices. Some of these best practices, such as backups, redundancy, and diversity, are perhaps so obvious that they are seldom mentioned;
however, they are often overlooked in practice. Traditional Internet security is a
broad field with many vendors. The new (to the Internet) financial risk management strategies and reputation systems have few Internet vendors as of yet.

   This chapter discusses many existing solutions and names some prominent
vendors. Apologies to any vendors not named: there was no room to mention
everyone, and new vendors appear all the time. Most strategic discussion is
left to Chapter 4.

Resilience: Backups, Redundancy, and Diversity

Three solutions may seem so obvious that they're hardly considered security
solutions at all: backups, redundancy, and diversity. Yet they are security solutions, and some of the most important. They help prevent loss of data and loss
of connectivity, or isolation. These resilience solutions thus help prevent loss of
productivity by making it hard for any given attack, failure, or accident to
affect all parts of the business system.

If you want agriculture that won't fail when a single insect attacks it, you plant multiple crops rather than waiting until something attacks and then using pesticides. If you want a healthy child, you build up the child's immune system by exposure to childhood diseases rather than waiting until disease strikes in adulthood and then calling an ambulance. If you want a healthy society, you encourage diversity. And if you want a healthy computing environment for a company, you implement redundancy and diversity.

Backups: Copy It or Lose It

Everyone knows that backups are necessary to prevent loss of information in case of hardware or software failure. Thus, it would seem that everyone already implements regular backups with tested retrieval methods. In fact, this is not the case:

> Computer systems at 19 department sites that served agencies like the Transportation Security Administration, Customs and Border Protection and the Coast Guard had no functioning backups or relied on obviously deficient or incomplete backups, the report by the inspector general of the department said. Even the Federal Emergency Management Agency, which is in charge of disaster recovery, was unprepared, the report said.[1]

If even the U.S. Department of Homeland Security does not keep real backups in many cases, should we expect private industry to be any better? Experience indicates not.

When you do keep backups, try to keep them encrypted. Citigroup's CitiFinancial division, Time Warner, and Bank of America found out the hard way what criminals already know: corporations tend to back up valuable material, and they don't usually encrypt it. Those three corporations lost data on 6 million people in 2005.[2] Even the best backup software from the most reputable vendors can have bugs,[3] so keep your backup software patched just like you would your operating system. Also consider Bank of America's solution and eliminate backup tapes entirely by copying directly to disks. Remember to encrypt the disks and transmissions across the intervening network, of course.

Offline backups are a form of redundancy intended to prevent loss of data. Live, online backups can provide further redundancy.

Redundancy: Separate Power, Connectivity, and Geography

Live backups can provide redundant access to information in case of network connectivity failure or loss of the original location due to fire, theft, or other reason. Disks are cheap these days, and it's not difficult to keep live off-site backups. It's not much more difficult to keep data accessible via the Internet from multiple locations, especially with many hosting services and Content Delivery Services (CDN) such as Akamai to assist.

There is cost involved, which increases with amount of data, degree of redundancy, and speed of access. However, a certain amount of redundancy is necessary to connect to the Internet at all: every domain served by the Domain Name System (DNS) must have at least two DNS servers. DNS servers translate from the domain names that people see such as example.com to numeric Internet addresses such as 192.0.34.166 that Internet software and protocols use to connect across the Internet.

Those redundant DNS servers should be on separate networks, but this point has often been forgotten by even the biggest corporations until they have a network outage and nobody can even look up their address to try to connect. Microsoft had this problem, which *Network World* called a rookie mistake, in January 2001, making inaccessible all of Microsoft.com, MSN.com, Expedia .com, CarPoint.com, and Encarta.com.[4] If Microsoft can make this mistake, so can your company, so check for it. Remember that even if you don't check, anyone on the Internet can, using simple tools available on every operating system release, so someone else can embarrass your company by revealing its DNS servers are on the same network, or even by attacking that network in hopes of knocking the company off the Internet.

Any redundancy is better than none, and the cost of redundancy should be compared to potential risk of loss of business without redundancy. Multiple backups and multiple DNS servers should be basic features of any Internet business; multiple mail servers and multiple web servers should be basic features of any such business of any size.

Diversity: Differing Targets Are Harder to Hit

Yet even redundancy can be useless if all the redundant sites are implemented with the same software and configuration, making them all vulnerable to the same type of failure or attack. Even the best content-delivery services can have DNS failures. As Lydia Leong of Gartner has remarked: "I don't think this is any reason to get gun-shy with CDNs, but my advice to clients regardless of whether they outsource their DNS is that they should have a contingency plan."[5]

Keeping live servers (web, DNS, and so on) available in case the CDN fails isn't that hard to do, especially since the CDN has to draw its content from somewhere. Yet companies may be reluctant to think about such things, much less implement them.

If companies are reluctant to ensure DNS diversity, which is comparatively easy, they are even more reluctant to deal with operating system (OS) or web or mail server or client diversity. Web and mail clients, in particular, are often standardized across entire corporations in the name of ease of use. Companies often standardize on a single operating system to get the same mail and web clients plus spreadsheet and other common software.

The U.S. Army did that, standardizing on Windows, until their web server was vandalized. Then they switched to Apple Macintoshes.[6]

The U.S. Department of Homeland Security (DHS) chose Microsoft as its preferred supplier of desktop and server software in July 2003.[7] As one reporter remarked at the time: "Microsoft's selection for such a wide range of software products would seem to indicate that officials have found those brands are used and favored by the majority of security agencies."

If that is true, it would seem that the majority of security agencies may be unclear on the concept of software diversity for security.

The risk today is not just of web servers being vandalized. Risks include botnet software taking over computers with similar software throughout an entire enterprise.[8] In the face of such a risk, DHS's goal is flawed: "Their ultimate goal has been to select one company as the sole supplier in each of several technology categories, such as e-mail or desktop computers."

Such a goal is like attempting to supply the widest possible growing conditions for a new disease. Yet companies and government agencies continue to think this way. Note that the Army did not avoid monoculture by switching from Windows to Macs. Macs may be harder to crack, but they're still a monoculture if the entire organization uses them. Monoculture in the name of ease of use and administration is the game too many companies continue to play.

Recent peer-reviewed research demonstrates that even minimal diversity has immediate benefits, benefits that outweigh the inconvenience of having to manage multiple operating systems or other software.[9] It turns out that diversification in information systems actually reverses the expected risk. This is different from financial instrument diversification as in portfolio management, or pooling as in insurance, neither of which usually reverses the expected risk. In other words, computer network diversification has better effects than one might have expected from diversification in other fields. As the paper says:

> *Exploiting externalities unique to information systems, we show that diversification can not only reduce loss variance but also minimize expected loss.*[10]

The paper takes into account both positive effects of fewer exploits and negative effects of less ease of use and administration because of less uniformity. It takes into account benefits to the firm that implements diversity, and benefits to society.

The paper concludes that benefits of diversity accrue even if a firm adds only one piece of software to its incumbent monoculture software, even if the new software is used by only a minority of computers in the firm, and even if the new software is not as secure as the incumbent software.

Of course, if you are talking operating systems, any of the alternatives to the incumbent monopoly OS have greater security, as the paper demonstrates.

So, software diversity in information systems would be good even in a world of worse alternatives to incumbent software and is even better in our actual world. For more on this, see also the material on open software in Chapter 8.

Fortification: Security Solutions

Traditional Internet security solutions are mostly methods of fortification, trying to prevent compromise of data or denial-of-service attacks. Security merges with performance where degradation of service is treated as a security problem, and where compromise, denial, or degradation cannot be prevented, insurance starts to come in. See Table 3-1.

Security is a popular market populated by many companies. Few of them are working in security of the Internet itself, beyond the intranet, firewall, web server, and extranet. Table 3-2 categorizes product areas in more detail. Note that the last row of this table covers the same space as the previous table.

As you move from intranets into the Internet, the number of owners, users, and the size of the networks involved increases, so the complexity of the problem increases. As complexity increases, predictability using traditional solutions decreases. Detection, categorization, localization, and management of perils in the Internet will increase the predictability of problems in the Internet and enable better security and performance, plus insurance.

IDC predicts a $7 billion dollar market in network security by 2005. This is 45 percent of a $15.6 billion dollar IT security market, distinguished from encryption, access management, perimeter security, and antivirus software. Network security in this sense is currently provided by firms that do intrusion detection and prevention, as well as vulnerability assessment.

Table 3-1 Internet Security, Performance, and Insurance

PAIN	SOLUTION	PREVENTABILITY
Compromise of data	Encryption	High
Denial-of-service	Intrusion detection + prevention, Internet peril detection and risk management, insurance	Medium
Degradation of service	SLAs, dynamic rerouting, Internet peril detection and risk management, insurance	Low

Table 3-2 Network Security

NETWORK	OWNERS	USERS	TYPICAL PAIN	SOLUTION	PREDICTABILITY
Intranet	Single enterprise	Employees	Viruses, Trojans, human compromise	Infection scanners, authentication	High
Internal firewall	Single enterprise	Employees	Permeability	Authorization	High
Web server	Enterprise + hosting	Employees + customers	Viruses, Trojans	Intrusion detection + prevention	Medium
External firewall	Enterprise + hosting	Employees + customers	Permeability	Authorization	Medium
Extranet	Enterprise + ISP	Employees + customers	Viruses, Trojans, human compromise	Scanners, authentication, intrusion detection + prevention	Medium
Outside perimeter	Enterprise + hosting + ISP	Employees + customers	Permeability, denial-of-service	Certificates, intrusion detection + prevention	Medium
Internet	Many	Diverse	Compromise of data, denial-of-service, degradation of service	Encryption, intrusion detection + prevention, SLAs, dynamic rerouting, Internet peril detection and risk management, insurance	Low

Encryption: Make It Useless to Steal

Redundant live backups implemented on diverse platforms can still fail spectacularly if data is stolen en route among them. Here is where encryption shines: in transfer of information along insecure channels. There is always still risk of compromise of the encryption, whether by technical means, by brute-force key searching, or by human error or sabotage. Nonetheless, information transfer is less risky with encryption than without.

Encryption is often used at the single application level. For example, PostX applies encryption to electronic mail using a variety of techniques. This makes the mail unreadable by someone without an appropriate decryption key. Encryption does not address the delivery time nor the path taken by the mail during delivery.

I&AM: Identity and Access Management

Security companies that are working in security of the Internet proper tend to be working in Identity and Access Management (I&AM). Identity management includes creation of an identity, such as a username, assigning privileges to it, and provisioning it on various computers. Access management includes authentication (who is it?), authorization (what can they do?), and audit (who did what?).

Typically, this involves two parts, those being each end of a transaction. On the corporate end, it involves certificates for web page access, and on the user end it involves verifying that the person initiating the transaction is who he says he is. The certificate authentication is solved with products from companies like Verisign and IBM with its CyberSafe.

Many antispam companies are involved in authentication and authorization for spam prevention. Common techniques include using one of content filtering, source filtering or source authentication.

Firewalls: Perimeter Defense

Perhaps the most common Internet authentication solution is the *firewall*. This is a hardware device with software that attempts to stop attacks as they enter an enterprise. Firewalls are very common. There are philosophical arguments about whether they should be used at all, since they limit what legitimate users can do, as well. Most businesses choose to use them anyway. A bigger problem with firewalls is that they no longer stop large classes of attacks, because so many attacks now enter through ports for services such as those for web servers that almost every enterprise has turned on. There are so many firewall vendors that there is no point listing them here.

VPN: Virtual Private Network

Many companies have turned to *Virtual Private Networks (VPNs)* for trusted communications between offices or between traveling personnel such as sales people and the office. VPNs are attempts to extend external access to intranets that run inside corporations. Corporations used to do this by actually buying leased lines to run their own networks between offices, but nowadays VPNs over the Internet are much more cost-effective. VPNs involve encrypting traffic between locations. They require special software not only inside the office but also on each client computer. They also typically provide access to the entire corporate network.

SSL-VPN: Secure Socket Layer VPN

A more recent I&AM solution is SSL-VPN, which leverages encryption that everyone uses anyway in secure web transactions. While this requires encryption software on the client end, every user already has it in their web browser. Because SSL-VPN goes through a web browser on the server end, the web server can limit access to just parts of the server, and can also permit access to certain resources beyond the server. Thus, SSL-VPN access is more convenient than VPN and more granular, thus limiting potential security breaches.

The leader of the SSL-VPN pack is Juniper, with its Neoteris Netscreen product. Juniper bought Neoteris, which seems to be a common pattern in this space; there have been so many acquisitions in recent years that there is no space to list them all in this book. Other SSL-VPN players include Aventail's Netifice, Netilla, Array Networks (SPX3000), F5 (FirePass), Nokia (NSAS), Whale Communications (eGap), Nortel (Alteon SSL-VPN), Cisco (SSL-VPN), Symantec (SafeWeb), NetSilica (EPN), and Citrix (Net6).

FIM: Federated Identity Management

If you have reserved an airplane ticket and also gotten a rental car or hotel reservation through the same web pages, you've used Federated Identity Management (FIM). Users like it because it decreases the number of passwords they have to remember; this aspect of FIM is called Single Sign-On (SSO). FIM also may reduce other information such as credit card numbers users have to enter online; this is simplified identity management. FIM also promises easy access to related products and their vendors. Finally, FIM may reduce identity theft because there is less identity information passing over the Internet from the user, and one can hope the vendors deploying FIM are doing so in a secure manner. While firewalls, VPN, and SSL-VPN are primarily concerned with providing and limiting access to a server or an intranet, FIM is focused on access across autonomous domains and across traditional internetwork boundaries.

Businesses want FIM for their products because it promises seamless partnering, more customers, more transactions, less overhead, and less identity theft.

The leader of the I&AM market is Computer Associates with eTrust + Netegrity, which implement a form of FIM. Other players include Trustgenix (Netegrity), RSA, PingIdentity, Microsoft (Passport), Oracle (Oblix), HP (Baltimore, Trulogica), BMC (OpenNetwork), M-Tech, IBM, Novell, and Sun (Waveset). There is an academic open source FIM project called Shibboleth that many universities use.

Managed Security Monitoring (MSM)

When running some security products isn't enough, and you need expert professional services as well, that's Managed Security Monitoring (MSM).

- **Counterpane: Simplify Network Security Concerns**—Counterpane claims to be the world leader MSM, including intrusion detection at the perimeter and within the customer's network.

- **CyberTrust: Is My Business Infrastructure Secure?**—CyberTrust includes the long-lived TruSecure certification product. TruSecure attempted to associate cost with the Slammer worm.

- **ISS: Internet Security Systems**—ISS of Atlanta is a leader in intrusion detection services to the extent that Atlanta seems to be the place new Internet security companies locate by choice. With their X-Force MSM, ISS is looking at the entire Internet beyond direct attacks on specific enterprises.

- **SecureWorks: Intrusion Prevention**—SecureWorks is an Atlanta firm that provides intrusion prevention. They detect intrusions via signatures, like other companies such as ISS, then they block the specific attacking packets, letting other packets through the same ports. Intrusion prevention is good, but will not deal with lost or degraded service due to perils farther out in the Internet.

- **SAIC: Science Applications International Corporation**—SAIC is interested in Internet security and quality, including how they affect federal government services. SAIC is the service provider for FS/ISAC.

- **InternetPerils: Risks Outside the Firewall**—With the customer's assistance, InternetPerils can determine the most likely dangers that the enterprise faces, given the geographic distribution of its employees and customers, the location and vulnerability of its Internet nodes, and the way it moves and uses data. InternetPerils monitors the global situation and employs proprietary data-fusion, deep-analysis, and pattern-recognition techniques. Incorporating geographic and historical data and

understanding of the topology of the Internet, InternetPerils extrapo-
lates the current risk elements, to pinpoint and monitor sources of trouble that are specific to the enterprise, presenting relevant information
and data about the enterprise's Internet-related risks and their probabilities in tables, graphs, and animations for analysis and further action.

Internet Hardware Vendors

Many of the vendors of the routers and servers that run the Internet also sell
security solutions.

- **Juniper: SSL-VPN**—As previously mentioned, Juniper is the leader in
  the SSL-VPN I&AM space.
- **Cisco: All About Routers**—Cisco has intrusion detection and prevention services, but not Internet peril detection and aggregation.
- **Sun: Internet Server Security**—Sun is dominant in Internet servers and
  thus has a vested interest in Internet security and performance.

Security and Performance

Some companies are working across the artificial boundary between security
and performance.

- **Mazu Networks: Passive Traffic Profiling and Blocking**—Mazu Networks is a startup, cofounded by an MIT professor, that passively taps
  incoming traffic, profiles it to determine normal versus anomalous traffic, and blocks anomalous traffic. This is an interesting approach,
  although like all intrusion detection and prevention, it will not deal
  with lost or degraded service due to perils farther out in the Internet.
- **NetScaler: Scaling Enterprise Internet Services**—NetScaler was
  founded by some former Sun employees to provide application-level
  route optimization and intrusion detection as part of an appliance that
  is intended to permit scaling of enterprise Internet services. They cross
  the boundary between security and performance.

■ **InternetPerils: Control Your Internet Business Risk**—InternetPerils, Inc. provides quantification and visualization products to help insurers, financial institutions, banks, telecommunications providers, government, and enterprises manage their Internet business risks. It finds perils and anomalies in topology and performance data for the edges and interior of the Internet. It delivers through the web topological models of the Internet focused on areas of particular concern to the customer enterprise, mapped to indicate their location and vulnerability, with drilldown for specific information. A worm, for example, would primarily affect enterprise servers and nodes that are topologically nearby, but a cut cable can affect critical nodes deep in the Internet, and have a far wider effect. Understanding how close a peril lies to your enterprise, and what its potential is for disabling your communications, can be critically important in risk assessment and in planning for disaster recovery, customer communications, and other essential operations.

Security Summary

There are many more companies in the security space. The ones briefly described in the preceding sections are a selection of some of the biggest and some of the most innovative players. Few of them are working on aggregated detail of perils in the Internet.

Consider the example companies, along with some others, in the table categories, drawn this time as a figure, Figure 3-1.

Note that Figure 3-1 also includes performance, risk management, and insurance companies; thus, it serves as a summary of the entire market landscape.

As can be seen, there are many companies looking at various aspects of an enterprise's security. Yet if a company cannot reach its customers and its customers cannot reach it easily and with alacrity, business and income are lost as surely as if there were a physical break-in or a loss of intellectual property. Problems on the Internet can affect traffic that appears to be confined to other portions of the network. Businesses need to be as aware of perils on the Internet as of theft or natural disaster.

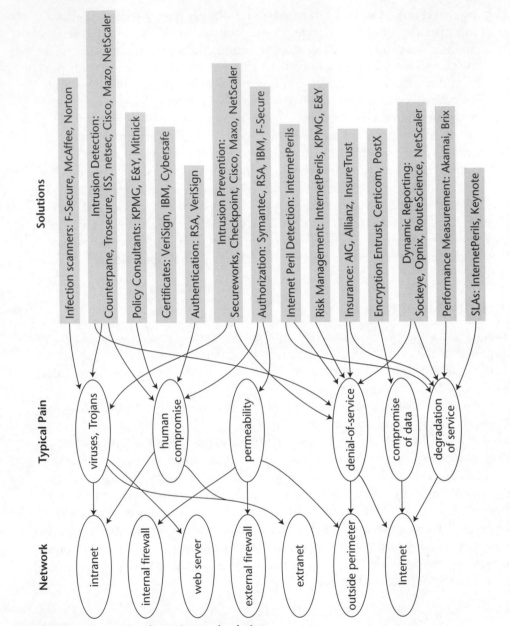

Figure 3-1:   Networks, pains, and solutions

Observation and Orientation: Performance Solutions

Knowledge is power, and observation of Internet performance can help one route around problems, deploy for redundant routes, and tell what failed, and when, where, and who was responsible. It may seem that Internet performance companies would in general be looking at performance of the Internet core, but in practice this is not the case.

For performance to be of real use, it is not enough to measure a few times. Ongoing measurements are needed to show baselines, anomalies, trends, and patterns. The scientist who discovered global warming, Dr. Charles D. Keeling, almost wasn't funded to continue climate measurements.[11] If he hadn't been persistent and gotten funded, we would have had even less warning than we do about one of the most far-reaching risks we all face. Internet performance is no different.

Performance Measurement

A few Internet performance measurement companies are looking at the interior of the Internet: InternetPerils, Akamai, and Brix. Akamai seems very focused on its core business of web server caching, and Brix requires placing devices to see near and between them.

Two other companies could, with significant effort, look at the core: Mercury Interactive and Keynote. Currently, they examine the Internet in an end-to-end fashion, not scrutinizing the interior of the Internet. Specific perils are, thus, not visible.

Route Optimization

At least two route optimization companies look at the interior of the Internet beyond paths directly leading to their customers: Sockeye and Opnix. A third one that could be of interest is RouteScience.

SLA: Service Level Agreements

Most ISPs these days have Service Level Agreements (SLAs). They mostly authenticate them themselves, which leads to a certain amount of skepticism on the part of customers, as is discussed in Chapter 8. Keynote has the highest profile in SLA measurement.

Internet Risk Assessment and Management

Risk management in general goes beyond technical solutions, resilience, and fortification. It also requires processes and procedures involving people.

- **Counterpane:** Counterpane has long included a professional services component in its offerings.

- **KPMG:** KPMG appears to be active in Internet Risk Management, judging by some documents from KPMG Slovakia. These documents regard Internet risk management as a combination of Internet security analysis, web risk management benchmarking, and Internet security policy development. Internet security analysis in this context seems to be defined from the point of view of penetration threats. Internet perils farther out from the enterprise do not seem to be addressed. KPMG Hungary has a list of engagements in various countries.

- **Ernst & Young:** Ernst & Young also does Internet risk assessment and management.

Decentralized Collective Action As Internet Management

Miscreants take advantage of the reach and power of the Internet to cause widespread damage. Legitimate users don't need to change the decentralized architecture of the Internet to respond with collective action. Aggregate damage demands collective action. Collective action is more of a social, political, and business question than a technical question. The decentralized reach of the Internet can be used to mobilize many eyes on problems and many resources to examine them.

Recall Bob Metcalfe's question from 1996: "Where are circuits inventoried, traffic forecasts consolidated, outages reported, upgrades analyzed and coordinated?"[12]

Metcalfe seemed to think that centralized management was necessary to produce such results. But centralization actually isn't needed to produce an organized process management of Internet operations.

Open Decentralization Is Strength, Not Weakness

As mentioned in the previous chapter, various centralizers have been proposed for the Internet, ranging from telephone companies to the UN and the ITU. Maybe they're all trying to solve the wrong problem. Bob Metcalfe sometimes said the Internet needs to be run like AOL. Maybe that's not what it needs. Maybe what the Internet needs is more cooperative decentralization, and new means to achieve it.

Metcalfe was right that the Internet is not a living system.[13] However, it is a scale-free network, which means it shares many properties with living systems. Scale-free networks emerge best without centralized control.[14] New connections get added as users need them. And they get infections that can be modeled and treated very much like those of living organisms.[15]

To quote David Weinberger, we have learned at least three things from the Internet:

> (a) Open standards work. Rather than building a network that connects A to B to C by touching copper to copper, the creators of the Internet built a network by establishing standards for how information is to be moved. It is because the Internet was not built as a thing that it has been able to bring the world many orders of magnitude more bandwidth than any previous network. . . .[16]

In other words, open standards may not be living things, but they do enable organic growth that resembles the way living things grow. Some closed standards, such as the Xerox XNS protocols or DEC's DECNET protocols, were about as capable as the Internet's TCP/IP standards, but only TCP/IP's standards and protocols were fully open, available to anyone who wanted to use them, produced by a process that invited participation from anywhere in the world and by anyone regardless of institutional affiliation, and with an early readily available reference implementation in Berkeley Unix.[17] For more about open standards and security, see Chapter 8.

> (b) Decentralization works. Keep the architecture clean and simple. Put the smarts in the devices communicating across the network rather than in centralized computers. In fact, central control and regulation would have kept the Internet from becoming the force that it has.[18]

To be specific, if the Internet had been centrally run, we never would have gotten electronic mailing lists (which first appeared for discussions about futurism and science fiction), anonymous FTP, the World Wide Web (WWW), point-to-point (P2P) file-sharing protocols such as BitTorrent, or numerous other protocols and applications that were authorized by no centralized authority and that probably would have been prevented by such an authority had it existed. We know this is true because none of those named items developed on centralized networks of the same time period, such as CompuServe, Prodigy, and Minitel. We almost certainly wouldn't have the Apache web server or the Linux operating system. We probably wouldn't even have the Domain Name System (DNS); we'd probably still be using a centralized host table that would require every host to be registered with a centralized authority.

(c) Lowering the cost of access and connection unleashes innovation beyond any reasonable expectation.[19]

This point has a corollary that ISPs competed each other into bankruptcy on price, because they weren't competing on the internals of the network, and they had no value-added services to sell; Scott Bradner has frequently mentioned this point. However, the same forces that caused that shakeout of ISPs can also produce new value-added services that will give ISPs a business model; see Chapter 9.

Meanwhile, don't throw the baby out with the bathwater. Decentralization is not a flaw of the Internet; it is one of the basic features that makes it work.

There are clearinghouses for security vulnerabilities and exploits, such as CERT and SANS. Some of them address specific industries, such as the ISACs.

Internet Research

Various U.S. federal agencies, including the National Institute of Standards and Technology (NIST) and the Department of Homeland Security (DHS) fund a variety of Internet security research projects. The National Science Foundation (NSF) has a Cyber Trust program that has granted at least $30 million to dozens of projects.[20] Here are a few of the highest profile projects; ones that enterprises concerned with security are likely to encounter. Apologies to any other projects that are not named.

DETER: Cyber Defense Technology Experimental Research

NSF has funded a digital simulation testbed called DETER:

. . . the digital model for the study of online attacks will be built by researchers at the University of California at Berkeley and the Los Angeles-based University of Southern California.[21]

Simulations are good; however, observation and examination of real perils and anomalies in the wild are also necessary. For example, laboratory simulations of the boll weevil never would have contained it without observations of its actual spread.

CIED: Center for Internet Epidemiology and Defenses

Vern Paxson has for years been calling for an Internet equivalent of the Centers for Disease Control (CDC), and in 2004 the NSF funded him to start one:

The CIED, led by Stefan Savage of the University of California at San Diego and Vern Paxson, a fellow principal investigator at the International Computer

Science Institute of the University of California at Berkeley, will receive $6.2 million from the NSF. The center will study ways to quickly analyze self-propagating programs and to develop techniques for stopping outbreaks before they spread worldwide.[22]

Paxson says CIED will be looking for ways to produce more general immunity than the case-by-case methods of most Internet security.

In addition to the NSF's funding, CIED will also receive support from Microsoft, Intel and Hewlett-Packard, as well as from UCSD's Center for Networked Systems, a recently-created $10 million research center funded by AT&T, Alcatel, Hewlett Packard and QUALCOMM.[23]

So, CIED is a public-private partnership; this kind of cooperation is part of the collective action the Internet needs to deal with aggregate damage. I would guess they (and probably others of these research projects) would be open to further funding from the private sector.

STIM: The Security through Interaction Modeling Center

While CIED appears to be aimed at software vulnerabilities and exploits, another NSF-funded effort, STIM, aims to categorize interactions inside the Internet:

The STIM Center, led by Mike Reiter of Carnegie Mellon University, will receive almost $6.4 million in funding from the NSF. The center will classify "healthy" network interactions to determine how to distinguish attacks and will study the interplay between different "species" of applications, such as e-mail and peer-to-peer networks.[24]

It will be interesting to see what STIM produces.

DNS-OARC: Domain Name System Operations, Analysis, and Research Center

DNS-OARC coordinates activities related to operations of the Domain Name System (DNS).

The 13 root DNS servers that do lookups for top-level domains, and the 13 top-level domain (TLD) DNS servers that do lookups for subdomains under TLDs, such as COM, EDU, NET, UK, FR, DE, JP, and the like, are mostly run by volunteer organizations, some for-profit, some nonprofit. In recent years, copies of the root DNS servers have been promulgated by further volunteers in countries around the world, responding to local DNS queries without having to traverse continents and oceans. While the original 13 root DNS servers are relatively widely distributed geographically and topologically, during

9/11 that distribution proved not to be accurate, because South Africa was cut off from root DNS service. That kind of problem should be much less likely to recur now. DNS-OARC helps coordinate such distribution work.

DNS-OARC has five key functions: incident response, operational characterization, testing, analysis, and outreach. In 2004, a year after its formation, DNS-OARC received a grant of $2.38 million from NSF, facilitated by CAIDA. This grant led to the first DNS-OARC meeting, which has been followed by another and appears likely to become a regular event. Members now include a broad range of participants from academia, nonprofits, industry, and government. Numerous preexisting DNS-related projects are now interacting more than before. For example, results of testing can now more easily reach large corporations, where many name servers that need upgrades of software or configuration reside.

CAIDA: Cooperative Association for Internet Data Analysis

CAIDA "provides tools and analyses promoting the engineering and maintenance of a robust, scalable global Internet infrastructure." CAIDA has for many years been a favorite of NSF for funding of Internet research tool projects. Its skitter diagram is very high profile; it shows interconnections among Internet Autonomous Systems (AS), which are groups of networks that are treated similarly for routing purposes. CAIDA organizes and participates in many workshops and conferences.

Clearinghouses

Various organizations serve as clearinghouses for incident reports and other security information.

CERT: Computer Emergency Response Team

CERT, begun in 1988 in response to the Morris Worm, is one of the most venerable organizations related to Internet security. It provides security alerts, keeps archives of past incidents, publishes papers about related topics, and gives seminars. It is housed at Carnegie Mellon University's Software Engineering Institute, which is federally funded. If we didn't have a CERT, we'd have to invent one, and that is precisely how CERT came to be. There are other emergency response organizations in various U.S. federal agencies and in other countries, but CERT is the archetype of such organizations.

US-CERT: United States Computer Emergency Response Team

US-CERT was established in 2003 as part of the U.S. Department of Homeland Security (DHS) as a public-private partnership. It distributes reports from

CERT and other organizations to the public and provides a way to contact the U.S. government about computer security incidents.

SANS: SysAdmin, Audit, Network, Security

SANS is a private organization providing information security training and certification; it claims to be the largest organization in the world providing such functions. SANS began in 1989, making it almost as old as CERT. SAS holds frequent for-pay tutorials in numerous locations and makes available a very large collection of security research documents. It provides a weekly vulnerability digest and a weekly news digest, plus an early warning system called the Internet Storm Center. Security professionals of all kinds are participants in SANS activities, from government, industry, and academia. So far as I know, SANS does not receive government funding and is an interesting example of how good coordination and reputation work can be funded by proceeds of the work itself.

NCFTA: National Cyber-Forensics & Training Alliance

This organization says it is an alliance of subject matter experts on Internet forensics from government, academia, and industry. It publishes some good papers.

InfraGard: Guarding the Nation's Infrastructure

InfraGard is a U.S Federal Bureau of Investigation (FBI) project for sharing security information among affected parties. It is organized around local FBI offices and has local and national conferences. Joining requires a background check, and online and meeting communications are confidential. Interestingly, InfraGard is not a result of DHS organization; it began in the local FBI Cleveland Field Office in 1996. As such, InfraGard is an interesting example of bottom-up emergent behavior in a government agency. One of its main benefits is that participants will discuss things that they would not say in a public forum.

EFF: Electronic Frontier Foundation

This is a nonprofit group concerned with civil liberties. Even if you think your business doesn't need EFF to defend it, reading up on the issues EFF addresses could help you avoid actions you weren't aware could be illegal. Even though civil liberties are often left off the agenda at business meetings, one of the best ways to damage a corporate reputation is to infringe on them, even inadvertently. Keeping up with EFF can help keep your company out of trouble.

Others

There are many other organizations that deal with various aspects of security, far too many to list here. Look on the web pages of some of the above organizations for further lists.

Anti-Exploit Groups

Some clearinghouses for vulnerabilities and exploits are organized around specific exploits.

Phishing

A promising avenue recently opened is the phishing repository project of the Anti-Phishing Working Group (APWG), www.antiphishing.org. The APWG repository collects reports from its many members of phishing mail messages and catalogs them in a database. This database provides raw material that can be used to demonstrate aggregate damage. Such material can be used in constructing evidence about compromised ISPs. It can even help with reputation systems, in which information about targets of phishing and compromised ISPs is made public so that customers of financial institutions can see which ones are being targeted and which ones are taking action against phishing, as well as which ISPs are compromised and which ones have done something about it.

Commercial Clearinghouses

Various commercial companies also operate in this space, such as Internet Security Systems (ISS) and InternetPerils. This all needs to be taken still further, to produce what the U.S. National Strategy to Secure Cyberspace called a holistic and synoptic view of cyberspace.[25] In other words, use many eyes to get the big picture and zoom in on problems related to specific stakeholders.

Beyond Protocols

Note that these organizations go beyond managing ISPs and Internet protocols. They also attempt to manage software and hardware vulnerabilities in servers and clients that are not owned or operated by ISPs, and they attempt to deal with business, social, and legal problems such as phishing, that aren't really even technical problems.

   This is a different approach from the old one of the FCC requiring telephone companies to report outages. Instead of trying to force ISPs to report information they are reluctant to reveal in public because it might make them look bad, third parties can discover important topological, performance, and vulnerability information and report it independently. Such a method produces a reputation system that draws ISPs in, rather than coercing them. Meanwhile, it does not depend on the ISPs to report on themselves; it gets independent outside views. And, even more important, it gets information that goes beyond what ISPs could provide. The result should actually be better than a centralized management system.

Hurricane History

The Galveston Hurricane of October 2, 1867 caused $1 million in damage ($12.3 million in today's dollars, or the equivalent of $1.3 billion in share of GDP). Also on the same day of the year, the Louisiana Delta hurricane of 1893 had winds of 100 miles per hour and a 12-foot storm surge that killed 1500 people. In 1882 on the same day a severe windstorm in northern California and Oregon did severe crop damage and blew down trees.

How do we (or, in this case, Intellicast)[26] know all this?

Take a look at the fourth major hurricane of this date: the one that struck the Georgia coast in 1898, washing away an entire island, Campbell Island, and killing 50 residents there, as well as all but one of the residents of St. Catherine's Island. The storm surge at Brunswick was estimated at 19 feet.

Worthy of note is the brief period of time which has seen the widespread deployment of remote sensing systems, which may accurately place the center of a landfalling storm in data sparse or lightly populated coastal regions.[27]

The relevant data was re-examined in 1998 by Al Sandrik, who provides a convenient table, which you can reference through the URL in the Note at the end of the chapter:

Technical Advances in systems for observing tropical cyclones, 1871 through 1980[28]

That table contains a significant overview of the history of a type of weather observation. Here are high points from that table. In 1898, there was some sort of Hurricane Watch Service; they had landline telegraph, and historians have access to ship's logs. Ships didn't get wireless telegraph until 1905, so ship's logs were no use to people on shore at the time.

Sandrik mines newspaper reports, personal letters, and measurements of buildings that are still standing, as well as finding some oaks that were blown down but still growing, providing wind direction at that point. With all this data he concludes that the wind only blew west north of Camden County (the Georgia coastal county just north of Florida), while it reversed and blew east there. So, the hurricane's eye had to have come ashore in Camden County, not

30 miles farther north as previously thought. Also, this was at least a category 3 hurricane, maybe 4, not a category 2 as previously thought.

He compares records for other hurricanes earlier and later, and concurs with another researcher that for nineteenth century hurricanes:

> *. . . the apparent low frequency on the Gulf coast between Cedar Key and St. Marks is not believed to be real. This area is very sparsely settled and the exact point where many of the storm centers reached the coast is not known, so there has been a natural tendency to place the track too close to the nearest observing point.*[29]

In other words, nineteenth century hurricanes were more common in places that were then sparsely populated but now are beach resorts. This has consequences for disaster planning. Not only that, but nineteenth century hurricanes were more severe than previously thought, which means that twentieth century expectations of hurricane severity in the U.S. southeast may have been too rosy (this is why the recent spate of hurricanes can't be used as evidence of global warming, although there are plenty of other pieces of evidence for that). Understanding the past has value for risk planning.

We don't have to do all this forensic research and statistical interpolation for modern hurricanes, because we never miss seeing one anymore, nor its track or intensity. This is because we have better means of observation and coordination.

A radiosonde network (weather balloons) was added in the late 1930s, and organized reconnaissance (hurricane chasing airplanes) in the 1940s. To draw an Internet analogy, if ship logs were somewhat like web server logs, weather balloons are perhaps like web monitoring companies.

The satellites and radar we are all used to seeing on TV and the Internet all date from the 1960s and later. The Internet analogy is what InternetPerils is doing regarding a holistic and synoptic view of the Internet.

Aircraft satellite data links were added in the late 1970s—sort of flying ship's log links. Ocean buoys were added about 1973; these are perhaps like honeypots and blacknets.

As Sandrik remarks, ". . . the more diverse and accurate the base information used to generate a storm track, the greater the level of confidence that can be ascribed to that particular track."[30]

This is why multiple sources of different types of data such as that collected by the DNS-OARC participants are important, as is the coordination being attempted by that body. We need both sensing buoys in the ocean of the Internet and ship, radar, aircraft, and satellite reconnaissance, with networks of coordination and display among them. Clearinghouse organizations such as CERT and SANS and the ISACs, help coordinate such information. The solution is neither a single source of information nor a single coordinator. More information is needed, from more sources, with more coordinators.

Hurricane Ivan Disconnects the Cayman Islands

On September 12, 2004, Hurricane Ivan damaged the undersea cable that connects the Cayman Islands to Florida, disconnecting Cable & Wireless' Internet connection to the Caymans.

Despite early news saying that Jamaica was also cut off, observations show Jamaica was connected all day. This is because the Jamaican node was on a different ISP and apparently a different undersea connection.

Observing the Internet directly can provide more information about some things than you will gather by asking ISPs one by one. Such information should be calibrated by information from the ISPs themselves; for example, Cable & Wireless says that their connection to the Caymans was back up within a day even though the central bank of the Caymans was not responding for 2 days.

Risk Transfer: Internet Insurance

What do we do about complicated attacks such as scob, for which there was no patch? Certainly we need to do all the usual things: apply patches, run firewalls, install intrusion detection, educate users, system administrators, and software vendors, plus some new things, such as software diversity, and competition on security. This is all due diligence and best practices.

But many users and companies won't do these things, because people tend to pay attention to security only when they suffer direct damage, and most people didn't this time. So, no matter how diligent you and your company are, the next attacks may still affect you because someone else was not so diligent.

You can have all the nonflammable insulation and sprinkler systems you like, and your office can still burn down in a wildfire, or your telephone or the power can go out due to a tornado or a system overload, all of which are beyond your control.

The time to buy insurance is before the building burns down.

Several companies offer business risk insurance, such as American Family Insurance, Farmers, Federal (Chubb), Kemper, Mutual of Omaha, and Nationwide. Those companies do not, however, offer Internet insurance.

I know of three companies offering Internet insurance products.

InsureTrust

InsureTrust is private, started in 1997, based in Atlanta, partnered with ISS and BMC. They deal mostly with intranets and with Internet connections. Their target customers are enterprises with less than $10 million/year. They're a managing general agency that does everything from underwriting to technical security, getting paid both for the insurance policy and for assessments.

AIG

American International Group (AIG) offers NetAdvantage. AIG says they will sell Internet insurance to any size company, and it seems generally accepted in the insurance industry that AIG has about 70 percent of the market. It appears that AIG does not examine perils beyond the firewall.

SafeOnline

This company, located a brief walk from Lloyd's in London, is starting to offer innovative insurance products. It even offers insurance forms online, something that other insurance companies usually (and surprisingly) still do not do.

Electronic Crime

As mentioned in the previous chapter, Internet attacks are no longer perpetrated primarily by script kiddies: It's criminals now.

Spam as Felony

At least one survey indicates that the great majority of spam as of August 2004 was perpetrated by a few hundred people, mostly located in the United States.[31] One group claims to know their names and has a list on the web.[32] This presents an opportunity for legal solutions to spam.

Legal solutions are sometimes preferable to the alternative. Consider what happened to one of Russia's biggest spammers:

> *Vardan Kushnir, notorious for sending spam to each and every citizen of Russia who appeared to have an e-mail, was found dead in his Moscow apartment on Sunday, Interfax reported Monday. He died after suffering repeated blows to the head.*[33]

Russia lacked laws against spam:

> *Under Russian law, spamming is not considered illegal, although lawmakers are working on legal projects that could protect Russian Internet users like they do in Europe and the U.S.*[34]

Government can successfully prosecute spammers, as illustrated by the case of Jeremy Jaynes, held on $1 million bond,[35] and sentenced under the new Virginia Computer Crimes Act[36] to a 9-year jail sentence.[37] He was alleged to have gained as much as $24 million in fraudulent assets through spamming,[38] not to mention all the resources of users, systems administrators, ISPs, and other organizations that he wasted, sending as many as 1.5 million mail messages on a single day. This was the first-ever U.S. felony conviction of a spammer, and one can only hope not the last.

For more about legal solutions and government, see Chapter 10.

Phishing and Spyware

New laws have recently been passed against phishing, and there are, as of this writing, bills in progress against spyware. Both the direct and indirect approaches of these bills have pros and cons. Meanwhile, industry, individuals, and other targets and marks need to deal with these problems. Collective action through organizations such as APWG, can help. Better observation, analysis, and reporting methods will also help.

Theft and Blackmail

In the MicroPatent case mentioned in the previous chapter, the company hired an ex-CIA profiler to help track down the perpetrator.[39] The perpetrator was sending messages from a wireless Internet connection while sitting in his car. Being able to determine the location of such transmissions would be quite useful in such cases. Such a solution presents many difficulties. For example, privacy: How do you tap such transmissions without interfering with other people's privacy or trespassing on their networks or premises? A bigger practical problem is if such a perpetrator moves around, sending from multiple different locations, then even if you could compel wireless operators in locations from Starbucks to houses to cooperate or sniff their networks anyway, you'd have a hard time getting physical access to all of them. A way is needed to determine who is sending from where in such cases without having physical access to the sending networks. That in turn presents problems of anonymity; anonymity has uses such as posting unpopular political opinions and whistle blowing that it would be best not to compromise. So, a technique needs to be found that walks through this minefield of complications and finds criminal perpetrators.

From Prevention to Management

Currently available solutions mostly deal with prevention, and mostly by resilience (redundancy and diversity) or fortification (encryption, firewalls, detection, etc.). There are some observation and orientation (mostly performance solutions), but there needs to be more. Prevention is good, but crisis management is also needed. Some traditional solutions extend into technical crisis management, but a business risk management plan must also include business procedures in case of crisis. Since it is not possible to prevent or ameliorate all risks of doing business on the Internet, it is necessary to include risk transfer instruments in a complete Internet business risk management plan. The next chapter is about constructing a risk management strategy.

Notes

1. Eric Lipton, "Audit Finds Security Dept. Is Lacking Disaster Backups," *New York Times.* (June 9, 2005). `http://query.nytimes.com/gst/abstract.html?res=FB0F14FA3B5C0C7A8CDDAF0894DD404482`

2. Jon Swartz, "Data losses push businesses to encrypt backup tapes," *USA Today.* (June 13, 2005). `www.usatoday.com/tech/news/2005-06-13-encrypt-usat_x.htm`

3. SANS, *Security Experts Issue Update (Quarter 2, 2005) Of SANS Top 20 Most Critical Internet Vulnerabilities List.* (SANS, July 25, 2005). `www.sans.org/press/q2-2005update_release.php`

4. "Microsoft's DNS eggs all in one basket," *Network World.* (January 24, 2001). `www.itworld.com/Net/3404/NWW0124msdns`

5. Jennifer Mears, "Akamai attack underscores DNS risks," *Network World.* (June 28, 2004). `www.networkworld.com/news/2004/062804akamaifolo.html`

6. Adam C. Engst, "U.S. Army Moves to Mac OS-based WebSTAR," *Tidbits.com.* (September 13, 1999). `http://db.tidbits.com/getbits.acgi?tbart=05552`

7. Shane Harris, "Microsoft chosen as exclusive Homeland Security contractor," *govexec.com.* (July 15, 2003). `www.govexec.com/dailyfed/0703/071503h2.htm`

8. Brian Krebs, "Hackers Embrace P2P Concept: Experts Fear 'Phatbot' Trojan Could Lead to New Wave of Spam or Denial-of-Service Attacks," *washingtonpost.com.* (March 17, 2004). `www.washingtonpost.com/wp-dyn/articles/A444-2004Mar17.html`

9. Pei-yu Chen, Gaurav Kataria, and Ramayya Krishnan, *Software Diversity for Information Security,* Fourth Workshop on the Economics of Information Security. (Kennedy School of Government, Harvard University, Cambridge, MA, 2–3 June 2005). `http://infosecon.net/workshop/pdf/47.pdf`

10. Ibid.

11. Kenneth Chang, "Charles D. Keeling, 77, Dies; Raised Global Warming Issue," *New York Times.* (June 23, 2005), Section C, Page 20, Column 1. www.nytimes.com/2005/06/23/science/23keeling.html

12. Bob Metcalfe, "From the Ether," *InfoWorld.* (November 18, 1996). www.infoworld.com/cgi-bin/displayNew.pl?/metcalfe/bm111896.htm

13. Ibid.

14. Steven Johnson, *Emergence: The Connected Lives of Ants, Brains, Cities, and Software.* (New York, Scribner, September 10, 2002).

15. "A Conversation with Peter Tippett and Steven Hofmeyr," *ACM Queue,* Volume 3, Number 5. (June 2005). www.acmqueue.org/modules.php?name=Content&pa=showpage d=314

16. David Weinberger, *Why Open Spectrum Matters: The End of the Broadcast Nation.* (January 21, 2003). www.greaterdemocracy.org/framing_openspectrum.html

17. Samuel J. Leffler, Marshall Kirk McKusick, Michael J. Karels, and John S. Quarterman, *The Design and Implementation of the 4.3BSD UNIX Operating System.* (Reading, MA: Addison-Wesley, 1989).

18. Op. cit. Johnson, *Emergence.*

19. Ibid.

20. Robert Lemos, "Schools to make model Net, then break it," *News.com,* (CNET, October 15, 2003). http://news.com.com/Schools+to+make+model+Net%2C+then+break+it/2100-7349_3-5092048.html?tag=nl

21. Ibid.

22. Robert Lemos, "Academics get NSF grant for Net security centers," *News.com.* (CNET, September 21, 2004). http://news.com.com/National+science+group+creates+Net+security+centers/2100-7348_3-5376474.html

23. "California Scientists Wage Joint War on Internet Plagues," *SDSC Press Release.* (San Diego Supercomputer Center, September 22, 2004). www.sdsc.edu/Press/2004/09/092204_Internet.html

24. Op. cit. Lemos, "Academics get NSF grant for Net security centers."

25. *National Strategy to Secure Cyberspace.* (U.S. Department of Homeland Security, February 2003). www.whitehouse.gov/pcipb

26. "Weather History," *Intellicast,* Intellicast.com. www.intellicast.com/Almanac/SouthCentral/October

27. Al Sandrik, Lead Forecaster, *A Reevaluation of the Georgia and Northeast Florida Hurricane of 2 October 1898 Using Historical Resources,* (National Weather Service Office, Jacksonville, Florida, October 8, 1998). `www.srh.noaa.gov/jax/research/hurricanes/history/1898`

28. Al Sandrik, Lead Forecaster, *Technical Advances in systems for observing tropical cyclones, 1871 through 1980.* (National Weather Service Office, Jacksonville, Florida, October 8, 1998). `www.srh.noaa.gov/jax/research/hurricanes/history/1898/fig1.html`

29. Op. Cit. Sandrik, *A Reevaluation of the Georgia and Northeast Florida Hurricane of 2 October 1898.*

30. Ibid.

31. Gregg Keizer, "Spam: Born in the USA," *TechWeb News,* Information-Week. (August 12, 2004). `www.informationweek.com/story/showArticle.jhtml?articleID=28700163`

32. Spamhaus Project, *Register of Known Spam Operations.* `www.spamhaus.org/rokso`

33. MosNews, "Russia's Biggest Spammer Brutally Murdered in Apartment," *MosNews.* (July 25, 2005). `http://mosnews.com/news/2005/07/25/spammerdead.shtml`

34. Ibid.

35. Stefanie Olsen, "$1 million bond set for alleged spammer's freedom," *News.com,* (CNET, November 9, 2004). `http://news.com.com/$1+million+bond+set+for+alleged+spammer's+freedom/2100-1028_3-5445486.html`

36. Todd R. Weiss, "New Law Makes Spam a Felony," *Computerworld.* (April 30, 2003). `www.pcworld.com/news/article/0,aid,110524,00.asp`

37. Linda Rosencrance, "Spammer Sentenced to Nine Years in Jail," *Computerworld.* (November 5, 2004). `www.pcworld.com/news/article/0,aid,118493,00.asp`

38. Op. cit. Olsen "$1 million bond set for alleged spammer's freedom."

39. Timothy L. O'Brien, 'New kind of criminal is prowling the Web," *The International Herald Tribune* (August 8, 2005). `www.iht.com/bin/print_ipub.php?file=/articles/2005/08/07/business/thugs.php`

CHAPTER 4

Strategies for Affected Verticals

. . . a catalyst or beacon around which to evolve those qualities that permit a collective entity or organic whole to improve its stature in the scheme of things.
—John R. Boyd

Complying with SOX, GLBA, and HIPAA, or PIPEDA or DPD, isn't enough for a risk management strategy. An Internet business risk management plan should include prevention solutions drawn from those discussed in the previous chapter, plus crisis management, and risk management, including risk transfer instruments. Appropriate plans will vary per industry and enterprise according to assets needing protection, risks to them, and resources available. Specific risks and solutions have already been discussed in the previous two chapters.

This chapter is about constructing such a strategy for risk management. It can be thought of as an executive summary of the rest of the book, which is about applications of the solutions. The chapter concludes with some discussions of how the structure of the Internet and some of its groups of users affects strategies that work, and some material on how an enterprise can fail like a country can collapse or succeed by coming to grips with the risks of Internet commerce.

Strategies

Some strategies are applicable to many different affected parties, yet are often overlooked.

Financial Instruments

The financial strategies available to most companies are self-insure or insure. Self-insurance is what companies that don't buy insurance are doing by default, whether they realize it or not. Some companies, especially banks, consciously self-insure and go to great lengths to quantify exactly how much capital they need to withhold to do that. The size of the risks of using the Internet indicate that most companies can't really afford to self-insure.

Don't depend on your existing traditional insurance policies to cover risks of doing business over the Internet. Many policies explicitly exclude such risks, and legal precedents indicate that even policies without such exclusions may be hard to use to collect.

Cyber-insurance of several kinds is currently available from a few insurers. The more companies that demand it, the more it will be available and the better it will be in price and coverage.

Insurers themselves need catastrophe bonds to provide the financial depth necessary to cover insurance policies in case of the kind of massive global aggregation that can occur on the Internet. A few of the largest enterprises may want to issue their own bonds. And certain types of enterprises, such as ISPs, may want to buy performance bonds.

Reputation Systems

According to PriceWaterhouseCoopers and the Economist Intelligence Unit in 2004, quantifying credit market, regulatory, and even IT risk isn't enough: "But what about those areas, like reputational risk, that are both harder to measure and more sudden and severe in their impact?"[1]

According to the report, which is based on a survey, while the internal corporate profile of risk management has increased in recent years, this has been not so much because of proactive measures as reaction to outside pressures from regulators and rating agencies. It seems most companies still see risk management as a relatively low-level activity having to do with crunching numbers of types they are already familiar with, rather than as a strategic activity that involves both quantifying additional areas of risk and making plans for types of risk that may never be quantifiable to the extent of some of the traditional areas. The report says that those companies that have made the shift to viewing risk management as such a strategic activity find it a source of competitive advantage.

"Such institutions accept that uncertainty cannot be tamed, only mitigated."[2]

The report recommends (echoing the Chairman of Lloyd's) that risk management plans be overseen at the board level; however, it notes that that mostly isn't happening yet. Reports like this are helping make lack of board oversight of such a plan a reputational risk.

If there is a reputation system for your company's industry, it would be prudent to participate in it. If there is not, perhaps your company should help start one. Proactive management of reputation will work better than passively waiting to see what reputation damage gets done.

Contractual Risk Transfer

ISPs typically have Service Level Agreements (SLAs) that provide some amount of reimbursement for outages or slowdowns. Those are a form of contractual risk transfer that covers some of your risk. It may also be possible to make contracts with users disclaim certain risks on the part of your company, as another form of contractual risk transfer. Which risks would depend on the company.

Other

It is possible to transfer some risk to external organizations. For example, many companies use hosting centers for their Internet servers, or use content distribution networks to pick up their served information and show it to users from servers closer to the users. Such arrangements may help with robustness, because a hosting center's core competence is running servers and thus may be expected to do better at its average business. They may help with resilience, because a hosting center may have multiple backups and a content distribution company has multiple servers.

Such arrangements can reduce the probability of a risk. However, if something fails anyway, such contracts may not have transferred any of the risk of lost business.

Developing a Strategy

Any given enterprise needs to examine what it is trying to protect, what risks apply, and choose solutions to deal with those risks. Solutions should be of three types: prevention, crisis management, and risk transfer.

Prevention: Resilience and Fortification

Most companies do at least something about prevention by using some traditional Internet security solutions. Most companies could do that better, simply by following standard security practices: patches, passwords, and encryption.

Firewalls are popular, but an important thing to remember about firewalls is that they do not provide complete security, no matter how good they are. A firewall at the perimeter will not protect against an intruder or an employee with physical access to the building walking down the hall and logging in on a computer with sensitive information. Nor will it prevent a user from taking an unpatched laptop home and bringing it back full of spyware and viruses. Use multiple layers of security: firewalls, per-machine passwords, encryption of sensitive material both inside and outside the company, patches, virus and spyware scans, and such other solutions as you need to protect your assets.

Crisis Management: Contingency Plans

If an exploit affects software at your company, what is your incident response plan? Are you ready to patch it immediately? If there is no patch, are you ready to take the affected computers offline? What will you use in their place meanwhile? What will you do if there is no replacement? Do you have backups and do you have a plan for how to find backup copies of the affected data and restore it or bring live backups on line quickly?

Do you have press releases drafted for common types of exploits, for downtime, for loss of information?

Do you know the appropriate contacts at your local police department, the FBI, the Secret Service, Interpol, and so on? Have you already talked to them about what resources they can bring to bear and what level of exploit they require before they will act?

Is your company a member of an appropriate information sharing or reputation system, such as InfraGard or AWPG so that you can quickly inform others who might have the same problems and find out what they have done to counteract such problems? Are your individual officers and other personnel similarly hooked into their corresponding professional groups and networks?

What else will you need to know and do when a crisis happens? Plan now so nobody panics then. If you had a fire in the building, you wouldn't want to have to figure out evacuation routes through the smoke. When a peril turns into an anomaly, you don't want to have to figure out what to do while customers are complaining.

Risk Transfer: Compensation for Loss

What will you do when all your technical security measures fail? I ask that question every time I give a talk about Internet business risk management, and every time the response is a dead silence. Eventually if it's a technical audience somebody will say: "Get a new job?" Or if it's an executive audience, somebody will say: "Find out where all that IT money went?"

Those are both appropriate answers, although not necessarily productive solutions.

Then I usually point at the ceiling of the room and ask them what the little nozzles are. Sprinklers. So, I ask why they are there. Most people look puzzled, but somebody usually answers: "Insurance?"

Exactly. Building codes require fire insurance, and you can't get fire insurance without a sprinkler system.

I don't know why almost nobody thinks of insurance in the context of Internet risk, considering that everyone uses insurance to transfer numerous other risks: fire, theft, flood, collision, casualty, medical, life. Insurance can be just as good at transferring Internet risk. And for the larger players, there are financial risk transfer instruments beyond insurance.

Value Drivers: What Is at Risk?

What are you trying to protect, anyway?

Money

The most obvious thing at risk is money: income lost through slow or disconnected connections, or capital spent on patching and repairing. Getting at least rough quantifications on financial risk can be most helpful in choosing which solutions to apply or buy. For example, how much would being off the Internet for a day cost your company in lost revenue? Two days? A week? The answer to that question may determine how much you would be willing to pay for Internet business continuity insurance.

Reputation

Perhaps even more important is reputation. As some companies learned during the Enron scandal, loss of reputation can sink a formerly well-respected company in a matter of months. Even without quite as dire consequences, reputation damage can cause loss of competitiveness and loss of customers. A bank or other financial institution cannot hide phishing from its customers because it's the customers who are being phished. An affected institution that does not take visible proactive steps to deal with the problem may lose customers to a competitor that does.

Reputation goes beyond just coming clean about attacks and vulnerabilities. It also has to do with how people and companies operate, and how they are perceived to do so.

> . . . e-marketplaces are media as much for social interactions as they are for financial transactions. That is, who you are and what you're doing are as important as what you want to buy or what you want to sell. It's no accident that eBay is still around and making money for both itself and its, ahem, community of auctioneers. Your reputation on eBay can—and often does—matter far more than what you are attempting to either buy or sell.[3]

As Howard Rheingold puts it:

The most long-lasting social effects of technology always go beyond the quantitative efficiency of doing old things more quickly or more cheaply. The most profoundly transformative potential of connecting human social proclivities to the efficiency of information technologies is the chance to do new things together, the potential for cooperating on scales and in ways never before possible.[4]

Rheingold's philosophical musings thus agree with PriceWaterhouseCoopers' hard-nosed survey-based business analysis[5] that some of the most important effects and risks of networks cannot be fully quantified or mitigated. However, if they are understood, they can be turned to business advantage.

Risk Assessment: Linking Risks to Value Drivers

It helps to be specific about which risks affect which things you are trying to protect.

What if someone gets through your Virtual Private Network (VPN) and gains access to your intranet? What sensitive documents or intellectual property could they steal? How much would that cost you?

Is your business susceptible to phishing? If so, what would it cost you?

If you are not familiar with such questions, you may want to get help from a Managed Security Monitoring (MSP) firm or other company that does Internet Risk Assessment and Management.

Risk Management Assessment: Choosing Solutions

If you can accurately map risks to value drivers, choosing solutions then becomes relatively straightforward because you can pick solutions to deal with the main risks you have identified.

Or you can take an approach of applying all the usual traditional security measures.

Either way, it would be prudent also to participate in a clearinghouse or reputation system for your industry and to look into financial risk transfer instruments.

Industries and Solutions

Strategies may be similar for enterprises in particular industries that have common problems. The rest of the book is organized into chapters per industry, in the order listed in the subsections that follow.

Banks: Quantification for Capital Withholding

Banks have all the same concerns of other enterprises (see the subsections that follow), plus because they deal with forms of money, they are favorite targets of some kinds of attacks, and they have their own peculiar regulations such as Basel II. Basel II, or the New Capital Accord, adds quantification of operational risk to a previous accord among large international banks that required quantification of credit risk. Such quantification feeds a formula that determines the amount of capital the bank has to withhold to deal with the risk. Banks are good at credit quantification, but are still working out how to deal with operational risk quantification, including quantification of Internet operational risks. They could apply the same sort of incident reports and management summaries as they do for credit risk. Basel II also goes beyond just quantification into attempts to use quantification to decrease probability of risk and to increase the ethical culture of the banks.

Financial Institutions: Favorite Targets

Financial institutions are tired of phishers fooling their customers into revealing information so the phishers can mimic identities and steal money. In 2004, banks and other financial institutions banded together to do something about phishing under the auspices of the Financial Services Technology Consortium (FSTC). The first phase of this initiative involved

> . . . *educating customers, outfitting customer desktop PCs with anti-spam-protection software, and working with law-enforcement authorities and Internet service providers to identify and stop phishing attacks while they're in progress.*[6]

There's a report out on Phase I,[7] in several documents ranging from definitions of terms (it wasn't even clear before what phishing was) to categorizing vendors solutions according to an FSTC Phishing Attack Lifecycle and Solutions Categorization.

Many of the FSTC recommendations sound like good risk management in general, for example:

> *Ensure that phishing preparedness plans (staff responsibilities, incident response plans, procedures, etc.) are appropriate, frequently reviewed, and updated as necessary. FSTC's Phishing Life Cycle Model and Attack Taxonomy can be used to structure concrete planning activities and assess adequacy.*[8]

The first of the next steps FSTC will be investigating illustrates a basic feature of this work: "Investigate and adopt better mutual authentication practices."

Although the FSTC report says that institutions acting alone can do these things, it's not clear that that is possible for something that is mutual. As the report also says, the industry acting as a whole can do these things.

In other words, collective action is needed for an aggregate threat. Financial institutions have to deal with threats they are not used to; even physical objects such as ATM cards and backup tapes are no longer safe. Meanwhile, financial institutions have business opportunities in issuing or trading catastrophe bonds and performance bonds related to Internet risk, and perhaps even derivative options.

Large Enterprises: Beyond Compliance to Competitiveness

Publicly traded companies have to comply with SOX, GLBA, and HIPAA in the U.S., or in Canada with PIPEDA, or in Europe with DPD. Educational institutions in the United States also have to worry about Family Educational Rights and Privacy Act (FERPA). The compliance alphabet soup isn't the half of it. Big businesses have to face no longer being able to control public perceptions the way they used to. Getting the big newspapers and conferences on your side isn't enough when 10,000 bloggers can post information quicker, drawing from millions of individuals as sources. Suing people doesn't even work as well as it used to, now that everyone knows you're doing it and reputation damage may exceed any gain. Fortunately, a company that shows some agility, an ability to plan ahead, and a willingness to participate in collective action can not only manage Internet business risk but can also find ways to turn it into a competitive advantage.

Small Enterprises: Risk As Opportunity

Small enterprises may not have as much concern with SOX and other laws because there are often exceptions for small enterprises. That doesn't make small companies immune to directed attacks, *force majeure* events, or accidents, yet small companies are often lacking the resources of big companies to deal with such perils. On the other hand, the Internet and the group communications and social connections it enables represent great entrepreneurial opportunities for small businesses.

Internet Service Providers: Bonded and Insured

ISPs providers often run on small profit margins and need to seek value-added services, while they are subject to all the same problems as other enterprises, plus they are expected to keep the bits flowing. They provide Service Level

Agreements (SLAs) to cover outages or slowdowns. Because customers are skeptical of ISP self-validation of SLAs, ISPs pay too many goodwill SLA payments. Performance bonds can turn SLAs into competitive advantages by reducing goodwill payouts and adding new forms of SLAs. That is, bonded SLAs can become value-added services that can improve an ISP's business model.

Government: Research before Guarantee

Governments have to defend themselves as enterprises, while being expected to pass and enforce laws to deal with severe problems, as well as help set social expectations and act as guarantor of last resort. In addition, government sometimes has to employ military force, while being wary of both physical and cyberspace attacks. Last but not least, government-supported research can open up areas that private industry can't or won't afford, and government purchasing can finance new industries resulting from such research. U.S. government investment of a few million dollars in the ARPANET supported by later purchasing decisions led to the Internet and the current worldwide boom in communications and commerce; a small research investment can have big payoffs. Such payoffs can help fuel a more robust economy, which will help everyone, from the military to industry, domestically and worldwide.

Insurers: A Range of New Products

Insurers increasingly use the Internet to sell and deliver insurance, and they are starting to sell insurance about the Internet itself. Such insurance can help drive more application of traditional Internet security in assessments and claims adjustment, while providing financial coverage when traditional security fails.

Insurers need to deal with the issue of global aggregation of risk that comes with the global reach of the Internet. One way to deal with that is to try to separate customers into groups that are not susceptible to the same risks at the same time. This may be possible by, for example, grouping customers by the type of software they use. However, some major risks such as disconnects or slowdowns outside the firewall are common to all enterprises regardless of what they run inside the firewall.

Thus insurers have to find ways to provide sufficient financial depth to cover their own potential losses in case of massive aggregated claims. Fortunately, ways to do that are already known in other industries. Internet business risk presents multiple business opportunities for insurers. As insurance becomes standard for doing business on the Internet, security will improve, because insurers will require it.

Force Is Not Security

In his book *Linked*, Albert-László Barabási remarks:

> *Real networks are not static, as all graph theoretical models were until recently.*
> *Instead growth plays a key role in shaping their topology. They are not as cen-*
> *tralized as a star network is. Rather, there is a hierarchy of hubs that keep these*
> *networks together, a heavily connected node closely followed by several less con-*
> *nected ones, trailed by dozens of even smaller nodes. No central node sits in the*
> *middle of the spider web, controlling and monitoring every link and node. There*
> *is no single node whose removal could break the web. A scale-free network is a*
> *web without a spider.*[9]

This is not news to those of us who were involved in USENET, the old store-and-forward Unix-based network that started in 1981 and was eventually absorbed by the Internet in the early 1990s. For example, in the mid-1980s I ran `ut-sally`, which was the second node in traffic behind `seismo`. And there were many other nodes of varying degrees of connectivity and traffic. The most connected node also changed from time to time; earlier it was `decvax`, and then `ihnp4`. The Internet also changes in such a spider web manner.

Both businesses and criminals take advantage of the scale-free nature of the Internet. The Internet's decentralized structure and global reach of communications attracts businesses. Unfortunately, it also attracts criminals to prey on that business. And many of the criminals deliberately organize themselves in a loose and decentralized way to evade detection as they take advantage of the Internet's global reach.

The Illicit Bazaar

Barabási[10] goes on to refer to Valdis Krebs' topological examination of the 9/11 hijackers' network,[11] which indicated that even if the most connected person involved had been apprehended, the rest could probably have proceeded. Barabási generalizes the point, noting that terrorist networks are themselves organized similarly.

This book is not about terrorists, but much thinking about illicit uses of networks has been about terrorists, so it is useful to examine some of that thinking to illuminate what businesses are up against when dealing with criminals in cyberspace. Both terrorists and criminals have illicit bazaars of information; they watch similar exploits, copy what works, and try out new modifications that feed back into the bazaar. Criminals are in many cases even more loosely organized than terrorists in that they have no common ideology other than making a buck.

John Robb has elaborated on this idea of an illicit bazaar in his *Global Guerillas* blog,[12] `http://globalguerrillas.typepad.com/globalguerrillas`,[12] in which he examines in depth how terrorist organizations thrive by decentralized funding and communications. One terrorist blows up something, and another terrorist sees it on the news and copies it. The two terrorists may or may not ever communicate directly, but they don't have to. The point of terrorist is terror, so the bomb that makes the biggest news splash is the most effective. Robb calls this stigmergic learning, after the way that ants learn by chemical signals they leave on their trails, even though they have no top-down command and control. Successful terrorists may get funding from any of several organizations that have money, and that provides them with the ability to make more attacks, which are then copied by others. This cycle of stigmergic learning and funding is what Robb calls the bazaar of violence. Nobody has to be in overall control, which means that there is no central organization or single head to take out to stop it.

Phishing is organized in a similar way. The original perpetrator may be a Russian gangster, who sets up attacks using machines in Korea and mails the actual phishing messages through computers on botnets in the United States, the United Kingdom, and elsewhere. He probably bought his botnet from a botnet herder who built it for sale to the highest bidder. Mules exchange money and goods among these illicit perpetrators. Most of these people never meet. Nor do they need to know each other before making deals; there are numerous online channels they use to communicate. Their methods evolve over time as they watch how various scams succeed, just as John Robb says global guerrillas learn through the bazaar of violence. There are some differences between the terrorist bazaar of violence and the cyberspace criminal illicit bazaar, of course. Phishing and other online scams are largely supported by funds derived directly from their illicit activities. But the main points of decentralization and learning by watching what others do are similar.

Force alone will not stop such organizations. This is not to say we can eschew force; in the best of all possible worlds that might be possible, but not in this one. Terrorists have to be hunted down, and phishers need to be apprehended and tried. Yet that won't stop more from springing up in their place. Something else is also needed.

Wealth Is Not the Solution

The solution is not as simple as Robert McNamara thought when he left the U.S. government to join the World Bank in 1967; poverty alone is not the cause of terrorism, and wealth alone is not the solution. Nor is lack of education the problem. Most of the 9/11 hijackers were not poor, and most suicide bombers are relatively highly educated by local standards.[13] Nor are terrorism or suicide attacks unique to Islam; the only organization in the world to kill two heads of state (Indira Gandhi and Rajiv Gandhi) with suicide attacks is the Tamil Tigers,[14] whose members tend to be Hindu.

There is a common cause of suicide attacks, according to a recent article in *New Scientist*[15] and the accompanying editorial:[16]

> *The decision to engage in suicide terrorism is political and strategic, Pape says. What is more, the aim is always the same: to coerce a government, through force of popular opinion (apart from a few isolated cases, modern suicide terrorism has only ever been used against democracies), to withdraw from territory the group considers its homeland.* [17]

This might indicate two ways of dealing with that particular problem: withdraw from the territory the terrorists consider occupied or change one's government to something other than a democracy. Not only do those options not seem terribly attractive, but suicide terrorism is only one form of terrorism, and withdrawal isn't the only demand of, for example, Al Qaeda.

Similarly, business can't just withdraw from the Internet and leave it to criminals. Nonetheless, in effect many businesses and individuals come close to doing that when they leave unpatched computers accessible on the Internet that bot herders then take over. Companies also sometimes overreact, suing people who they consider to be infringing on their intellectual property even though such people may actually be offering constructive advice or indicating a lucrative market opportunity.

There is no single simple tactic that will do away with terrorism; neither attacking terrorists nor conceding to their demands will work. The former is often necessary, but not sufficient, and the latter is usually unacceptable. Crime on the Internet also has no simple single tactical solution, although part of the answer is to increase use of tactics we already know and to add some new ones.

What strategy can organize such tactics?

A Radical Solution

Barabási proposes eliminating the "underlying social, economic, and political roots that fuel the network's growth."[18] and to offer "a chance to belong to more constructive and meaningful webs."[19]

This is literally a radical solution, since the root of the word *radical* is *radix*, the Latin word for root. Such a solution may work to some extent for some terrorists. But for it to work constant application would likely be required, and most of the change would emerge from inside rather than be imposed from outside.

Such a solution may work for some crackers; there are many cases of former crackers now working in security companies, other industrries, government, or academia. Then there are spammers whom nothing except jail time stops.

And there are phishers who appear to be members of longstanding criminal gangs in countries far removed from those of their victims. Dealing with Internet crime can't wait on fixing the political, economic, and legal infrastructures of every country in the world.

Yet we need a strategy.

To Fix a Broken Network, Make It More Connected

Here's another view on that, by Dr. Steven Everts, Senior Research Fellow at the Centre for European Reform in London:

> In the past few years, something has gone wrong in the broader relationship between the so-called West and the countries of the Arab and Muslim world. Distrust, recriminations and resentment have mounted. Minor misunderstandings or disagreements have taken on highly symbolic importance and fed the cycle of suspicion.[20]

He continued:

> More dialogue per se may not guarantee better relations, but it can help and would at least reduce the barriers of ignorance. Thus we need a dramatic expansion of scholarship programmes and workplace exchange schemes so that more people know about life on the other side. Europe has been transformed through political and market integration, driven by supranational institutions. But the most successful EU programme has been the Erasmus scheme, which gives tens of thousands of students the chance to do part of their university degree in another EU country. Similar schemes also operate for professors and other categories of workers. Together with low-cost airlines, they have probably done more for European unity than the deadweight of the common agricultural policy. We need a similar scheme to link educational establishments in the West to those of the Arab and Muslim world. And, why not, we must also explore the possibilities of introducing low cost air travel on routes to and from the Middle East. There is no reason, other than politically inspired protectionism, why a ticket from London to Beirut or Jeddah should cost twice as much as one to New York. The overwhelming evidence suggests that if people are exposed to more factual information and different experiences, they moderate their views and factor in greater complexity. We may still differ on many things, but at least we should get the facts straight.[21]

And of course the Marshall Plan and the Eurail Pass have probably had effect on United States–European relations because they involved many Americans and Europeans interacting. It wasn't enough to win World War II; then it was necessary to win the peace.

Sometimes you have to fight force with force, but that alone leads only to more fights. The best way to fix a broken world network may not be to break it further. It may be better to make it more connected.

The Marshall Plan may seem far removed from Internet crime, yet given the way phishing works, businesses are now directly affected by conditions in remote countries. Yet businesses still can't try to fix numerous countries to deal with cybercrime in the near term. However, what businesses can do is to increase their communication and interaction with peers and even competitors, as well as law enforcement, monitoring and forensic companies, the public, and, of course, first and foremost their customers. A business whose customers have reason to believe their vendor is honest with them, pays attention to them, and is being proactive in dealing with peril such as phishing is a business that is more likely to thrive than one that does not give its customers reason to believe those things.

Influence the Uncommitted

As McNamara said in 1966: "The decisive factor for a powerful nation already adequately armed is the character of its relationships with the world."[22]

This opinion matches that of many military strategists, especially those who draw from the work of John R. Boyd, one of the most influential strategists of the past century, who recommended "isolating adversaries from physical, mental, and moral support,"[23] while at the same time saying we should "influence the uncommitted or potential adversaries so that they are drawn towards our philosophy and are empathetic toward our success."[24]

In other words, the key to grand strategy is communications.

In a scale-free networked world, isolating adversaries from information is not going to be as effective as it used to be: "With the growth of satellite television and the Internet, censorship is not a realistic option."[25]

So, it is necessary to emphasize even more influencing those who may be drawn away from being adversaries. This would seem to include assisting in their own success as well as our own. That's a tall order to accomplish without adversely affecting one's own organization. It requires ones own organization to be up to snuff, to have a unifying vision, which Boyd described as:

A grand ideal, overarching theme, or noble philosophy that represents a coherent paradigm within which individuals as well as societies can shape and adapt to unfolding circumstances yet offers a way to expose flaws of competing or adversary systems. Such a unifying vision should be so compelling that it acts as a catalyst or beacon around which to evolve those qualities that permit a collective entity or organic whole to improve its stature in the scheme of things.[26]

The Constitution is the definitive statement of such a thing for the United States. Other countries or organizations need their own.

This may sound like the stuff of corporate mission and vision statements, and that is not coincidental; there is a thread of derivation leading back to Boyd. The important thing here is not only to have a vision but also to match it with actions. A vision contradicted by actions is an opening for the kind of tactics Boyd recommends for attacking an adversary.

Hypocrisy: A Real and Present Danger

Actions that don't match words are a real and present danger a corporation can produce for itself in a networked world:

> Look what happened to Nike—from being "the spirit of sports" in the early 90s, the campaign against its use of atrocious sweatshops in developing countries led CEO Phil Knight to confess in 1998 that his shoes "have become synonymous with slave wages, forced overtime, and arbitrary abuse." When it's no longer just about trainers, when the corporations have promised so much more—a way of life!—they have very much more to lose.[27]

It is even possible to overdo the vision thing:

> What's more, says Klein, people start to resent the colonization of their lives. Fine, they say, I'll buy my shoes from you, but I don't want you to take over my head.[28]

That is an opinion from Naomi Klein, a former mallrat brand maven turned international protest organizer and successful author of a book called *No Logo*[29] about the ill effects of brands. Hypocrisy can turn your best customers into adversaries.

Nations are not alone in needing to deal with the character of their relationships with the world. Sometimes hiring more lawyers, lobbyists, and publicists and spending still more on security fortifications isn't the right solution for corporations, either. In today's interconnected world, building bigger fortifications around one's own network and company and brands is no longer a strategy that is likely to succeed. Nor can counterstrikes against cybercriminals succeed alone, especially if they are made by individual businesses acting alone. Businesses also need to improve the character of their relations with the world. Two means of such improvement are risk transfer and new means of reputation management. All these means need to be coordinated in a general risk management plan that not only talks the talk but also walks the walk.

Motivation: Overcoming Inertia

Even if you have thought out a risk management strategy, there is still the need to decide to turn it into a plan, and to convince your people to help.[30]

Companies Can Collapse Like Societies

Jared Diamond's book *Collapse: How Societies Choose to Fail or Succeed*[31] examines societies from the smallest (Tikopia) to the largest (China) and why they have succeeded or failed, where failure has included warfare, poverty, depopulation, and complete extinction. He thought he could do this purely through examining how societies damaged their environments but discovered that he also had to consider climate change, hostile neighbors, trading partners, and reactions of the society to all of those, including reevaluating how the society's basic suppositions affect survival in changed conditions.

For example, medieval Norse Greenlanders insisted on remaining Europeans to the extent of valuing the same food animals and plants in the same order, even though the local climate was not propitious for hogs and cows and grain crops, and the sea nearby was full of fish and seals. When the climate became colder, their marginal way of life became even more so. Meanwhile, colder weather led the Inuit to move southward until they contacted the Norse, who reacted adversely, producing hostile relations. And cold weather stopped the trading ships from Norway. The Greenland Norse never learned to use kayaks, harpoons, ice spears, or dogs. In the end, they all died.

Europeans are capable of learning all these things, as the Danes who rediscovered Greenland several hundred years later demonstrated. The medieval Norse Greenlanders stuck so slavishly to their presuppositions that they doomed themselves. It's true that they survived for more than 400 years, which is a long time as civilizations go, but they didn't have to die; all they had to do was to become a bit more flexible.

Many corporations are larger than the tiny island nation of Tikopia, where the inhabitants are almost always in sight of the sea. Many have more people than the entire population of Norse Greenland. And many corporations operate in cultural straitjackets as severe as that of the Norse Greenlanders: stovepiped departments, top-down command-and-control hierarchy, and fast profit instead of long-term investment, to name a few.

To get a bit more concrete, take a look at a few of the one-liner objections Diamond says he encounters to the importance of environmental concerns. I'll translate them into their contemporary corporate equivalents, which you will probably recognize:

- **Diamond:** "The environment has to be balanced against the economy."

  Corporate corollary: Risk management has to be balanced against near-term profit.

  Indeed, no corporation can spend all its profit on risk management, but if it doesn't spend enough on risk management, it risks there being no profit because there may be no corporation. Plus, risk management can be a competitive advantage. With the London Stock Exchange requiring corporations to have risk management plans to be listed, and the U.S. Securities and Exchange Commission (SEC) considering the same thing, at the least risk management is becoming a requirement to play capitalism. The first corporations to have good plans can also gain marketing advantages. In addition, the kinds of information a corporation needs to make a good plan can also be used to improve connectivity, lessen risk, and improve customer satisfaction, all of which should have some positive benefit on the bottom line.

■ **Diamond:** "Technology will solve all our problems."

Corporate corollary: Buying more Internet security technical solutions will solve Internet security problems.

This is what corporations have been assuming, but recent history indicates otherwise. Yes, every corporation needs some forms of technical security, just as every building needs fire control mechanisms, but a building can still burn down and Internet connections can still fail, so insurance is also needed.

■ **Diamond:** "If we exhaust one resource, we can always switch to some other resource meeting the same need."

Corporate corollary: We can always fall back on something other than the Internet.

This is the attitude I've seen with people who think that if the United States is attacked via the Internet, we'll just cut off Internet connectivity at the edges of the continental United States (CONUS). I've heard such a thing proposed at government-sponsored conferences and in the press. One analogy that is sometimes used is with the authority of the Federal Aviation Administration (FAA) to ground every aircraft within U.S. airspace, which they used after 9/11.

Such an attitude ignores the basic fact that there is no way to do that successfully with the Internet. During the 1980s, the ARPANET and USENET supposedly didn't extend beyond the Iron Curtain into eastern Europe. In fact, USENET did, and much ARPANET traffic was relayed, as was well known to many network administrators in Europe. For that matter, the U.S. government supported a network from Virginia to Moscow that transferred seismological data between the United States and the Soviet Union. Also in the 1980s, South Africa applied to network after network (BITNET, EARN, UUCP, ARPANET, and so on) and was denied access because of the apartheid policies of its government, never mind that the entity applying was a university. The University of Cape Town proceeded to connect via FidoNet anyway. Back when the Chinese government was still trying to prevent the Internet from entering China, I saw links going in from Hong Kong. Shortly afterward, the Chinese government decided to adopt and co-opt the Internet in country, supporting connections while requiring registrations. Nowadays there are so many methods for Internet connectivity, ranging from landline telephone dialup to cell phone to satellite and others, that there is always a way in or out of any sizable country.

The Internet's potential for cascade failure is also because of its organization as a scale-free network with many hubs of various sizes. Yet this is also what makes it so robust unless the hubs are directly targeted. Much of the Internet would interpret an attempt to shut it off at national borders as an attack to be routed around; there are always more ways in or out than any government can prevent. Meanwhile, a great deal of U.S. commerce and even emergency communication measures would suffer. In addition to many of those things being intertwined with the rest of the world, you still have to take into account Alaska and Hawaii, which are part of the United States. Finally, while any airplane crash risks loss of life, not every Internet exploit does, so there isn't a close analogy between air transport and the Internet.

Some corporate executives think they'll find something to replace the Internet so that they don't have to deal with Internet problems; for example, they'll put up private communication links to their business partners, or they'll build perfect Virtual Private Networks on top of the Internet. Both of these approaches have certain applications, but neither of them can replace the Internet as a globally accessible communications medium. Replacing the Internet with something else is about as likely as replacing electricity.

Not all of the one-liners Diamond lists are so obviously parallel with Internet problems and denials, but these three may be sufficient to illustrate the point. The point is that business as usual isn't enough for Internet business risk management planning. Traditions need to be reexamined in order to construct and implement new strategies that will work.

Denial Can Be Managed

Denial causes damage, and managing denial can be hard. It requires paying attention to both your supporters and your critics, and considering that they may both be right. For that matter, they may be the same people; it is essential not to consider a critic to be an enemy because it is too easy not to listen to enemies.

In the case of the Internet in the event of a terrorist attack, why not use the multiplicity of communications as an advantage? Don't limit communications; instead use all available methods, from IM and cell phone text messages to government web sites, to facilitate outgoing advisories, two-way communications, and group coordination.

The same applies to corporations. Don't try to hide behind intellectual property, press releases, and secrecy. Tell your customers what's really going on, give them what you can to handle problems, admit it when you don't have the solution to a problem, and keep them talking to you and each other.

Risk Produces Fear, Reason Can Manage Fear

The best way to prevent irrational fear-based reactions to risk by your company is to make a risk management plan in advance. This should include being clear about what is and is not a risk. People often become frightened of things because they are unexpected, and they don't know what they are.

The rational response to risk is to determine what the risks are to decide how much risk to accept. People who don't need to do something, such as ride a bus or visit a cafe, probably won't do it if they think it's risky. But people who see concrete benefits in the activity usually decide whether the risk is worth it to them, and, if so, they continue the activity.[32] Cornell has made available a study by two economists of reactions to terror in Israel.[33] The study notes that casual ridership of buses or casual users of cafes goes down markedly after a terrorist incident that strikes a bus or cafe, while regular patrons don't vary their usage much. One could argue that bus riders don't have much choice, but cafe patrons could eat at home or go down the street to another cafe, and regular patrons don't; they continue what they were doing.

So, a corporation that rationally decides to accept a risk would seem less likely to react out of fear when the risk occurs, and that would seem to be a competitive advantage.

If your organization decides to accept a risk, another rational response is to determine how to lessen the effects of the risk.

Act before Damage

Talking about risk management strategies for the Internet is often like talking about backups: people don't want to deal with it until they see significant damage that directly affects them. Companies don't want to spend money on insurance or time on preparing a risk management plan until they've experienced undeniable damage.

In July 2004, CNET announced:

Internet-based business disruptions triggered by worms and viruses are costing companies an average of nearly $2 million in lost revenue per incident, market researcher Aberdeen said on Tuesday.

Out of 162 companies contacted, 84 percent said their business operations have been disrupted and disabled by Internet security events during the last three years. Though the average rate of business operations disruption was one incident per year, about 15 percent of the surveyed companies said their operations had been halted and disabled more than seven times over a three-year period.[34]

Of course, everyone has also heard about people and companies that didn't have adequate backups when their equipment failed. Sometimes people listen to such stories and start making backups before their computers fail.

Backups are a risk management strategy. Other risk management strategies are like backups: they're best put in place *before* they're needed.

From Fear to Advantage

It's no longer enough to apply the usual technical fixes; we still need them, more than before, but they're not enough. It's no longer possible to try to ignore the problem; commerce is too dependent on the Internet. Crooks are trying to compromise your computers and steal your money and your customers' information. Plus, many kinds of failures can happen beyond your firewall that you can't control. Going it alone won't work in a networked world of aggregate damage. Internal and external coordination is needed to turn Internet risk management from a fragmented fearful reaction into a core business competence that builds competitiveness.

Notes

1. *Uncertainty tamed? The evolution of risk management in the financial services industry,* PricewaterhouseCoopers and the Economist Intelligence Unit (July 29, 2004). www.pwc.com/images/gx/eng/fs/072704eiurisk.pdf

2. Ibid.

3. strategy+business, "Network theory's new math," News.com. (CNET, 1 January 2003). http://news.com.com/2009-1069-978596.html

4. Howard Rheingold, *Smart Mobs: The Next Social Revolution.* (Perseus Publishing, 2002). www.smartmobs.com/book

5. Op. cit. *Uncertainty tamed?*

6. Steven Marlin, "Phishing Expedition Set to Enter Second Phase," *InformationWeek.* (October 29, 2004). `http://informationweek.com/story/showArticle.jhtml?articleID=51201465`

7. Zach Tumin and Jim Salters, Financial Services Technology Consortium Counter-Phishing Initiative: Phase I, Financial Services Technology Consortium (December 2004). `www.fstc.org/projects/counter-phishing-phase-1`

8. Ibid.

9. Albert-Laszlo Barabási, *Linked: How Everything Is Connected to Everything Else and What It Means.* (New York: Plume, April 2003).

10. Ibid.

11. Valdis Krebs, "Social Network Analysis of the 9-11 Terrorist Network," orgnet.com (2004). `www.orgnet.com/hijackers.html`

12. John Robb, Global Guerrillas, "Typepad." `http://globalguerrillas.typepad.com/globalguerrillas`

13. Ellis Shuman, "What makes suicide bombers tick?," *IsraelInsider* (June 4, 2001). `www.israelinsider.com/channels/security/articles/sec_0049.htm`

14. "Suicide Attacks," Jewish Virtual Library, A Division of the American-Israeli Cooperative Enterprise (2003). `www.jewishvirtuallibrary.org/jsource/Terrorism/suicide.html`

15. Michael Bond, "The making of a suicide bomber," *New Scientist*, Volume 182, Issue 2447 (May 15, 2004). `http://archive.newscientist.com/secure/article/article.jsp?id=mg18224475.900`

16. "All it takes to make a suicide attacker," *New Scientist*, Volume 182, Issue 2447 (May 15, 2004). `http://archive.newscientist.com/secure/article/article.jsp?rp=1&id=mg18224470.200`

17. Ibid.

18. Op. cit. Barabási, *Linked*.

19. Ibid.

20. Dr. Steven Everts, "Why We Do Not Get On? And What to Do About It?," Dar Al-Hayat (September 25, 2004). `http://english.daralhayat.com/opinion/contributors/09-2004/Article-20040925-37643810-c0a8-01ed-002c-03ffd3b01174/story.html`

21. Ibid.

22. Robert S. McNamara, U.S. Secretary of Defense, "Security in the Contemporary World," before the American Society of Newspaper Editors, Montreal, Canada (18 May 1966). www.oldcolo.com/McNamara/mcnamara.txt

23. Dr. Chet Richards, "Grand Strategy," Defense and the National Interest. www.d-n-i.net/fcs/boyd_grand_strategy.htm

24. Ibid.

25. Ibid.

26. Ibid.

27. Katharine Viner, "Hand-to-Brand-Combat: A Profile Of Naomi Klein," Guardian (23 September 2000). www.commondreams.org/views/092300-103.htm

28. Ibid.

29. Naomi Klein, No Logo: No Space, No Choice, No Jobs, (Picador, 30. John S. Quarterman, "Rethinking Internet Risk Management," Phone+ Magazine (December 2004). http://phoneplusmag.com/articles/4c1soap.html

31. Jared Diamond, Collapse: How Societies Choose to Fail or Succeed. (New York: Viking Adult, December 2004).

32. "The rational response to Terrorism," *Economist* (July 23, 2005). www.economist.com/finance/displayStory.cfm?story_id=4198336&tranMode=none

33. Gary S. Becker and Yona Rubenstein, "Fear and the Response to Terrorism: an Economic Analysis" (August 2004). www.ilr.cornell.edu/international/events/upload/Beckerrubinstein Paper.pdf

34. CNET News.com Staff, "The attack of the $2 million worm," News.com. (CNET, July 6, 2004). http://news.com.com/The+attack+of+the+%242+million+worm/2100-7355_3-5258769.html?tag=cd.top

Banks and Basel II

Given the extraordinary magnitude of international financial transactions—which amount to some $4 trillion per day moving through the New York clearance system alone—the opportunities for fraud are huge, the rewards great, and the systems put in place to protect against them, far from adequate. . . .

—The BCCI Affair[1]

Complementary to SOX, Basel II is a banking agreement that imposes operational controls on participating organizations. While Basel II applies directly only to a relatively small number of large international banks (initially only the 10 largest in the U.S., for example), it will eventually spread to more banks, and it contains some methods that are useful for non-banking organizations. Some of its methods may be competing with SOX for resources even within banks. However, SOX and Basel II do not have to compete, since some of the methods of Basel II, in particular some implementations of its Advanced Measurement Approaches (AMA), should incorporate methods of peril and anomaly measurement and control that enterprises may be required to implement anyway, for example, in order to get Internet business continuity insurance. Further, many of those methods prove beneficial to enterprises in the form of reduced costs, customer retention, and overall competitiveness, regardless of external requirements. Thus Basel II is worth consideration by all enterprises because it is an attempt to codify a culture of risk management.

What Is Basel II?

Big international banks meet periodically in Basel, Switzerland, and sometimes impose requirements upon themselves via the Basel Committee on Banking Supervision (BCBS). In 1988 they made the Capital Accord, now known as Basel I[2], which required them to quantify credit risk so that they could use it in a formula to determine how much cash overhead each bank needs to keep. Even though Basel agreements have no force of law, every big international bank and many smaller ones now follow the Basel I procedures for quantification of credit risk.

In the 1990s, there were a number of unfortunate banking incidents involving rogue traders and illegal activities. In 1991, the Bank of Credit and Commerce International (BCCI) collapsed under $10 billion in losses, resulting from illegal activities ranging from money laundering to sale of nuclear technologies to tax evasion and illicit purchase of real estate, involving many corporate officers and government officials in many countries. The U.S. Senate Foreign Relations Committee report on the BCCI Affair, sometimes known as the world's worst financial scandal, runs to many pages.[3] In 1995 Barings collapsed after more than two centuries because of a single rogue derivative trader, and in the same year Daiwa New York lost $1.1 billion through unauthorized trading.[4]

These incidents indicated a need to detect illegal and unethical bank cultures and to prevent them. While governments can play a role in this, they cannot do it alone, given that such banks often operate in multiple countries simultaneously.

In 2001, the BCBS produced the New Capital Accord, or Basel II, which requires large international banks to quantify operational risk, in addition to credit risk. Basel II was codified in June 2004 in a document entitled *International Convergence of Capital Measurement and Capital Standards: A Revised Framework* (The Basel II Framework, or the Framework). It is to take effect in 2006.

Since every bank uses the Internet these days, to reach customers, suppliers, outsourcers, other offices, and so on, Basel II thus requires quantifying Internet operational risk. This is outside the core competencies of banks, and also of the Federal Reserve, to judge by the 308-page paper the Federal Reserve staff put out in fall 2003 in conjunction with three other federal agencies, outlining a proposed U.S. implementation of Basel II: *Advance Notice of Proposed Rulemaking* (ANPR).[5] The ANPR does not mention networks or the Internet specifically as sources of operational risk. Nonetheless, it mentions applications such as e-banking that use the Internet, and it mentions outsourcing, automation, natural disasters, terrorism, and vandalism. Outsourcing requires networks; automation requires automated monitoring; the last three (natural disasters, terrorism, and vandalism) are all examples of Internet perils. The Internet figures prominently in real-world applications of at least four of the seven types of operational risk specified in the documents, especially those involving relations with trade counterparties or vendors. And the documents require ongoing operational measurement, monitoring, alerting, and reporting.

Two-thirds of the ANPR details the additional credit risk requirements of Basel II and how to implement them. The other third attempts to do the same for operational risk yet says in several places that the banks do not know how to do it and it will have to be worked out in practice.

The Internet is central in modern international banking; international banking needs to quantify (measure, test, verify, maintain, administer) Internet risk. Neither Basel II nor the ANPR actually specify how to do that in enough detail to implement it from those documents. However, those documents and others related to them do spell out how to set up an organizational culture that should be conducive to quantification of Internet risk, and even more conducive to quantifying and controlling operational risk in general. This chapter discusses the operational risk approaches recommended by Basel II and fills in some of the gaps for Internet operational risk. Both parts should be complementary to SOX.

Operational Risk Approaches

Basel II provides three methods for dealing with operational risk, two of which are ways of calculating that risk for purposes of determining how much capital to withhold, and the third of which involves additional measurements that may reduce risk. All quotations in this section are from the Basel II Framework of June 2004[6] except where otherwise noted.

Basic Indicator Approach

In this approach, the bank uses a single indicator such as average gross income to calculate withholding. There are some fine points, such as how to deal with years with negative gross income, and gross income has a precise definition: net interest income plus net non-interest income. Nonetheless, this is a simple method that requires no changes to existing operations. Thus, even the smallest banks could apply this method with little effort. Any bank is permitted to use this method.

Standardized Approach

This second approach is similar to the first, except this one involves calculating capital requirements for each of eight lines of business and then applying a formula to produce an overall result for capital withholding. The eight business lines are: corporate finance, trading and sales, retail banking, commercial banking, payment and settlement, agency services, asset management, and retail brokerage. The formula simply takes gross income for each business line and multiplies it by a fudge factor (called *beta*) specific to that business line;

beta is supposed to be set (by BCBS) to indicate the relationship of risk to gross income for each business line. The resulting amount for capital withholding could be significantly smaller than for the Basic Indicator Approach.

However, there are some prerequisites a bank must meet before it can use the Standardized Approach. The bank must have an operational management system in place that can track operational risk data for each business line, with reports all the way up to the board of directors, and with processes ensuring compliance with documented internal policies, controls, and procedures. All this must be subject to regular independent review and validation.

There is also an Alternative Standardized Approach (ASA) that simplifies calculations for two lines of business, retail banking and commercial banking, by replacing gross income with loans and advances multiplied by a fixed factor. ASA is otherwise the same as the Standardized Approach.

The main point of the Standardized Approach seems to be to use lines of business to provide some degree of granularity for calculating risk without actually modifying the bank's business. Nonetheless the Standardized Approach requires tracking operational risk. If a bank has such a tracking and reporting system, it may get better results (less capital withholding and more control of risk) by using the third approach.

Advanced Measurement Approaches (AMA)

This third method permits the bank to make up its own operational risk measurement system, "provided it is sufficiently comprehensive and systematic." Going beyond simply averaging what is already occurring for the whole bank or per business line, with AMA the bank can perform other statistics on its history of losses and related factors to derive more sophisticated versions of probability of loss.

The bank could phrase such calculations in the terms used for credit risk, for example, Probability of Default (PD), Loss Given Default (LGD), Exposure at Default (EAD), and effective Maturity (M), or it could use other terms in its calculations.

Not every bank can use AMA; such use requires supervisory approval. Many banks will want to, because AMA could yield significantly lower withholding. AMA could conceivably also yield significantly lower risk, because careful measurement of risks as they occur could result in small and large operational changes that could ameliorate current risks and help prevent future ones.

The main advantage of AMA over the other two approaches is flexibility. However, that flexibility raises some large questions.

1. If banks are to make up their own AMA, how are they to know what to construct?

2. If each bank makes up its own AMA, how is the supervisory body to know which AMAs to approve? It is easy for the BCBS to say that an AMA must be sufficiently comprehensive and systematic, but what does that mean in practice? Is an AMA that quantifies and analyzes business losses resulting from Internet outages sufficiently comprehensive if it does not also quantify losses resulting from slow access?

3. If each bank has a different AMA, won't that make independent review and validation difficult, since any review organization will have to review each bank differently?

4. Finally, if each bank has a different AMA, won't that make data sharing in the manner of, for example, FS-ISAC difficult, because data collection, format, and analysis may be different per bank, and thus not commensurable for determining vulnerabilities and incidents across the industry?

Or, to summarize these questions, since Internet operational risk involves dealing with phenomena that affect many enterprises (banks or not) and their customers, wouldn't it be more effective and cost-effective to have as much as possible of the AMA produced by or derived from third-party methods common to the entire industry?

The BCBS has recognized this point to some extent by, for example, providing a list of ten principles for an appropriate risk management environment, in its *Sound Practices for the Management and Supervision of Operational Risk* of February 2003.[7] These principles say what various corporate personnel should do, not how they should do it. Each principle in the *Sound Practices* document is stated as a paragraph, so the following summary is an oversimplification; for the full details, it is best to read the *Sound Practices* document.

Principles 1–3 say the board of directors should periodically review and approve the bank's operational risk management framework, that the board should ensure that framework is subject to internal audit by operationally independent staff, and that senior management should have responsibility for implementing the framework, including making sure all personnel at all levels are appropriately involved and for establishing appropriate policies, processes, and procedures. Principles 8–9 say that banking supervisors should ensure that banks they supervise have an operational risk framework and that supervisors should conduct regular independent evaluations of those frameworks. Principle 10 says that banks should make sufficient public disclosure to allow market participants to assess their approach to operational risk management.

Principles 4 to 6 say a bit more about implementation of the framework, so I want to quote them in full:

Principle 4: Banks should identify and assess the operational risk inherent in all material products, activities, processes and systems. Banks should also ensure that before new products, activities, processes and systems are introduced or undertaken, the operational risk inherent in them is subject to adequate assessment procedures.

Principle 5: Banks should implement a process to regularly monitor operational risk profiles and material exposures to losses. There should be regular reporting of pertinent information to senior management and the board of directors that supports the proactive management of operational risk.

Principle 6: Banks should have policies, processes and procedures to control and/or mitigate material operational risks. Banks should periodically review their risk limitation and control strategies and should adjust their operational risk profile accordingly using appropriate strategies, in light of their overall risk appetite and profile.

Principle 7: Banks should have in place contingency and business continuity plans to ensure their ability to operate on an ongoing basis and limit losses in the event of severe business disruption. Since the AMA must deal with forms of risk that are new to banks (most banks weren't even using the Internet at the beginning of the 1990s, when some of the incidents occurred that provoked Basel II), there are devils in the details of Internet operational risk beyond those ten principles. The *Sound Practices* document acknowledges this point in a general way:

The Committee recognises that operational risk is a term that has a variety of meanings within the banking industry, and therefore for internal purposes (including in the application of the Sound Practices paper), banks may choose to adopt their own definitions of operational risk.

In addition to the question of what is operational risk, there is the question of how it affects the organization. The kind of operational risk that caused Basel II to be written had to do with rogue traders or other personnel engaging in inappropriate activities within a single line of business. Using the corporate hierarchy to deal with such matters makes perfect sense. But an Internet outage or slowdown usually is not caused by explicit action of a particular person and may affect multiple lines of business all at once, since many lines of business use the Internet. Basel II includes the idea of internal audit by operationally independent personnel, but there is some complication with Internet operational risk since there may be no line of business or department that is actually independent of it. External audit may be required for Internet operational risk to perform some of the functions that for other operational risk would be performed by internal audit.

Meanwhile, the U.S. supervisory agencies have said that:

*The Framework contains several alternative measures for calculating minimum
regulatory capital requirements, but the U.S. Agencies are planning to adopt
only the most advanced approaches for credit and operational risk for U.S. financial institutions.*[8]

In other words, they plan to adopt AMA. Yet they have not said what AMA
means for Internet operational risk.

There is also some doubt that many banks will have AMA approved by
2006, because they are supposed to have 3 years of historical data and a couple
of years of experience with their AMA methods before supervisory approval.
However, the earlier they start, the earlier they will receive approval. And
many appropriate techniques for AMA are appropriate for enterprises of all
kinds to be using regardless of banking supervision.

Implementation of AMA

This section is about implementation of AMA. In particular, it is about the
implementation of AMA for Internet operational risk. As previously mentioned, Internet operational risk can cross lines of business and may need
external audit.

Incident Reports

If your bank has a firewall, intrusion detection, and patched software, is it safe
from Internet security problems? No, because there are perils outside the firewall in the Internet that can interfere with customers reaching the bank.

The subsections that follow identify some Internet perils related to banks
that were found by InternetPerils, Inc., using its GAIN technology and displayed using its PerilScope interactive display interface.

Slow Links

The third hop before the Kansas City bank node depicted in Figure 5-1 is slow
(the line between the nodes in Topeka and Kansas City), with latency at 13:45
GMT July 15, 2004, of more than a second.

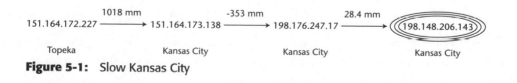

Figure 5-1: Slow Kansas City

Latency of a second is more than enough to cause the Internet's Transmission Control Protocol (TCP) to back off on its sending rate, slowing down web and other transactions. Since setting up a web retrieval typically takes several round trip communications, the delay perceptible to the user is probably several times the one second underlying delay, and quite likely with intermittent longer delays. That hop is between two cities (Topeka and Kansas City), which would result in some slowness simply due to geographical distance, but it isn't normally that slow. Figure 5-2 shows normal behavior, at 12:45 GMT.

The latency shown in Figure 5-2 on that hop is less than 100 milliseconds, which is not unusual for a loaded router on a geographically separated link.

Maybe the slowness is something to do with the camera in Austin that was used to draw that graph? No, because the anomalous latency is also visible, shown in Figure 5-3 at 13:45 GMT, from a camera in London.

A *camera* in this sense is a data collection device, that is, a computer sending probes and collecting responses. This camera in London shows 618 milliseconds on the Topeka to Kansas City hop. Again latency that high is not normal for that hop; see Figure 5-4 for 12:45 GMT from London.

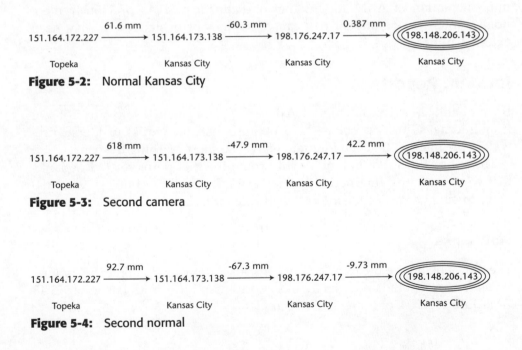

Figure 5-2:   Normal Kansas City

Figure 5-3:   Second camera

Figure 5-4:   Second normal

The London camera shows 93 milliseconds on the hop of interest during normal times. Multiple cameras show the anomalous latency at the same time, and the normal latency at the same time. The exact value of the latency is somewhat different from the different cameras, but they all show a large rise in latency when the anomaly starts. Thus, it is unlikely that the anomaly is some sort of artifact of a single camera or its location; the anomalous rise in latency really is out there in the Internet.

Multiple scans show that the anomalous latency is sustained and is enough to cause slow transactions. The longer a problem like this persists, the more likely a customer will give up for the day, or give up on the transaction completely. It takes only 8 seconds for the average Internet user to give up on the average web page. Some bank transactions are even more time-sensitive.

All the user normally knows in such a situation is that transactions are slow. The user will most likely suspect the bank's server of being slow. The bank may check its server and determine that it is running fine. The bank would look better to the customer if it could say where the problem is. And such knowledge could help in avoiding the problem in the future.

Nonredundant Routes

The focus node in Figure 5-5 (the five-sided node a bit above and to the right of center), apparently in Phoenix, Arizona, appears to be the main way to several bank nodes. The three ellipses to the right of the focus node and one above the other are three Schwab nodes. They each have addresses apparently in different netblocks, which might lead one to believe they were routed differently; actually, they are all routed the same, as the figure demonstrates. A routing or performance problem that affects one of these three nodes will probably also affect the other two. This figure shows just such a performance anomaly. These nodes were noticed by the software because they all showed a performance anomaly at the same time. The other two ellipses above the focus node are two Wells Fargo nodes, also in different netblocks, and thus apparently widely separated, but actually with similar routing. They are somewhat more widely separated than the Schwab nodes but still susceptible to being affected by the same routing or performance problems. And that is what actually happened: the Wells Fargo nodes, like the Schwab nodes, were detected as having anomalous performance at the same time.

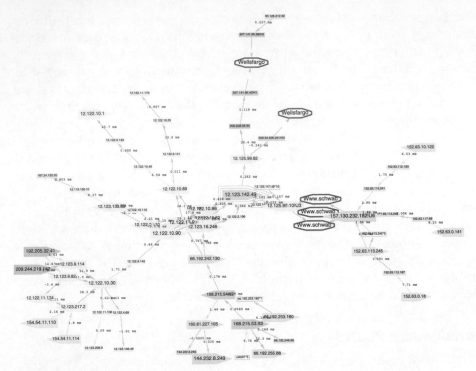

Figure 5-5: Nonredundant routes

This graph is for July 22, 2004 at 6:30 a.m. GMT, using data from three cameras, in London, Virginia, and Texas.

There could be other paths not detected in this dataset, but it is also possible that the focus node is a single point of failure—what InternetPerils calls a PerilPoint. If such a PerilPoint were to fail, it could cause lost connectivity, leading to lost business, in this case for several businesses.

Neither the banks nor the users normally know about any of this topology, nor the nonredundant routes shown in Figure 5-5. If such a bank did know, it could choose its server locations to be more redundant.

Congestion

Figure 5-6 depicts 27 bank nodes having a problem on Thursday, July 22, 2004. These bank destinations did not show a huge spike in latency; however, they did show repeated smaller variations in latency. And they all showed their latency changes at near the same times, which is usually an indication of something deeper in the Internet on paths leading to the several nodes. The graph shows that the slow hops are mostly several hops before the destinations.

Figure 5-6: Congestion

What if this set of links were hit by a significant worm, causing much more latency? Many banks would have connectivity problems at the same time. None of them would normally know why, and they would be even more unlikely to know that multiple banks were affected at the same time.

In this graph, the bank destinations are the ellipses. This is a single frame for 7:45 A.M. GMT from an animation of the entire span of the anomaly, which lasted 6 hours from 6:30 to 12:30 GMT, as seen from three cameras. The animation shows many routing changes; it is also in color and shows frequent red lines striking like lightning.

A Path of Action

Banking, and all other businesses that use the Internet, could suffer from network problems such as slow links that can cause lost transactions, nonredundancy that risks outages, and congestion that could affect multiple enterprises simultaneously. Individual banks need to know about such incidents as they occur. The financial industry needs to know how such incidents affect multiple institutions.

Remember the *Sound Practices*:

> *Principle 5: Banks should implement a process to regularly monitor operational risk profiles and material exposures to losses.*

Banks and other businesses need to track anomalies such as slow links and congestion because they interfere with customer access, as well as various other uses of the Internet, ranging from coordinating traveling sales forces to distributed offices to supply chains to outsourcers.

This is in addition to tracking more traditional Internet security concerns such as patches, intrusions, and denial-of-service attacks that can be seen by the enterprise itself.

Anomalies outside the firewall can best be seen using multiple vantage points, which may require using a third party to do the measurement.

When anomalies affect multiple enterprises simultaneously, it is useful for each affected enterprise to know that, but even harder for each enterprise to see such aggregation. Collective action is needed, involving one or more third parties.

Perils such as nonredundant links may be better dealt with in management summaries (see the next section).

Management Summaries

Remember the rest of *Sound Practices* Principle 5:

> *There should be regular reporting of pertinent information to senior management and the board of directors that supports the proactive management of operational risk.*

What is pertinent information to report for Basel II? Among the list of seven operational risk categories in the ANPR are four that include Internet perils and anomalies. Those are discussed in the next four sections. Each section begins with the operational risk category as outlined in the ANPR and is followed by examples of how those categories include Internet perils management must be concerned about.

Obligation Failure

iv. Clients, products, or business practices: an unintentional or negligent failure to meet a professional obligation to specific clients (including fiduciary and suitability requirements), or from the nature or design of a product.

This operational risk category in the context of Internet perils and anomalies could include at least the following:

- Picking the wrong Internet Service Provider (ISP), as in picking an ISP that has a single point of failure to multiple customers or that has a history of periodic congestion that if exacerbated, for example, by increased traffic from a worm, could interfere with customer access. Suppose that the congestion illustrated by Figure 5-6 recurred every afternoon between the bank and its customers. The bank would then want to contact the ISP to determine if something could be done, or possibly consider connecting to a different or additional ISP. Similarly, even if only a single link is slow, as in Figure 5-4, if it is slow repeatedly and is on the way to multiple customers, the bank needs to know that and to consider appropriate action. Note that just because an ISP may be suboptimal for a particular bank to use to reach its customers does not mean that the same ISP is suboptimal or wrong in general. But the bank needs to know how the ISP performs in reaching the bank's customers.

- Similar considerations apply to siting distributed servers. Figure 5-5 illustrates some apparently nonredundant links and routes to several servers. The bank that is paying for those servers needs to know that, and to consider whether to ask the hosting ISP to route them differently, or to move some of them to different hosting locations on the same ISP, or to move some of them to other ISPs. Geography as well as topology will play a role in such decisions: three servers on different netblocks that turn out to be in the same room, or even the same city, are at risk of failure due to the same electrical outage, earthquake, or tornado. In addition to nonredundant routing or nondiverse siting, which are perils, the bank needs to know when actual anomalies result, such as the one illustrated by Figure 5-5, and how often. Management summaries should compile such information.

- Other considerations to include in management summaries include hardware and software monoculture. Even if a bank has multiple servers which are each sited on a different network run by a different ISP in a different city, they can still all be vulnerable to the same exploit if they are all running the same version of the same software.

All these cases and others like them could lead to failure of obligation to clients.

Physical Damage

> *v. Damage to physical assets: the loss or damage to physical assets from natural disaster or other events.*

This could include a variety of types of physical damage, such as:

- Hurricane Floyd flooded a datacenter in the Washington, DC, area, taking thenode of that ISP offline.

- 9/11 caused numerous problems with the Internet, many of them *after* the time of the attack, such as datacenters losing power days later due to running out of fuel or air filters clogging up and causing overheating. Many of these datacenters were far away from Manhattan, as far as Finland, Italy, Hungary, and South Africa.

- Hurricane Ivan disconnecting the Cayman Islands by disturbing the undersea cable carrying connectivity there. Yet nearby Jamaica was not completely disconnected.

A bank will want to know how often such problems have occurred, how long they took to fix, and whether there is alternative service. In addition, there is at least one court case involving an electric utility that determined that loss of service amounted to physical damage: *American Guarantee & Liability Insurance Co. v. Ingram Micro, Inc.* 2000.[9] To summarize and possibly oversimplify, a company in Arizona that did not receive electrical power for a day made a claim against insurance for physical damage and won in the courts, including on appeal. For more about this case and successors, see Chapter 11.

The distinction between physical damage to assets owned by a bank, or damage to a facility owned by someone else that damages a system such as the Internet that the bank uses, or sufficient system damage to count as physical damage is not as clear as it once may have been. Management summaries should report such cases and where possible elaborate on the gray areas.

System Failure

> *vi. Business disruption and system failures: disruption of business or system failures.*

This could include, in addition to some of the items already mentioned in the previous sections, numerous traditional and new Internet security problems, including but not limited to:

- Denial-of-service (DoS) attacks
- Worms

- Other operating system failures due to lack of application of patches
- Phishing

Since so many systems in banks and other enterprises these days depend on the Internet, an Internet failure is a system failure that can lead to business disruption. This is one of the essential ways that Internet perils and anomalies differ from what Basel II was mainly designed to prevent: rogue activities by humans inside the banks. Internet perils and anomalies aren't necessarily deliberately instigated by any person in the bank. (Some of them may be deliberately instigated by persons *outside* the bank, but that's no different from traditional theft, except in the leverage across geography, enterprises, and time provided by the Internet.) Nonetheless, Basel II's focus on policies and procedures as a solution is appropriate, because appropriate policies and procedures such as incident reports and management summaries can help prevent, contain, and ameliorate Internet-related system failures.

Process Failure

vii. Execution, delivery, and process management: failed transaction processing or process management, from relations with trade counterparties or vendors.

This could include:

- Congestion (see Figure 5-6)
- Routing flaps
- Other degradation of service between an institution and counterparties such as suppliers or outsourced call centers, as well as in the ISPs conveying the service
- Failures of specific application protocols, as in the Slammer worm, which attacked a specific application server and among other effects took a well-known international bank card company's servers off the Net

Because the Internet is the conduit for connecting so many different groups, such as distributed offices, traveling sales forces, joint venture partners, supply chains, outsourcers, and customers, the Internet can be involved in process failures involving any of those groups. In addition, the bank may not know even which countries are traversed by Internet connections to counterparties such as outsourced call centers or software development shops; a proper assessment of Internet connectivity would show that, and thus reveal which political and legal regimes might be likely to get involved.

A Path of Action

Such management summaries have several purposes, including, but not limited to:

- Assessments such as recommended in *Sound Practices* Principle 4. These should happen not just once, at the beginning of an Internet service, but also periodically. Two of the main purposes of such assessments are choosing ISPs and server siting, as discussed previously.

- Reviewing which lines of business were affected by which outages and slowdowns.

- Reviewing the appropriate delivery mechanism for a service. Should it be via web pages, through a special-purpose Internet application, or not through the Internet at all?

- Determining ISP Service Level Agreement (SLA) violations for reporting to the ISP.

- Determining ISP performance bond claims for reporting to the bond holder.

- For incorporating into a risk management plan for reporting to shareholders or stock exchanges (the London Stock Exchange already requires such a risk management plan).

To summarize the purpose of the management summaries, they are to help determine things that can't necessarily be seen through individual incidents, yet can be seen through aggregations of incidents and of perils.

With incident reports and management reports, and further materials prepared from them for use by executives, boards, shareholders, and oversight bodies, Internet-specific operational quantification such as required for Basel II can be implemented and used. (Basel II also has implications for other industries, as we shall see in other chapters.)

Notes

1. Senator John Kerry and Senator Hank Brown, *The BCCI Affair: A Report to the Committee on Foreign Relations*, United States Senate, 102d Congress 2d Session Senate Print 102-140 (December 1992). www.fas.org/irp/congress/1992_rpt/bcci

2. Basel Committee on Banking Supervision (BCBS), *International Convergence of Capital Measurement and Capital Standards* (July 1988). www.bis.org/publ/bcbs04a.htm

3. Op. Cit. Kerry and Brown, *The BCCI Affair: A Report to the Committee on Foreign Relations.*

4. Bruce Moulton, *Basel II: Operational Risk and Information Security,* (Symantec, January 27, 2004). `http://ses.symantec.com/Industry/Regulations/article.cfm?articleid=3270&EID=0`

5. Office of the Comptroller of the Currency, Dept. of the Treasury, Board of Governors of the Federal Reserve System, Federal Deposit Insurance Corporation, and Office of Thrift Supervision, Dept. of the Treasury, *Advance Notice of Proposed Rulemaking* (July 3, 2003). `www.federalreserve.gov/boarddocs/press/bcreg/2003/20030804/default.htm`

6. Basel Committee on Banking Supervision (BCBS), *International Convergence of Capital Measurement and Capital Standards: A Revised Framework* (June 2004). `www.bis.org/publ/bcbs107.htm`

7. Basel Committee on Banking Supervision (BCBS), *Sound Practices for the Management and Supervision of Operational Risk* (February 2003). `www.bis.org/publ/bcbs96.htm`

8. Office of the Comptroller of the Currency, Dept. of the Treasury, Board of Governors of the Federal Reserve System, Federal Deposit Insurance Corporation, and Office of Thrift Supervision, Dept. of the Treasury, *Proposed Agency Information Collection Activities: Comment Request* (August 2004). `www.federalreserve.gov/BoardDocs/Press/Foiadocs/2004/20040810/default.pdf`

9. U.S. District Court, Arizona, *American Guarantee & Liability Insurance Co. v. Ingram Micro, Inc.* 2000 U.S. Dist. Lexis 7299 (D. Ariz., April 19, 2000). `www.phillipsnizer.com/library/cases/lib_case155.cfm`

Financial Institutions Beyond Quantification

. . . a tsunami is going to occur for sure.[1]
—**Smith Dharmasaroja**

Financial institutions face many of the same risks as banks, plus perhaps broader concerns related to finance. Delays in options trades or other financial transactions may significantly reduce their value. Many financial institutions also have the same concerns of other big businesses; see Chapter 7.

Some of the most difficult challenges finance faces are difficult if not impossible to quantify, yet paradoxically they may require further quantification in order to enable qualitative decisions. These include both events that affect the financial institutions directly, and financial risk transfer instruments that they can issue or trade to assist other enterprises.

People not in financial services companies may want to read this chapter to get some ideas on what they can ask their financial services company to do. The more companies that ask for catastrophe bonds and other financial risk transfer instruments, the more likely they will be issued.

Qualifying the Unquantifiable

According to a 2004 survey by PricewaterhouseCoopers and the Economist Intelligence Unit (EIU), financial services companies have put increasing emphasis on risk management in the corporate agenda. However, they are doing so mostly by continuing to concentrate on credit and market risk, perhaps because they know how to quantify those risks, and perhaps because of regulatory requirements. The report says they see the biggest risk to their market value as reputational risk, which is not so easy to quantify.[2]

The survey indicates four reasons why risk management in financial services companies has not yet shifted to focus on protecting and improving the value of the enterprise:

- A culture of risk awareness has yet to emerge.
- Compliance is not being turned into competitive advantage.
- The importance of governance is underestimated.
- Quantifiable risks are still the focus of too much attention.

Some of these reasons sound more like symptoms rather than causes. For example, why are quantifiable risks still the focus of too much attention?

Part of the answer may be in what the report does *not* mention. It mentions geopolitical risks beyond the control of the corporation, such as regime change, and it emphasizes the importance of risks outside the corporation involving supplies, outsourcers, and the like. Yet the report does not mention Internet continuity problems that could come from such sources and affect business.

Perhaps financial institutions have not yet realized that in a world of scale-free communications built on scale-free networks, it no longer makes sense to try to calculate only typical risks when there is no limit on the size of risks. It is possible to protect against large numbers of small near-term risks and still be wiped out by a single big rare risk. And that big rare risk could be reputation, rather than credit or market.

The report says that some companies have made the shift to viewing risk management as a strategic activity that involves both quantifying additional areas of risk and making plans for types of risk that may never be quantifiable to the extent of some of the traditional areas. Those companies that have made the shift find risk management a source of competitive advantage.

Such institutions accept that uncertainty cannot be tamed, only mitigated.

And such institutions that can handle uncertainty, quantify where they can, and mitigate where they can't, may also be able to develop, sell, or trade risk transfer instruments for use by other organizations.

Physical Security May Not Be Secure

Formerly relatively safe physical security systems such as ATMs are no longer safe. Assuming that they can be expensive; Gartner estimates $2.75 billion in ATM and debit card fraud in the 12 months ending May 2005, with an average loss of $900 affecting 3 million people. The actual losses are usually covered by the financial institutions involved.[3] Those institutions may face further losses beyond the direct financial costs, however.

The Something You Have Needs to Be Different

Physical systems require a physical object for access: something you have, in addition to something you know. But that object adds security only if it provides information that cannot be obtained without having the object in hand. ATM or debit cards can provide such additional information such as a card identifier number beyond the customer's name, account number, and personal identification number (PIN). The additional information is not known to the customer, so the customer cannot reveal it in a phishing attack. However, some banks found it inconvenient to have the customer come into the bank to have the ATM card reprogrammed each time the customer changed a PIN, so they stopped reading the additional information when the customer used the card for transactions.[4] Gartner estimates that perhaps as many as half of U.S. banks do not verify the additional card information.[5]

So, a customer who gets phished, that is, who is conned into providing account number and PIN in response to a phishing message, or who has information stolen by keylogging spyware, is vulnerable to a related ATM attack. The perpetrator makes up a physical ATM card and uses the phished information along with it to withdraw funds. This may be possible even with ATMs that do check the additional information on the card, if the perpetrator knows what that information should be, as well. This can happen if insiders at the bank are involved, or due to theft of such additional information, for example, during transfer to a backup repository.[6]

Anomaly Profiling and Longer Codes

Gartner recommends watching for anomalies:

> *"The best defense is a transaction anomaly detection system that compares incoming transactions with profiles of what is expected from the user," Ms. Litan said. "Anomalies are flagged for further investigation and/or subsequent interactive authentication of the user, perhaps through a phone call to the user."*[7]

Monitoring one's own transactions is almost always a good idea. In this case, it would also help to check the additional information on the cards, and encrypting in-house repositories of such information, as well as any backup or transfer media for them.

As Gartner points out, it also wouldn't hurt to lengthen the codes involved. Four-digit PIN and three-digit card codes may have served well enough in an unnetworked world, but not when perpetrators are willing to try brute force tests, or when they can collect information on thousands of customers or cards and look for patterns.

Prevention and monitoring would be a good combination. Adding financial risk transfer in case of big losses would be even better.

FedLine: Advantage or Menace?

Moving away from the semi-physical security of leased lines to using the Internet could be an improvement in security, but it can also be confusing to many people.

This story in the *New York Post* on August 15, 2004, was all over the Internet:

With little fanfare, the Federal Reserve will begin transferring the nation's money supply over an Internet-based system this month, a move critics say could open the U.S.'s banking system to cyber threats.

The Fed moves about $1.8 trillion a day on a closed, stand-alone computer network. But soon it will switch to a system called FedLine Advantage, a Web-based technology.[8]

The story is quite confused. What is "a Web-based technology"? Is it one that uses web pages for entry? Or is this typical confusion of the web with the Internet? And does FedLine actually run over the public Internet, or does it simply use Internet protocols over private leased lines?

The story doesn't answer any of these questions. It also says:

Patti Lorenzen, a spokeswoman for the Federal Reserve, said the agency is taking every precaution.

"Of course, we will not discuss the specifics of our security measures for obvious reasons," she said. "We feel confident that this system adheres to the highest standards of security. Without disclosing the specifics, it is important to note that our security controls include authentication, encryption, firewalls, intrusion detection, and Federal Reserve conducted reviews."[9]

Somehow I'm not comforted by the first and most frequently mentioned method, security by obscurity. And the mention of firewalls would seem to indicate that this service does run over the public Internet.

The Fed has this to say about FedLine Advantage:

In recent years, we have announced our strategy to provide access to all Financial Services using web technology. We are pleased to announce FedLine Advantage, the Federal Reserve Banks' next generation of service access, is on the horizon.

FedLine Advantage will extend the use of web technology to provide access to critical payment services such as Fedwire Funds Service, Fedwire Securities Service, and FedACH Services. In addition, FedLine Advantage will also enable the use of financial services that are currently accessible via FedLine Web, making it the access method of choice for Federal Reserve Financial Services.[10]

FedFocus May 2004 defines Virtual Private Network (VPN) and Frame Relay, notes how the former works over a public network and the latter does not, plus various kinds of encryption, such as Secure Sockets Layer (SSL), and various kinds of user authentication, such as passwords.[11] However, it never quite seems to say which of these technologies FedLine Advantage will use.

That issue of *FedFocus* does emphasize conversion from an MS/DOS earlier version.[12] So, it seems to be largely a user interface move, which would indicate a change to a web interface, perhaps using the same underlying physical links as before.

Perhaps they will start with Frame Relay (FR) and offer VPN service to those who want to risk it. As convenience increasingly wins out, the result should be many more VPN customers than FR ones.

Even if FedLine stays completely on leased lines, there's still the issue of the computers that are used to using the web interface. The *Fedfocus* issue mentions that an old version of Internet Explorer (IE) will no longer be supported for FedLine Web (a service currently in use), but newer versions of IE will be supported. What if someone compromises IE on such a computer?

Some transactions may be compromised. The same thing can already happen if you use IE to access your bank account over the Internet, although the scale may be bigger. It's the usual tradeoff of more convenience for somewhat more risk. Maybe this change will promote enough additional commerce through convenience to offset any losses from the increased risk.

This creates many smallish risks, not one huge risk of the entire Federal Reserve system being compromised all at once, as the newspaper article might lead one to believe. However, I wonder if the Fed practices software diversity and topological and physical distribution of resources? Emphasizing IE rather than recommending a variety of web browsers indicates that they do not take diversity seriously. Near-term convenience will draw slightly longer term criminals, and software monoculture exacerbates the problem. I'm sure the Fed doesn't want preventable failure of the financial system. There is more they could do to prevent it. I don't want to move further into Tom Clancy territory. Suffice it to say that this is yet another case where technology alone will not completely manage risk, and nontechnological means are also needed.

Risk Transfer Instruments beyond Insurance Policies

Several risk transfer instruments exist beyond insurance policies. Most of them are discussed in other chapters, as indicated in the following subsections, while this chapter provides some more detail and more strategic discussion.

Insurance Policies

Insurance is discussed more extensively in Chapter 11.

Warren Buffett explained insurance for earthquakes to his shareholders:

A few facts about our exposure to California earthquakes—our largest risk—seem in order. The Northridge quake of 1994 laid homeowners' losses on insurers that greatly exceeded what computer models had told them to expect. Yet the intensity of that quake was mild compared to the "worst-case" possibility for California. Understandably, insurers became—ahem—shaken and started contemplating a retreat from writing earthquake coverage into their homeowners' policies.

In a thoughtful response, Chuck Quackenbush, California's insurance commissioner, designed a new residential earthquake policy to be written by a state-sponsored insurer, The California Earthquake Authority. This entity, which went into operation on December 1, 1996, needed large layers of reinsurance—and that's where we came in. Berkshire's layer of approximately $1 billion will be called upon if the Authority's aggregate losses in the period ending March 31, 2001 exceed about $5 billion. (The press originally reported larger figures, but these would have applied only if all California insurers had entered into the arrangement; instead only 72% signed up.)[13]

If $5 billion loss is enough to require reinsurance, what about $50 billion for a worst-case Internet worm?[14] Buffett reiterated his distrust of computer models and stated flat out that he didn't know what the odds were of having to pay out on a California earthquake:

So what are the true odds of our having to make a payout during the policy's term? We don't know—nor do we think computer models will help us, since we believe the precision they project is a chimera. In fact, such models can lull decision-makers into a false sense of security and thereby increase their chances of making a really huge mistake. We've already seen such debacles in both insurance and investments. Witness "portfolio insurance," whose destructive effects in the 1987 market crash led one wag to observe that it was the computers that should have been jumping out of windows.[15]

It sounds like the models weren't taking into account large previous occurrences such as the 1929 stock market crash or the Netherlands tulip bulb craze or the South Pacific Bubble. I know at least one very successful stock market analyst who did predict the 2000 crash. Perhaps those who underwrote portfolio insurance in the 1980s weren't listening to the stock market equivalents of Tsunami Smith (see that discussion later in the chapter).

At what point does the risk become so large that even the biggest risk takers need some sort of model before assuming the risk? Warren Buffett had the means to take on California earthquake insurance, but even he can't insure every hurricane, tsunami, wildfire, worm, software bug, or phishing attack. More methodical companies such as Swiss Re are moving into catastrophe bonds to provide retrocessional coverage of the reinsurance needed for insurers to issue insurance policies. Some of the biggest insurers can afford to gamble on issuing Internet business continuity policies without actuarial tables, as AIG is doing (see Chapter 11), but most cannot, and AIG can't do that forever. Each of these levels of insurance needs financial models so that none of them exceed their financial capacity.

Catastrophe Bonds

Hurricane Ivan of 2004 prompted the *Wall Street Journal* to publish an article about catastrophe (cat) bonds:

> *Cat bonds first began to appear in the 1990s after insurers and reinsurers suffered financially from storms such as Hurricane Andrew that struck Florida in 1992 and the Northridge Earthquake that hit California in 1994. From 1989 to 1995, total insured property losses in the U.S. were $75 billion, 50% more than the property losses from the prior 40 years, according to Standard & Poor's.[16]*

The *Wall Street Journal* didn't mention Buffett's role in reinsurance for California earthquakes, which actually precluded a role for cat bonds in that instance. Nonetheless, cat bonds have increasingly caught on since then.

Live Cats

Cat bonds did catch on, though:

> *Reinsurance giant Swiss Re, for example, is a major issuer of catastrophe bonds. A year ago, under its Arbor program, Swiss Re issued six catastrophe bonds with four-year maturities and total protection for Swiss Re of $205 million.[17]*

Still, nobody is as yet issuing cat bonds for Internet outages, even though a single Internet worm[18] could cost more than Hurricanes Charley, Frances, and Ivan combined, and $50 billion is much more than the $5 billion trigger for Berkshire Hathaway to have to pick up where the California Earthquake Authority leaves off.

Stripped Cats

One way of spreading the risk of a cat bond is by stripping it, that is, by splitting it up into multiple securities, each of which is assigned its own proportion of the total bond's principal payments and interest payments,[19] and with different ratings.[20] The ratings can come from a rating agency such as Moody's or Standard & Poor's. Such ratings are already standard practice for completion bonds that guarantee completion of a mortgaged building on time, so the building can be used as collateral for a mortgage. One strip might have a 13 percent coupon (interest) with a AA rating, while another might have a 10 percent coupon with a AAA rating. The higher interest strips for a cat bond would normally be used first if the catastrophe happens.

Popular Cats

Cat bonds have become increasingly popular in recent years. Artemis' Alternative Risk Transfer (ART) Deal Directory shows four in 2004 and four in the first half of 2005.[21] The subjects covered are all over the map. Perhaps the most popular subjects are earthquakes in California and Japan, hurricanes in the United States, typhoons in Japan, and windstorms in Europe. Another is based on indexes of mortality in five countries (United States, United Kingdom, Germany, Japan, and Canada).

In one unusual example, in 2003, "FIFA, world football's governing body, is set to issue a so-called catastrophe bond to protect its investment in the 2006 World Cup in Germany."[22]

Not a small one, either: 400 million euros or $437 million U.S. dollars. This cat bond is for postponement or cancellation, including because of risk of terrorism, but excluding world war or boycott.

> *FIFA conscientiously opted for this arrangement having carefully evaluated the traditional insurance market, which no longer covers FIFA's needs as required. As a result of the attacks in the USA on 11 September 2001 and the subsequent withdrawal by insurers from the 2002 FIFA World Cup cancellation insurance policy, FIFA requires any future protection to be immune from such risk. The proposed transaction meets FIFAs requirements in this respect.*[23]

This FIFA cat bond, co-managed by Credit Suisse First Boston and Swiss Re Capital Markets, was apparently a triple first, for transferring credit risk of an event, for covering terrorism risk, and for combining man-made and natural catastrophe risk.

This cat bond appears to have been stripped:

> *The bond was rated A3, or mid-investment grade by ratings agency Moody's Investors Service. It came in four tranches denominated in three currencies via a special purpose vehicle called Golden Goal Finance Limited.*[24]

These are all examples of how cat bonds are one way capital markets are increasingly assuming risks that were formerly covered by insurance.

In addition, the deals listed by Artemis seem to be evolving from various ad hoc structures to mostly cat bonds.

If cat bonds can cover cancellation of a sporting event and indexes of mortality, they ought to be able to cover a worst-case Internet worm and Internet slowdowns.

Exceptional Conditions

It is worth looking at a few exceptional conditions to see if some of them may be appropriate for cat bonds.

Tsunami Insurance

The tsunami of December 2004 raises a number of interesting questions. It appears that insurers usually exclude tsunamis from flood coverage, considering them more like earthquakes. Whether there is such an exclusion in a given earthquake or flood insurance policy seems to depend on the policy. As is the case with Internet outages and other cyber risks, you can't depend on standard insurance coverage being enough without checking it. See Chapter 11 for more on this.

Insurers don't seem very worried about excess claims for the tsunami,[25] possibly because of exclusions like those mentioned previously, and also because the insurers are often covered by catastrophe reinsurance.

2004, Record Year for Disasters

According to Swiss Re, 2004 was the most expensive in modern history for natural and man-made disasters, with $123 billion in total losses and $49 billion in property insurance claims.[26] The December Indian Ocean tsunami claimed by far the most lives, the most since the Bangladesh floods of 1970. But the most in dollar amount of property insurance claims was from hurricanes in the Americas, topped by Hurricane Ivan with $11 billion, and from typhoons in the Pacific, topped by Typhoon Songda with $4 billion in Japan and South Korea. The big discrepancy between where lives were lost and where financial claims were most would seem to indicate that many of the people affected by the tsunami probably weren't insured. With more reinsurance, backed by cat bonds, maybe more people would be insured.

Global Warming Insurance

Canadian TV presented a three part series at the end of 2004 called The Great Warming,[27] which compares global warming, especially the challenge of the coming period as it increases, to the Great Depression or a Great Plague.

The TV series is sponsored by Swiss Re.[28] That reinsurer and financial services company (one of the largest in the world) is sufficiently interested in this issue that it is reducing its own emissions by 15 percent, and the remaining 85 percent will be offset by investing in "clean development mechanism" instruments as described in the Kyoto protocol.[29]

Big reinsurers and financial services companies are working to meet the challenges of a warming world. Can they also meet the challenge of monetizing financial risk transfer instruments for Internet security?

It seems to me that one of the biggest problems with the recent tsunamis has been assessing the damage. Hundreds of islands hadn't even reported in days later. Investing in improved communications and monitoring might also be a good idea. This idea also applies to cyberhurricanes.

Insurers don't know who is affected by a given worm incident: which companies, which industries, whether they group that way, what does cause them to group, or how the probability of being affected changes with which security measure. Insurers need to avoid the peril to them of aggregation; they don't want to issue many policies and have claims come in on all of them at the same time. Nobody wants to be Lloyd's left holding the bag for the 1905 San Francisco Earthquake. Avoiding that goes beyond just looking at companies that are currently insured by a given insurer. Remember the boll weevil and what it took to contain it (see Chapter 2). What is needed is ongoing examination and analysis of the whole Internet all the time.

Cumbre Vieja Submerging Florida

The losses of the year 2004 could be small compared to what may happen if part of the volcano Cumbre Vieja falls off the island of La Palma in the Canary Islands.[30] An eruption could cause a block of rock twice the size of the Isle of Man to fall into the sea, releasing energy equal to half that of the electricity consumption of the United States in a year, and causing a tsunami that would produce waves at the western Sahara 300 feet high, smaller at Spain, Portugal, France, and Britain, at Brazil 120 feet high, and at Florida and the Caribbean 150 feet high.[31] Many of the most densely populated areas of Florida are only a few feet above sea level, so damages are expected to be in the trillions of dollars, at least 10 times greater than all the catastrophe losses in the record year of 2004.

Western Sahara may not have much insurance coverage, and maybe not Brazil, but the other places do. Or do they? Insurers have known about Cumbre Vieja since 2001 and have probably written exceptions into their policies.

Cumbre Vieja most recently erupted in 1949 and 1971. On the one hand, 1970 was the year of the most recent natural catastrophe at least as large as the 2004 Indian Ocean tsunami in loss of life, so it would not be wise to discount such an eruption just because it hasn't happened for 30 years. On the other hand, there has never in recorded history been an instance of a volcano falling into the sea such as is projected for Cumbre Vieja. (Although in 1958 a magnitude 8.0 earthquake caused a landslide into Lituya Bay in Alaska, producing a wave 1720 feet (a third of a mile or 524 meters) high on the other side of the bay.)

Further, the report remarks:

> The collapse will occur during some future eruption after days or weeks of precursory deformation and earthquakes. An effective earthquake monitoring system could provide advanced warning of a likely collapse and allow early emergency management organisations a valuable window of time in which to plan and respond.[32]

It's a little hard to imagine half of Florida and most of the U.S. East Coast as far north as Boston being evacuated. Florida is at least used to similar warnings due to hurricanes; Boston is not, although downtown Boston is not many feet from Boston Harbor and the Back Bay is landfill that would probably subside if inundated. Long Island would be another evacuation nightmare; it has no more protection from the sea than the Mississippi coast did during Hurricane Katrina. With enough warning perhaps it could happen. Still, in any case, early warning would not save many buildings from being washed away. Nonetheless, given the small likelihood of such an event actually happening, combined with the huge consequences if it did, perhaps this is an opportunity for a very large catastrophe bond that might not ever have to be used yet could be quite worthwhile if it did.

Cumbre Vieja is an interesting analogy to the kind of disasters that could happen on the Internet as more people and companies use it. Catastrophe bonds could be a way to handle such a disaster. As insurers increasingly issue Internet business continuity insurance and other cyber-insurance, they need better coverage themselves in case of aggregate claims. The potential aggregate risk is so large that reinsurers of cyberhurricanes also need coverage. Cat bonds are a likely financial risk transfer instrument that could provide sufficient financial depth for such retrocessional coverage.

Local Losses Covered by Global Investment

One thing about tsunamis is that they can affect many countries. The Indian Ocean tsunami originated in Indonesia and caused significant damage as far away as Africa. A Cumbre Vieja tsunami could affect perhaps even more countries. Ordinary insurance may seem unable to deal with such disasters, since premiums are normally paid in a single country. However, Lloyds of London covered much of the damage of the 1905 San Francisco earthquake in the United States, so risk can be spread across countries even with insurance. Catastrophe bonds can spread the risk even further, since they can be bought anywhere. They are an appropriate vehicle for Internet risk, which can spread worldwide in seconds.

Performance Bonds beyond Outages

While catastrophe bonds are generally for coverage of large-scale destruction, performance bonds are for slowdowns, brownouts, and other performance problems. Performance bonds have been used for some time by electric power utilities to cover them in case of brownouts. They can also be applied to Internet Security Provider (ISP) Service Level Agreements (SLAs). Performance bonds are discussed further Chapter 9.

Reliability over Price in ISP Selection

According to a 2004 survey by In-Stat/MDR:

> *Seventy-three percent of respondents said service quality/reliability was the most important criteria in selecting an Internet service provider.*
> *Sixty-nine percent selected price.*

Twenty-one percent of respondents selected company reputation, knowledgeable customer service staff, and availability at multiple locations/national footprint.[33]

It seems that performance and reliability have moved ahead of price in picking ISPs, and availability, reach, and topology are also significant criteria. Apparently Scott Bradner has been right all these years he's been saying that ISPs need to have a business model beyond price competition.

Given this situation, it would also seem that an ISP with a risk management plan and a performance bond would have a competitive edge. That sounds like a market for issuers of performance bonds.

Tsunami Smith: Mad Dog or Prophet?

In 1998 the former chief meteorologist of Thailand said ". . . a tsunami is going to occur for sure."[34]

Smith Dharmasaroja was called a mad dog for that. On Sunday December 26, 2004, after the earthquake but before the tsunami hit Thailand, he tried again to warn the Thai meteorological department but could not get them to respond. This is a case of denial and damage, just as happened years before in the United States regarding tornados, as we have seen back in Chapter 2.

How Did He Know?

How did Mr. Smith know? He didn't accept the received wisdom that earthquakes off Indonesia would happen only on the other side of Sumatra from Thailand. He studied seismology and discovered there was a fault line that would put the Thai tourist resort Phuket in the direct path of a tsunami. His public warning in 1998 was after a tsunami from the same fault hit Papua New Guinea (the Aitapa tsunami of Friday July 17, 1998). There was no tsunami warning system for that part of the Pacific at that time, either.[35]

"You'd really have to go digging into very old historical records and the scientific literature and extrapolate from what's there to find that yes, there could be effects (leading to tsunamis) in Thailand," says Phil Cummins, a seismologist who studies the region at Australia's national geological agency. "But he was correct."[36]

Such an earthquake did occur and the resulting tsunami hit Phuket.

Two weeks after the 2004 tsunami, the Thai government called Smith Dharmasaroja out of retirement to head its new tsunami warning system.[37]

The economic damages of the 2004 tsunami are estimated at $14 billion by Munich Re, the world's largest reinsurer.[38] Maybe it would be prudent to do some historical exploration and to set up an early warning system for Internet events that could cause $50[39] to $100 billion[40] in economic damages.

Tsunami Early Warning System

It seems likely that tsunami insurance would be easier to get if there were an early warning system. There is one for the Pacific[41] but none for the Indian Ocean.

Australia, which participates in the Pacific warning system, may have been the first country to volunteer (on December 27) to help set up a tsunami warning system for the Indian Ocean. Since then, India has announced it is building one to be operational within 3 years, Prime Minister Koizumi has ordered one for Japan, the United States has come out in favor of one, Thailand is lobbying to be the location for one, and there's been a meeting in Indonesia about the need for one. Early warning and tracking systems would be useful for other fields of likely major economic damage, such as the Internet. The next section discusses forms that such Internet early warning and tracking could take. Some of these forms are already in process; others need to be started and continued.

Internet Analysis: Beyond Information Sharing

There are several kinds of Internet analysis. One is simply gathering together existing sources of information and presenting them in a coherent manner, which is a major service. Two organizations specifically related to financial services that do this are FS/ISAC and APWG. Then there are questions of incidence of risk, including extent of risk, economic consequences, disaster accounting, and costs of breach of confidentiality, all of which require further analysis.

FS/ISAC: Financial Services Information Sharing and Analysis Center

FS/ISAC, which began in 1999, is reputed to be the most active of the ISACs. As the name indicates, FS/ISAC is for sharing information among companies in the Financial Services industry. Sharing in this case mostly consists of information detected by various Internet monitoring firms and presented via the FS/ISAC web pages to the member companies from the industry. It is not clear how much information the member companies actually volunteer.

FS/ISAC is operated by Science Applications International Corporation (SAIC). The current very nice web pages were funded by the U.S. Treasury Department. Further work is funded by membership fees.

The information presented is as timely as possible, showing effects on the industry. In-depth examinations of effects on specific enterprises are mostly left for individual information providers to provide directly to those specific enterprises.

APWG: Anti-Phishing Working Group

APWG collects information on incidents of phishing and publishes statistics and reports frequently. Its lively invitation-only meetings approximately quarterly draw participants from finance, banking, Internet application vendors, security vendors, government, and law enforcement. Its phishing repository collects phishing reports from its members in a database that is being mined by various parties to pull out useful aggregate information, such as evidence about compromised ISPs. It can even help with reputation systems, in which information about targets of phishing and compromised ISPs is made public so that customers of financial institutions can see which ones are being targeted and which ones are taking action against phishing, as well as which ISPs are compromised and which ones have done something about it.

Incidence of Risk beyond the Firewall

How probable are cyberhurricanes? What are their probable effects or duration, and who or what are they most likely to affect? To answer those questions requires data collection about the Internet outside the firewall, between the user and the server.[42] Rough data can be collected using mechanisms such as routing announcements, but the granularity is very coarse; similarly, packet intercepts can provide fine detail but from a very limited perspective.[43] Ongoing collection and analysis of the actual paths taken by packets and changes in their topology and performance is also needed.

Extent of Risk: Local Causes, Effects a World Away

By far most Internet events are small and produce only transient ripples. However, some local events can have other local effects a world away, as happened when physical damage in New York City on September 11, 2001, caused side effects as far away as Finland, Hungary, Italy, and South Africa.[44] An increasing number of large events, some global, some local, often have uneven effects, because of different software, different precautions, differently provisioned ISPs, different paths, or other reasons. The task is to quantify such unevenness in order to tilt the table and reap the rewards just ahead of the risk curve.

For this reason it may be useful to track odd events at the fringes, such as when the United Arab Emirates (UAE) froze over in 2004.[45] The whole country didn't freeze, but there was snow in the mountains, which was sufficiently unusual that the crown prince went to see it. A resident of the UAE reports:

Although the amount of rain (30 mm over 3 days) wasn't unusual, the cold weather was definitely unusual. Temperatures were 6–7 degrees below normal (avg high max 24, actual high temp 17–18, with cooler nights) So, it was much colder in the mountains. And because rain continued, it has turned into snow in the mountains.

What is the Internet equivalent of being able to see a combination of rain and cold that will produce snow in the mountains? Perhaps it is increasing variance in latency by time of day combined with increasing software monoculture or nonredundant routes. Add a worm or a big sporting event that produces more traffic, and response times may spike above what users are willing to tolerate, causing businesses to lose custom for the moment, and to lose customers if the snow in the Internet mountains continues very long.

To be able to see detail over time in the big picture requires a data collection technique that can resolve individual routers, and preferably paths, and do it frequently. Detection and characterization of particular types of anomalies must be tuned in conjunction with customers.

The Economic Consequences of Anomalies

For ISP performance bonds (see Chapter 9), the economic consequences of anomalies are largely defined by ISPs SLAs, plus probabilities of occurrence.

Cat bonds will be more like insurance policies, requiring building up from the bottom. In addition to incidence of risk, we need to know the value of the risk to the affected parties. To determine such economic consequences requires additional data beyond what can be collected directly from the Internet. It requires data fusion of historical and contemporary data from carriers, enterprises, news media, and others for verification and calibration. Such external data is used to determine costs of loss of transactions, sales, or customers, which can then be aggregated per affected party. In addition, for policies or bonds dealing with complete business interruption, one can also factor in how much a day of lost business is worth to a given class of business. This involves estimating how much business would just move to a different day. If every lost day were a catastrophe, Sundays would be disasters, yet a stock transaction tomorrow (that was meant for today) can be an economic disaster.

Disaster Accounting

This process of data fusion, verification, and calibration can be seen as a form of disaster accounting, just like determining what happened after a hurricane hits Florida (or Boston). As such, it feeds into pricing. The same data on incidence of risk and economic consequences can be used to reduce adverse selection by providing an external view of the likely value of insurance to a customer. It can be used to reduce moral hazard by keeping track of actual perils and anomalies related to a customer.

Costs of Breach of Confidentiality

Failing to keep sensitive consumer financial information confidential can be quite expensive in publicity, legal fees, and other costs.[46] See CardSystems and other examples discussed in the next chapter. If your company is going to outsource a financial process such as credit card collection, it would be prudent first to discover how the outsourcing agency is connected to the Internet, what sort of encryption they use, whether they in turn outsource to backup agencies, and what sort of connectivity and encryption those backup agencies have.

Early Warning and Tracking

Many people are jaded with the idea of early warning for Internet exploits because the time from discovery of a software vulnerability to exploit has shrunk from months to hours. So-called zero-day exploits happen now. This makes people think that early warning is not possible.

Yet it is possible. Software diversity can greatly decrease the likelihood of an exploit affecting all of a company's computers. Redundant paths can greatly reduce the probability of a company's customers being unable to reach it. Topological performance analysis can help predict how vulnerable a company's connections are to various kinds of perils. Increase or decrease in these factors can serve as early warning and as a form of tracking. In addition, while software exploits may be zero-day, they often in practice take effect according to local working hours, which differ by country and time zone. Thus a global mesh of up-to-date ongoing Internet analysis can see a zero-day exploit happening in Asia and warn likely targets in the Americas and Europe hours in advance. Hours may not be a long time, but they are more than zero time. And diversity, redundancy, and performance analysis can be applied now to reduce or prevent perils of days or months from now.

Traditional Security: The Arthashastra

According to tradition, around 300 B.C. Vishnagupta Kautilya wrote a book called the *Arthashastra* in which he spelled out in exhaustive detail the methods of statecraft, economics, law, war, and so on that he recommended, and that he had used to make Chandragupta Maurya emperor of India. Missing nothing, he identifies *force majeure* events in much the same way we do today:

> *Calamities due to acts of God are: fires, floods, diseases and epidemics, and famine.*
> *Other calamities of divine origin are: rats, wild animals, snakes, and evil spirits. It is the duty of the king to protect the people from all these calamities.*[47]

He recommends the government be the guarantor not only of last resort but of first resort: "Whenever danger threatens, the King shall protect all those afflicted like a father and shall organize continuous prayers with oblations."[48]
And he recommends specific measures:

All such calamities can be overcome by propitiating Gods and Brahmins. When there is drought or excessive rain or visitations of evil, the rites prescribed in the Atharva Veda and those recommended by ascetics shall be performed. Therefore, experts in occult practices and holy ascetics shall be honoured and thus encouraged to stay in the country so that they can counteract the calamities of divine origin.[49]

He provides a handy table of which deities to propitiate for which calamity, for example Agni the god of fire for wildfires. The book doesn't say whether he recommends posting different risk level colors from time to time.

To be fair, he also includes practical instructions for specific calamities, such as the following: "During the rainy season, villagers living near river banks shall move to higher ground; they shall keep a collection of wooden planks, bamboo and planks."[50]

In addition, the King is to keep stores of food and seeds to distribute in case of famine. So, Kautilya advises some collective action as practical insurance.

He also discusses relative seriousness of calamities, dismissing irremediability in favor of breadth of effect. Some previous pundits had ranked fire as the most serious, because it burns things up irremediably, but Kautilya ranks flood and famine as most serious because they can affect whole countries, followed by fire and disease, and then by local problems such as rats. So, the concept of aggregation as used by modern insurers is apparently at least 2300 years old.

Nonetheless, Kautilya does not mention pooling finances in a form that would be recognizable as insurance. That was a risk management strategy yet to be invented in India.

Modern Risk Management?

Ancient India under the Guptas had *force majeure* events such as flood, fire, and famine just like we do today, and Kautilya in his *Arthashastra* expected the king (government) to step in, because insurance apparently hadn't been invented yet. Recent news indicates that apparently insurance still isn't much applied, not only in India but also on the Internet:

Residents in the Middle East who are sweltering in the heat and humidity must be baffled by the scope and ferocity of flood waters lashing huge parts of South Asia, including India, Bangladesh, reports of which are now being televised daily.

How can nature be so discriminating that it punishes one part of the world with drought and penury while forcing evacuations elsewhere with floods?

While billions of dollars are lost in these countries, which affects their national economies adversely, the insurance industry is left almost untouched as most of the goods and lives lost are uninsured.

Conversely, in the United States, Canada, Western Europe and Japan, for instance, the insurance industry generally plays an active role in providing financial protection against such miseries.

For this reason, natural calamities such as earthquakes and floods, even when they strike with their full might in the subcontinent and South-East Asia, do not hugely impact the global economic outlook.[51]

Insurers in countries that do try to insure natural disasters support an index called the Tropical Storm Risk (TSR) that predicts how many hurricanes to expect.

According to a research report released in February by Munich Re, the largest reinsurance company, insured losses from natural catastrophes totalled $15.8 billion last year, up 37.4 per cent over 2002.[52]

That's a lot of money. But it's less than the $50 billion worst-case Internet worm risk for just the U.S.[53]

If it is wise to insure against fire, flood, and storm, shouldn't it also be wise to insure against cyberhurricanes that could cause even more economic damage?

No-Go Areas for Commerce?

1998 was a previous record year for damage from weather; for example, Bangladesh flooded again. In November of that year the *Times* of London published an article about no-go areas for insurers shown on a climate disaster map, available from Munich Re:

Vast areas of the world are becoming uninsurable as global warming triggers devastating and costly rises in sea levels, as well as droughts, floods and increasingly violent storms.

Experts fear that some nations, especially those in the Caribbean, parts of Asia and the Pacific, face greater economic hardship. They believe insurance cover, vital for attracting inward investment to develop tourist resorts and protect homes and businesses, will become prohibitively high. In some areas it may disappear entirely as insurers protect themselves from multibillion-pound claims.[54]

The map didn't show anything that wasn't available through various public sources, but it showed it graphically and compiled all on one map.

While the article says that insurers will not want to say publicly that they will not insure certain geographical areas, one has to wonder how easy it is to get insurance in, for example, Bangladesh,[55] or tsunami-prone coasts of the

Indian Ocean. Bruce Sterling speculates further on what the results could be for such geographical areas,[56] but I want to apply the analogy to the subject of this book.

Do we want the same thing to happen to the Internet? Will we write off chunks of it as uninsurable no-go areas for commerce? Some steps in that direction have already been taken; for example, many companies block electronic mail from South Korea entirely because so much spam and phishing is staged through there. And Korea is not a poor Pacific island nation slowly sinking into the ocean; it is one of the most developed countries on the planet. In fact, it is one of Korea's most developed features that facilitates this problem: fast broadband everywhere, with plenty of inadequately secured home and business computers. Thus blocking mail from Korea looks like blocking mail from many potential customers. I don't think that's a good solution.

No-go areas on the Internet are not going to segregate readily according to wealth, and they aren't all going to separate out by geography, either. Should a large corporation that doesn't secure its systems be blacklisted? This already does happen with antispam lists. Should such a corporation be able to get Internet business continuity insurance? Actually, it probably shouldn't, until it cleans up its act, anymore than a homeowner who insists on building on a beach in a historical hurricane path should be able to get insurance.

Even with cleaner acts, we will all still be at risk, due to the unpredictable scale-free nature of the Internet. Thus far, such apparently unlimited risk has frightened off most insurers.

For physical world insurance, catastrophe bonds have emerged as a way to provide sufficient financial depth to cover huge catastrophes. Will insurers continue to treat the entire Internet as a no-go area, or will financial services companies step forward with catastrophe bonds for the Internet? I think we'll see cat bonds for the Internet once companies increase their demands for cyber-insurance, as they are already doing.

Turning Externalities into Profits

The PriceWaterhouseCoopers survey of 2004 said, "Compliance is not being turned into competitive advantage."[57]

Compliance may be seen as an attempt by governments and oversight bodies to turn externalities into costs for financial institutions. Yet even compliance can be turned to competitive advantage, starting with doing it first and best and advertising that.

Why not go beyond compliance and find ways to leverage externalities produced by the Internet into competitive advantages?

Bandwidth Futures

Looking backward a couple of years, here's an interesting article about carriers hedging risks by taking out options on future bandwidth prices, among various other forms of risk management (anything except bandwidth trading, which got a bad name because of Enron). One of the most interesting passages I think is this one about carriers not necessarily knowing themselves:

> *Ciara Ryan, a partner in the bandwidth team at global consulting firm Andersen, agrees. Ryan explains the lack of visibility is due in part to mergers and acquisitions creating carriers that are an amalgam of many parts. The information pertaining to these assets has been integrated poorly, making it difficult to employ risk-management tactics, she says.*
>
> *Ryan says carriers must be able to extrapolate key bits of information from their databases to manage their network assets properly. This would include how much they have sold on a particular route, from which point of presence (PoP) it was sold, what the service level agreement (SLA) entailed, whether an option was sold on the contract, whether a contract was a short-term lease or indefeasible rights of use (IRU) agreement and what the definite and projected sales include on particular routes.*
>
> *"Very, very few of them would be able to give you this information," Ryan adds.*[58]

And that's before considering paths all the way from the carrier's customer to its customers. If the carriers don't even know what their own networks consist of, it would appear they can't be expected to provide a holistic and synoptic view of the Internet, neither one by one or all together. Third-party risk assessment companies will have to fill this gap. Performance bonds may be the path forward to such an actionable view of the Internet and its constituent ISPs.

Collateral Shredding

One effect of the privacy requirements of HIPAA has been an increase in shredding of documents. According to a 2005 news article:
"The number of U.S. shredding companies belonging to the National Association of Information Destruction trade group has doubled to 550 over the past three years."[59]

This shredding growth is due to several reasons, including the dot.com bust (all those companies going out of business needed documents shredded) and HIPAA coming into effect in April 2003. Yet another compliance concern arose in 2004:

> *Then, a new rule issued by the Federal Trade Commission last October under the 2003 federal Fair and Accurate Credit Transactions Act began requiring more businesses than ever to destroy credit reports or information derived from them. The act*

was intended to prevent identity theft, where crooks hijack someone's personal, credit or bank information and use it to steal cash or make fraudulent purchases.[60]

The new FTC rule went into effect in June 2005, with a grace period until December 2005 for compliance. What other firms have benefited from the new regulations, and which of them need financial instruments? This is a question that financial institutions could pursue to their profit.

Smart Connections

As Howard Rheingold noted in his book, *Smartmobs*:

When you piece together these different technological, economic, and social components, the result is an infrastructure that makes certain kinds of human actions possible that were never possible before: The killer apps of tomorrow's mobile infocom industry won't be hardware devices or software programs but social practices. The most far-reaching changes will come, as they often do, from the kinds of relationships, enterprises, communities and markets that the infrastructure makes possible.[61]

He was talking about mobile telephones and texting in particular, which have numerous effects, apparently including swaying a presidential election in South Korea. That technology increasingly interacts with the Internet, for example, in mailing pictures from phones to people. And technologically mediated group interactions have also been taking place without mobile devices, and will increasingly do so, as displayed by eBay, Google, P2P file sharing, and the sales, customer, and supplier interactions of many businesses. So, the important criterion here is not mobile, but social.

Social changes aren't all as large as completely new behaviors or changes of government. Some are small mutations to existing practices, often business practices. For example, even Warren Buffett delivers his shareholder letters online these days,[62] which makes them much easier to file, find, and search. Rheingold's book is available in HTML online, which makes finding appropriate passages and quoting them far easier, and much recent experience indicates that such online availability increases sales of the same books on paper.

Probably more new businesses and business practices will emerge from such small pieces loosely joined.[63] The question to ask is then what financial risk transfer instruments would help facilitate them. I'm sure there are further answers beyond the ones I've already given in this chapter, answers that will address lucrative niche markets.

Economic Derivatives

Goldman Sachs and Deutsche Bank are offering options markets for economic derivatives based on indicators such as jobs, housing, inflation, and consumer sentiment.[64] Their method avoids basis risk by not requiring buyers or sellers to be precise about prices; they can trade options on ranges of values of specific indicators.

Financial Derivatives of Network Laws

As mentioned in Chapter 1, Reed's Law is about options. Reed has elaborated on that point:

> And if you look at my original notes on the subject, I have always pointed out that you have to consider this value in the context of what people can spend to "exercise" these options (denominated in $ or minutes of attention, the actual realizable value should be linear in the number of users, once their spending power or attention is saturated). Utility (value) in economics is essentially a formal quantity, and is used only to rank choices—the actual price of an object turns out to be monotonic in utility, but not a direct function of utility.
>
> Metcalfe's Law and Reed's Law, in the end, are about assigning comparative value to an "architecture" independent of the end-user's utility functions. As such, it is appropriate in thinking about architecture to weight each option of a class equally. However, real user preferences are likely to be both heterogeneous and complex, so one would have to weight both the options created, but also alternatives "outside" the network that compete for users' resources of money and attention.[65]

Is there room for financial derivatives that can hedge on the growth of new product offerings according to how quickly Metcalfe's Law and Reed's Law will enable them to grow and then saturate? Or how quickly security exploits will cause financial problems for their vendors and customers, or for that matter for the rest of the Internet?

Who will offer markets similar to Goldman Sachs' economic derivatives that also take into account changes in the effects of Reed's Law according to the current size of the Internet and of the connectivity of certain types of products? Or amount of traffic for certain services, for example P2P services? How about options on security effects according to Internet growth and communications media or security options based on the prevalence of factors such as nonredundant links or routers near overload or known unpatched servers in certain ISPs, or topographical or geographic sections of the Internet, or industries, or individual enterprises?

Innovation Will Outmode Specifics

A document published by the Basel committee called "Risk management principles for electronic banking" has an interesting passage in a section about legal and reputational risk management:

To protect banks against business, legal and reputation risk, e-banking services must be delivered on a consistent and timely basis in accordance with high customer expectations for constant and rapid availability and potentially high transaction demand. The bank must have the ability to deliver e-banking services to all end-users and be able to maintain such availability in all circumstances. Effective incident response mechanisms are also critical to minimise operational, legal and reputational risks arising from unexpected events, including internal and external attacks, that may affect the provision of e-banking systems and services. To meet customers' expectations, banks should therefore have effective capacity, business continuity and contingency planning. Banks should also develop appropriate incident response plans, including communication strategies, that ensure business continuity, control reputation risk and limit liability associated with disruptions in their e-banking services.[66]

The document also says that the reason it sets forth principles instead of rules or even best practices is that it expects that innovation will outmode anything even as specific as best practices.

Hindsight Is 10/20

Tsunami forecasts may be all the rage after the Indian Ocean tsunami and the record natural disaster year of 2004. One correspondent remarks that hindsight is better than 20/20:

Regarding media, my prediction is that the 2005 Super Bowl will do a natural disaster pregame show feature this year. Corporate sponsors often influence what goes on with regard to environment, business, and natural disaster followup.[67]

And he wrote that *before* Hurricane Katrina demolished the U.S. Gulf Coast. Which financial institutions will be the first to pioneer new financial risk instruments for the Internet such as catastrophe bonds and performance bonds? Who will be the first to be able to brag about its increased credibility and authority with Internet risk as Swiss Re CEO John Coomber did with environmental risk:

I think you know that Swiss Re is committed to being a socially and environmentally responsible company. Because of that, we're taking a leadership role by putting strategies in place that will deal with the risks (and the opportunities) of our changing climate.[68]

The climate of corporate connectivity is undergoing a sea change, rising with the tide of Internet use. Which captain of industry will make the first fortune monetizing commerce for that new sea?

Notes

1. Patrick Barta, "Thai official once reviled for tsunami prediction back in charge: Disaster warning came in '98 speech," *The Wall Street Journal*. (Bangkok, Thailand, 11 January 2005). www.signonsandiego.com/uniontrib/20050111/news_1n11smith.html

2. "Financial Institutions still grappling with less quantifiable forms of risk." (PricewaterhouseCoopers and the Economist Intelligence Unit, Singapore, July 29, 2004). www.pwc.com/extweb/ncpress release.nsf/docid/28247DC2B0EB6CC8CA256EE00025E617

3. Gartner, "Gartner Says ATM/Debit Card Fraud Resulted in $2.75 Billion in Losses in Past Year." (Stamford, Connecticut, August 2, 2005). www.gartner.com/press_releases/asset_133138_11.html

4. Brian Bergstein, "Analysts say ATM systems highly vulnerable to fraud." (Associated Press, August 2, 2005). http://politics.yahoo.com/s/ap/atm_vulnerabilities

5. Op. cit. Gartner, "Gartner Says ATM/Debit Card Fraud Resulted in $2.75 Billion in Losses in Past Year."

6. Op. cit. Bergstin, "Analysts say ATM systems highly vulnerable to fraud."

7. Op. cit. Gartner, "Gartner Says ATM/Debit Card Fraud Resulted in $2.75 Billion in Losses in Past Year."

8. Hilary Kramer, "Cyber Fears On Fed's Web Plan." (August 15, 2004). www.interesting-people.org/archives/interesting-people/200408/msg00183.html

9. Ibid.

10. "FedLine Advantage," *Federal Reserve Financial Services* (2004). www.frbservices.org/Electronic-Access/Fedline Advantage.html

11. *Fedfocus*, Volume 2, Issue 2 (May 2004).

12. Ibid.

13. Warren Buffett, *Chairman's Letter.* (Berkshire Hathaway, Inc., February 28, 1997). www.ifa.com/Library/Buffet.html

14. Nicholas Weaver and Vern Paxson, "A Worst-Case Worm," *The Third Annual Workshop on Economics and Information Security (WEIS04).* Digital Technology Center, University of Minnesota (May 13–14, 2004). www.dtc.umn.edu/weis2004/weaver.pdf

15. Op. cit. *Chairman's Letter*.

16. Carrick Mollenkamp and Christopher Oster, "Investors Who Bet On Storms, Disasters Gauge Trade Winds," *The Wall Street Journal* (September 13, 2004). `http://finance.baylor.edu/weblogs/riskmgmt/docs/catbonds.pdf`

17. Ibid.

18. Op. cit. Weaver and Paxson, "A Worst-Case Worm."

19. "Types of Bonds," *InvestingBonds.com.* (The Bond Market Association, 2005). `www.investinginbonds.com/learnmore.asp?catid=5`

20. Christopher McGhee, "Catastrophe Bonds Come of Age," *MMC Views,* 2 (2000). Originally available at `www.mmc.com/views/00wintermcghee.shtml`

21. *ART Deal Directory,* Artemis, The Alternative Risk Transfer Portal (July 2005). `www.artemis.bm/html/dealdir/index.htm`

22. Ibid.

23. Ibid.

24. Ibid.

25. "Insurers May Have Some Tsunami Claims Exposure," *Forbes.com,* (December 27, 2004). `www.forbes.com/markets/equities/2004/12/27/1227automarketscan08.html`

26. Swiss Re, "New Swiss Re sigma study on catastrophes in 2004: more than 300,000 fatalities, insured losses reach nearly USD 50bn." (Zurich, March 1, 2005). `www.swissre.com/INTERNET/pwswpspr.nsf/fmBookMarkFrameSet?ReadForm&BM=../vwAllbyIDKeyLu/bmer-6a2auz?OpenDocument`

27. *The Great Warming.* (Stonehaven CSS Canada, December 2004). `www.thegreatwarming.com`

28. Alex Steffen, "The Great Warming and The Greening of the Reinsurance Industry," *Worldchanging.com* (December 25, 2004). `www.worldchanging.com/archives/001795.html`

29. Ibid.

30. Steven N. Ward and Simon Day, *Cumbre Vieja Volcano—Potential collapse and tsunami at La Palma, Canary Islands.* (University of California, Santa Cruz, August 31, 2001). `www.es.ucsc.edu/~ward/papers/La_Palma_grl.pdf`

31. Patrick Edwards, "Mega-tsunami to devastate US coastline." (University College London, August 31, 2001). `www.eurekalert.org/pub_releases/2001-08/ucl-mtd082301.php`

32. Ibid.

33. Daryl Schoolar and Kirsten Fischer, "Despite Price Erosion, Business Internet Access Service Revenues Continue to Grow," In-Stat/MDR. (Scottsdale, Arizona, September 27, 2004). `https://www.internet perils.com/risk.php#Schoolar1`

34. Op. cit. Barta, "Thai official once reviled for tsunami prediction back in charge."

35. George Pararas-Carayannis, "The Earthquake And Tsunami of 17 July 1998 In Papua-New Guinea (Png)," *The Tsunami Page of Dr. George P.C.* (2000). `www.drgeorgepc.com/Tsunami1998PNG.html`

36. Patrick Barta, "A meteorologist who alerted about a possible Asian tsunami recovers his prestige," *Dow Jones Newswires* (January 12, 2005). `www.sentidocomun.com.mx/articulo.phtml?id=5272`

37. Op. cit. Barta, "Thai official once reviled for tsunami prediction back in charge."

38. Tsucost and Reuters, "Insurer puts tsunami cost at $14bn," *Climate Ark - Climate Change Portal* (December 29, 2004). `www.climateark.org/articles/reader.asp?linkid=37698`

39. Op. cit. Weaver and Paxson, "A Worst-Case Worm."

40. mi2g, "Silently preparing for the $100 billion cyber-catastrophe risk," *News Alert.* (mi2g, February 16, 2004).

41. NOAA, "Pacific Tsunami Warning Center," *NOAA's National Weather Service*, NOAA (June 25, 2004). `www.prh.noaa.gov/ptwc`

42. John S. Quarterman, Peter F. Cassidy, and Gretchen K. Phillips, *Internet Risk Bonds: Essential Reinsurance Proxy for CyberHurricane Risk Management.* (InternetPerils, Inc., July 2004).

43. John S. Quarterman and Peter H. Salus, "Why Do the Graphs of the Slammer Worm Differ So Much?," *Proceedings of TPRC 2003.* (Telecommunications Policy Research Conference, 2003).

44. John S. Quarterman, "Reachability of four representative sets of Internet hosts on September 11 and 12" in *The Internet Under Crisis Conditions: Learning from September 11,* Computer Science and Telecommunications Board (CSTB), National Research Council of the National Academies (2003).

45. "Cold snap brings Gulf rare snow: Snowfall in Ras al Khaimah," *BBC* (December 30, 2004). `http://news.bbc.co.uk/2/hi/middle_east/4135857.stm`

46. Robert McMillan, "Court orders CardSystems to retain breach information," (IDG News Service, August 4, 2005). `www.computerworld.com/securitytopics/security/story/0,10801,103666,00.html`

47. L. N. Rangarajan, ed., Vishnagupta Kautilya, *The Arthashastra.* (New York: Penguin Books, 1992).

48. Ibid.

49. Ibid.

50. Ibid.

51. V. A. Tommy, "Managing Risk: Natural disasters: It is wise to prepare for worst," *Gulf News.* `www.gulf-news.com/Articles/Business2.asp?ArticleID=129344`

52. Ibid.

53. Weaver and Paxson, "A Worst-Case Worm."

54. Nick Nuttall, Environment Correspondent in Buenos Aires, "Climate disaster map pinpoints 'no-go' areas for insurers," *The Times.* (London, November 9, 1998).

55. Bruce Sterling, "The World Is Becoming Uninsurable, Part 2," *Viridian Note,* 00022. `www.viridiandesign.org/notes/1-25/Note%2000022.txt`

56. Ibid.

57. Op. cit. "Financial Institutions still grappling with less quantifiable forms of risk."

58. Josh Long, "Carriers Seek Rewards of Risk Management," *Phone+ Magazine* (January 2002). `www.phoneplusmag.com/articles/211trade1.html`

59. Sue McAllister and Michele Chandler, "Identity Theft a Boon for Document Shredding Business," *Mercury News* (San Jose, California, August 4, 2005). `www.siliconvalley.com/mld/siliconvalley/12302178.htm`

60. Ibid.

61. Howard Rheingold, *Smart Mobs: The Next Social Revolution.* (Perseus Publishing, 2002). `www.smartmobs.com/book`

62. Op. cit. *Fedfocus,* Volume 2, Issue 2.

63. David Weinberger, *Small Pieces Loosely Joined: A Unified Theory of the Web.* (Perseus Books Group, May 2003). `www.smallpieces.com`

64. Goldman Sachs, *Economic Derivatives*. (Goldman Sachs, 2005). `www.gs.com/econderivs/`

65. David P. Reed, "I'm happy to comment on the Odlyzko and Tilly paper, briefly," *Dewayne-Net Digest*, #1526, Dewayne Hendricks (March 8, 2005).

66. "Risk management principles for electronic banking," *Basel Committee Publications*, No. 98 (July 2003). `www.bis.org/publ/bcbs98.htm`

67. John C. Griffin, "Hindsight is 23/22," *Perilocity* (January 14, 2005).

68. Alex Steffen, "The Great Warming and The Greening of the Reinsurance Industry."

CHAPTER 7

Large Enterprises: Big Risks, Big Solutions

Companies' margins are thin, and risk management is a huge part of running a big business these days.[1]

—Terry Duffy, Chair of the Chicago Mercantile Exchange

Unlike banks, many large enterprises are not averse to all risks. This is one reason that the average Fortune 500 company is not likely to completely implement a strategy like Basel II. However, the size of the risks inherent in using the Internet has come to the attention of big company CEOs, some of whom now think that such a risk big enough to wipe out their company requires some risk management.

Big companies are the main targets of SOX and other legislation such as Canada's PIPEDA and Europe's DPD. Beyond compliance with such higher legal standards of diligence, the CFO needs insurance and possibly cat bonds, engineering needs information beyond the firewall and beyond the local ISP, and both need visualizations that facilitate cost containment, deployment, and customer support.

Risk Management As Corporate Management

Consider what risk management means as a type of corporate management.

EWRM: Enterprise-Wide Risk Management Systems

Jennifer Cartmell, chief risk officer at Texaco, told the World Insurance Forum in Bermuda in December 1999 that Enterprise-Wide Risk Management

(EWRM) was the next big thing. Six months later, she resigned. Why didn't EWRM get the uptake she expected?

> *Establishing an EWRM system is expensive, she said. Firms have difficulty establishing centralised risk management controls because most companies are organised into silos and division heads don't like having power taken away from them, she explained. And according to one source close to the situation, these elements played a part in making things come unstuck at Texaco.*[2]

People remaining at Texaco mentioned other reasons, such as an impending merger with Chevron and that an oil company could and even wanted to accept some risks that banks could not.[3] Nonetheless, trying to get an entire big corporation to subscribe to EWRM may be difficult.

Fortunately, since 1999 Moore's Law has shifted availability of EWRM software away from big box in-house solutions requiring consultants to babysit them towards Application Software Provider (ASP) solutions that cost less and are easier to deploy.

> *"We're componentising what we offer as a product suite," says Paul Smetanin, senior director of product strategy and marketing at Algorithmics in Toronto. "Clients are now able to be far more selective in their choice of functionality. Rather than having to buy a new car with all the extras, we can now allow clients to be selective as to what extras they require."*[4]

This sounds a lot like the type of fifth wave product described Chapter 8. In other words, while an all-company risk equation such as that Basel II defines may be just what banks need, that style of risk management may be too structured for other big businesses.

Of course, this is not to say there can't be enterprise-wide risk management solutions for big businesses. Insurance and bonds can be such solutions, for example, even if capital withholding in the Basel II style is not.

EWRM in the sense discussed here is mostly about credit risk and market risk. Operational risk, especially Internet operational risk, is new not only to Basel II, but it is also a new wildcard in big business.

Profits Up the Stovepipe

One reason some large corporations have not done much about risk management is that they are organized in stovepiped departments whose heads want no power taken away from them for any reason. As Vladislav Surkov, deputy head of Russia's presidential administration said:

> *In this case, we are retarded in our conception of the authorities. Because the notorious power vertical is a primitive interpretation. Today, it is not the vertical that is ruling. The conception that there is a telephone above, the second telephone below, and the third far lower, is stupid. Unfortunately, many of our bureaucrats*

base themselves on those principles, not feeling and not understanding the current processes. This is a problem of the education and the retarded political culture.[5]

Top-down command and control alone isn't enough to win anymore. Surkov continued:

These are the reasons why the Soviet Union collapsed. Russia, too, may collapse because of it. But while the Soviet Union crashed kinglike, a catastrophe worth filming, we will decay slowly and everything will finish at this stage.[6]

That last sentence reminds me of AT&T's long, slow, demise. Of course, a big company not adequately prepared for a worst-case worm could meet a swifter demise. Many other large companies will choose an upward path, using risk management to prepare before the worst comes.

Agility for New Connections

Dealing with Surkov's "notorious power vertical" doesn't mean giving up corporate hierarchy; it means making it flexible and its workers agile. One of the most flexible and agile organizations around is the U.S. Marines, and they have ranks, uniforms, and salutes. They also have training in which they learn to operate on their own even in small groups, so that they don't have to have specific orders for every little thing they do.

Frederick Winslow Taylor[7] was wrong; John R. Boyd was right; the Marines got to be agile partly by studying Boyd.[8] The key to efficiency is not in specifying every move of every worker; it is in making sure every worker knows what the organization is trying to do and what they can do to help it. There isn't necessarily any one most efficient way to do anything, and efficiency isn't everything. Some things may be more important to do inefficiently than other things are to do efficiently. The key to grand strategy is communications, especially in a networked world. Networks can provide access to the information knowledgeable workers need to make many of their own decisions.[9]

Personal Empowerment and Group Connections

It may seem that agility is about personal empowerment, and it is.[10] However, it is even more about groups and connections. Sufficient agility should permit emergence of new ideas and behaviors that can assist with the corporate purpose even though they may not have previously been envisioned. Emergence occurs when local behavior produces observable macro phenomena[11]—in other words, when individuals or groups are flexible enough that they together do new things or do things in new ways.

Flexibility to permit new behavior is especially important in a networked world, where competitive advantages are to be gained from new uses of networked communications. Some of the most important emergent ideas may come from connections among groups of people who are not formal work-groups, and who may not even know each other.

Focus, Emergence, and Research

Corporate focus is good. But it needs to be, in Stephen R. Covey's terms,[12] more on Quadrant I (urgent and important) and less on Quadrant III (urgent but not important), with some time for Quadrant II (not urgent yet important), because that's where planning gets done. Exclusive focus on Quadrant I items may be good for the short-term bottom line, but it is not so good for long-term competitiveness.

Some time should even be spent in Quadrant IV (neither urgent nor important), because things may be found there that were not yet known to be important. Such Quadrant II and IV activity may be considered research; see Chapter 10 for more on why research is good for the economy. Government can't be expected to fund all research; corporations need to help, and by doing so they will help themselves.

However, emergence doesn't require formal research. It can happen with salespeople using camera phones to record customer's situations, or engineers organizing technical teams as needed across geographically disparate offices, or in the CTO's blog drawing interest in the company's products. Or it could even be as simple as the famous case of Sony chairman Akio Morita inventing the idea of the Walkman by noticing that Sony made cassette tape recorders and stereo headphones, and that if it combined the two, while omitting the speaker and the record function, Sony could make a wearable tape player. Connect two existing things and leave a few features out: an invention results.

The Pattern That Connects

With networks the connection doesn't even have to involve new physical things; it can be a new pattern of communication among people. A device can promote such a pattern, as well. The Walkman and the iPod don't get people to communicate directly very much, but cell phones and the Internet do. The more important question then is what people will use such communications to do. Emergence isn't so much about inventing a device as about multiple people doing things in a different pattern that none of them may have previously anticipated.

Google encourages engineers to spend 20 percent of their work time on personal projects.[13] Several of these projects are now visible as features on Google's web pages. Other companies may find other ways to encourage research and emergence. Software monoculture impedes emergence, and diversity of software and communications encourages it.

Deeper Than Mission

Of course, for all this to work the corporation needs a purpose beyond profit and deeper than mission, or the workers won't be able to focus on it without more specific instructions. Such a deeper purpose has long been a hallmark of successful long-lived companies.[14]

Even the banking industry's Basel II isn't really about ever more baroque details of quantification of credit and operational risk. It is about organizing the corporation in such a way that the various parts know what they need to do and some parts watch other parts so as to produce a sufficient combination of agility and oversight so that many risks are prevented and others are caught quickly. See Chapter 5 for more on Basel II.

Risk Management As Agility

Risk management is assisted by contingency plans, just as a good fire management plan needs exits and evacuation routes posted. But there may be more than one exit, and more than one way to put out a fire. Plus, you don't know which part of the building will fall down. Everyone needs to be able to act appropriately when the time comes. The right way out may be found by many people trying different exits and reporting back, and that is emergent behavior. A risk management plan needs to encourage sufficient agility for emergence to be possible.

New Responses to Risk

As Lord Levene, chairman of Lloyd's said:

> The impact of factors like business interruption and the rising importance of intangible assets means that we need to respond to risk in a new way. It also means that traditional risk management processes aren't always possible or desirable, let alone adequate. Business interruption often isn't covered by the traditional insurance policy. And few standard policies protect businesses from loss or damage to their intellectual property. But a growing range of insurance solutions are available. Take product recall insurance, where coverage has been designed not just to cover the cost of the recall, but also to provide the policyholder with access to risk management advice and services—and business interruption costs including marketing and publicity needed to restore the company's image.[15]

What can big business do about these new risks?

$100 Billion Cyberhurricane Risk

In the Introduction I mentioned the $100 billion cybercatastrophe risk some big company CEOs think they face,[16] and the reputable researchers' estimate of $50 billion in economic damage just in the United States from a single worst-case worm.[17] In Chapter 2, I described even more risks, some of which have reached the attention of major company CEOs:

> Lord Levene, Chairman of Lloyd's, the world's leading specialist insurance market, addressed U.S. business leaders about new global risks that threaten corporations including, but not limited to, business interruption costs, corporate fraud, and increased liability claims.[18]

As described in Chapter 3, there are steps any corporation can take to help prevent data theft, attacks, and loss of service. However, there are still risks beyond the control of any corporation, such as outages or slowdowns beyond the firewall, that can interfere with communications with customers, salespeople, suppliers, and outsourcers.

If you had known the likelihood of these events, and their extent and impact on the Internet, how would you have done things differently? You need to assess and track your organization's unique vulnerability to Internet-related risks, with specific information about the dangers that most threaten you and your customers so that you can best deploy your planning and security dollars.

Incident Reports

When something goes wrong in your enterprise network, your system administrators can try to figure out what's happening within your firewall. Your ISP monitors its own network and can usually identify problems there and plan contingencies for its customers in the event of an outage or interruption in their service. But the major perils facing Internet users lie outside local networks and outside ISPs. You need to extrapolate risk over the entire Internet.

Management Summaries

Individual incident reports need to be summarized daily and weekly for management reports. Because of the way the Internet is constructed, as a matrix of redundant, interconnected routes, no one else shares exactly the same risks with your corporation. You need to know the most likely dangers that your enterprise faces, given the geographic distribution of its employees and customers, the location and vulnerability of its Internet nodes, and the way it moves and uses data.

Risk Aggregations

Determining enterprise strategy also requires aggregations and predictions of frequency, duration, and probable effects of trouble and its sources, such as cable cuts, bad routing, worms, and terrorist attacks. See Chapter 6 for more detail.

Basic Security

These basic security methods have already been discussed in Chapters 3 and 4, but recent examples of big companies not using them indicate that it is worthwhile to reemphasize them here.

In early 2005, the company ChoicePoint, which assists employment applicant background checks by providing information on applicants, "confirmed that suspected criminals posing as legitimate businesses had gained access to some 145,000 of its own profiles of American consumers."[19]

In March 2005, crackers broke into a company called Seisint:

... gaining access to the personal data of an estimated 32,000 U.S. citizens, the Reed Elsevier Group said in a statement on Thursday. Seisint is a unit of Reed Elsevier's business information subsidiary LexisNexis. The break-in exposed names, addresses, Social Security numbers and driver's license information, the company said.[20]

Vermont Senator Patrick Leahy remarked:

"This is the latest window on security weaknesses that jeopardize the personal information that data brokers hold about every American, and the view is a chilling one," he said. "We are vulnerable not only to run-of-the-mill thieves but also potentially to sophisticated scams, organized crime or even terrorists. If criminals can breach these security arrangements, there is a danger that terrorists may also be able to."[21]

I don't know whether he was aware of the ATM and debit card exploits described in the Chapter 6, but they would seem to classify as sophisticated scams that could be facilitated by this kind of information leak.

Don't be surprised if these sorts of events result in new legislation. California Senator Dianne Feinstein had already the previous year introduced a bill that would require businesses to notify people whose personal information had been compromised.

The risk of such leaks is not theoretical: "In the ChoicePoint leak, some 750 cases of related identity fraud have already been reported to law enforcement officials, and a California man has pleaded no contest to felony charges related to the heist."[22]

And that was just the start of such problems in 2005.

Backups and Encryption

When employee data on 600,000 current and former coworkers of a Fortune 500 firm can go missing,[23] something is amiss in big business backup strategies. This happened with Time Warner, the world's largest media company, in 2005. The lost information included names and Social Security numbers, which could be very useful in phishing or other scams.

While the backup company, Iron Mountain, perhaps could have been more careful with the 40 lost tapes, storing them unencrypted nevertheless was not a good idea. While the Secret Service did not find any immediate misuses of the missing data, perpetrators of ID theft sometimes wait quite a while before using such information. A little encryption can prevent a lot of corporate and individual worry and federal investigation.

Shipping and Encryption

2005 seems to have been a bumper year for data losses: "In February, Bank of America said computer tapes containing data for some 1.2 million U.S. government employees, including U.S. senators, disappeared."[24]

Another happened in May 2005: "Citigroup Inc. (C) Monday said computer tapes containing account and payment history data, including Social Security numbers, on 3.9 million customers were lost by United Parcel Service Inc. (UPS)."[25]

Citigroup shipped the tapes via UPS from Weehawken, New Jersey, on May 2 to the credit bureau Experian in Texas. Apparently nobody noticed a problem until Experian asked Citigroup for a tracking number on May 20. Better controls could also be useful.

The tapes were not encrypted in any of these cases. A popular alternative suggestion was heard:

> Nick Akerman, a partner at Dorsey & Whitney LLP who represents companies whose data are lost, said: "If you're Citigroup, you'd want to ask if UPS is the proper way to deliver such information, and whether you should be using private deliverers to transport sensitive data."[26]

I've also heard this suggestion from bankers, who are used to sending cash between banks in the pockets of bank officers. But cash when stolen does not compromise customer's personal information. Stolen tapes do.

The bigger the business, the more important it is to remember: backups are good, but encrypted backups are better. Tapes still have very high throughput for shipping long distances, but that makes them very attractive to thieves: encrypt them before shipping.

Don't forget that most electronic mail is unencrypted, so be careful not to send personal information that way, either.

Outsourcers Also Need Security

In July 2005, 40 million MasterCard, Visa, and other credit card accounts were compromised due to a Trojan horse in software at credit card processor CardSystems Solutions.[27] Even if MasterCard International was secure and all the merchants and financial institutions for which CardSystems processed were secure, nonetheless aggregating all those card numbers at one processor permitted a successful exploit. MasterCard and CardSystems said that *only* "68,000 MasterCard accounts, 100,000 Visa accounts and 30,000 accounts from other card brands" were actually exported by the Trojan software. That's still a lot of unhappy consumers having to get new credit card numbers and hoping that the crackers aren't saving up ancillary data such as Social Security numbers for other exploits.

Both MasterCard and CardSystems claim they separately detected a problem and pursued it. According to both their accounts it seems to have taken them several months to identify the problem. Meanwhile, it became clear that CardSystems was holding information about accounts after transactions were complete, contrary to policy. CardSystems promised to comply with policy. At the same time, a court ordered CardSystems to retain information related to the security breach.[28] That would seem to make compliance with the policy difficult. Maybe the retained data will be encrypted.

It is easy for outsourcers and their customers to think that such policies are not important, because who would ever try to break in? This example indicates that sometimes someone will. Crooks are quite capable of figuring out who holds the most data or who is under the least security and attacking there. Better to be safe than sorry.

Passwords and Humint

Encryption is no good if the passwords are easily guessable or if they are written down where someone can easily find them or if people tell them to others who are unauthorized. These points may seem too obvious to state, but experience indicates they are seldom taken seriously. Humint (human intelligence as contrasted with sigint or signal intelligence) or social engineering (see Chapter 2) is among the most common ways of compromising security. People from secretaries to executives give out their passwords to unknown parties via the telephone, write them on their whiteboard, or use their pet's or spouse's or child's name as a password. Stories by real crackers such as Kevin Mitnick indicate social engineering is the most common means used in break-ins.[29]

Even a Little Diversity Is Good

Business cost saving and efficiency improvements via standardization may seem to indicate that it is best to standardize on one operating system, one electronic mail system, one database system, or so on. Recent peer-reviewed academic research[30] agrees with real-world experience that even a small amount of diversity in such software (and hardware) systems gains benefits.

Don't be fooled by thinking that running Macs or Linux or FreeBSD or another operating system in addition to Windows will cost too much in additional user inconvenience and administrative expense. The recent study, published at a Harvard security conference, shows that the overall benefits outweigh the costs. While it is theoretically possible to write a worm that will affect several operating systems equally and simultaneously, doing so is much harder than writing a worm that affects a single OS. So, a worm can still take down all of the computers running one OS, but the others will probably still be up. Being partly up is much better than being all down.

Layers of Security

Depending on a single layer of security such as a firewall alone is inviting a cracker to attack the one layer. It is better to have multiple layers, including per-machine passwords, firewalls, intrusion detection, intrusion prevention, SSL-VPN, and external monitoring. And don't forget patching, especially on individual users' computers, plus virus scans. Many companies have found out the hard way that no amount of internal corporate security measures will keep a worm out if users take unpatched laptops home at night and bring them to work the next day.

Don't forget password protection and encryption in-house for sensitive information. Encrypting backups and external communications won't be enough if an employee puts a current unencrypted copy of corporate files on a laptop or data stick and walks out the door with it.[31] In any company, there may be disgruntled employees or ex-employees who still have access. In a big company, the probability doesn't have to be high for one among thousands of employees to be that one. Plus, the bigger the company, the more valuable the data, and the more likely someone can be compromised by payments from other parties.

Security or Loss of Confidence?

As John Pescatore of Gartner has said: "Consumer confidence is now dropping faster than more security would ever have done."[32]

I've never trusted ATM cards, and I'm sure not starting now (see Chapter 6). I do use credit cards, but I'm not happy about it. A cash economy sounds better all the time, but that just isn't possible using the Internet.

Frank Smith, vice president at Capgemini, sums up the situation: "They don't supply due diligence to the whole system."[33]

The whole system includes tapes and passwords and outsourcers and shippers.

The big companies that get their security act together will be the ones consumers will want to use. Losing consumer data is a big reputation problem. Security is a competitive advantage.

Don't Try to Secure Alone

Big companies may think they can solve their security problems alone, or with a few security vendors. This isn't enough to deal with *force majeure* events and electronic crime. Your outsourcer may not be secure, or your shipping company. The next company on your same ISP Point of Presence (PoP) may not be secure and may slow down your customers by spewing excess traffic during the next worm. Electronic criminals try to hide, and often their tracks can be inferred only from seeing how they reach multiple targets. Collective action is needed for aggregate risk. Such action can include cooperation via clearinghouses such as FS/ISAC or APWG financial risk transfer, and even law enforcement. For clearinghouses see Chapters 3 and 6. For law enforcement, see the Chapter 10. Here, I will mention financial risk transfer instruments again.

Financial Risk Transfer Solutions

When risk becomes too large for a single organization to handle, insurance and other financial risk transfer instruments can spread the risk more widely.

Self-Insurance

If a large enterprise doesn't do anything about financial risk transfer, essentially it is insuring itself. An enterprise may also choose to self-insure. Banks do this with Basel II. Yet even Berkshire-Hathaway seeks reinsurance, and that's just for earthquakes. Internet risk can be even bigger, so it is probably best to look into external financial risk transfer instruments rather than trying to go it alone.

Insurance

Traditional insurance usually does not cover many Internet or computer-related problems. As discussed in Chapter 11, it is best to get coverage for Internet business continuity insurance and for risks related to the ever-higher standards of diligence required by SOX, GLBA, HIPAA, PIPEDA, DPD, and other laws and requirements.

Bonds

The largest companies may want to issue their own bonds, but most companies will use bonds indirectly because insurers will use them to provide sufficient capital for reinsurance and retrocessional coverage, as discussed Chapter 6.

Vulnerability Disclosure Hurts Share Price

A vulnerability disclosure is an announcement about a software defect. Academic researchers have demonstrated that vulnerability disclosure correlates with loss in share price of the vendor of the software. According to Robert Lemos of *SecurityFocus*, the study analyzed the release of 146 vulnerabilities and found that a software company's stock price decreased 0.63 percent compared to the tech-heavy NASDAQ on the day a flaw in the firm's product is announced. The study assumed that the stock of a company would have the same trend as the stock index, and that any departure from the index would be due to the disclosure.[34]

Such a share difference is enough for investors to see it and could be enough to make them think about more long-term judgments of the quality of the vendor's product. Lemos writes further:

> However, the paper also suggests that immediate disclosure of vulnerabilities, before a patch is available from the software maker, punishes companies to a higher degree. If the patch is available, a company's stock price falls 0.37 percent below the NASDAQ on average, while disclosing a vulnerability before a patch is available signaled a decrease of 1.49 percent, according to the paper.

The study itself notes that, somewhat counter intuitively, the market does not punish the vendor any more if a third party discloses the vulnerability than if the vendor makes the disclosure.[35] So apparently it pays to try to find a patch before announcing.

The study does not say what happens if miscreants meanwhile find the vulnerability and exploit it before a patch is announced. Nor does it say what the effect on share price is of missing a ship date while waiting for a fix to a vulnerability. The study used correlation, which does not necessarily imply causation, and showed a correlation with share price lasting only a few days.

Nonetheless, the effect was observable, and your shareholders will probably also be able to see it. Security affects the bottom line.

Vulnerability Bounties

TippingPoint (owned by 3Com) and iDefense (owned by Verisign) are both offering bounties for disclosure of vulnerabilities. Both firms apparently intend to reveal the disclosures to the affected vendors, rather than to the public.[36] Mozilla has for some time been paying $500 per bug found.[37] This is similar to paying for what open software gets for free: more eyes looking for flaws in the product.

Vulnerability Restraints?

At the same Black Hat Conference in Las Vegas at which TippingPoint announced its disclosure bounty, disclosures made the news for a slightly different reason on July 27, 2005:

> *Vulnerability disclosure was also an issue for the Black Hat Conference itself when former Internet Security Systems (ISS) research analyst Michael Lynn quit his job to provide information on a serious Cisco Systems router vulnerability at the conference. ISS decided not to give a presentation on the flaw, but Lynn quit so that he could give the presentation.*[38]

The vulnerability had already been fixed months before, so public disclosure would have seemed the normal course. Nonetheless, neither Cisco nor ISS wanted the talk about it given; Cisco actually had some of its employees physically remove the 10-page presentation from the printed proceedings books. Then Lynn quit his job with ISS less than 2 hours before the scheduled talk time and gave the presentation anyway, wearing a white hat labeled Good.[39]

> *During his presentation, Lynn outlined an eight step process using any known, but unpatched flaw, to compromise a Cisco IOS-based router. While he did not publish any vulnerabilities, Lynn said that finding new flaws would not be hard.*[40]

Lynn did not reveal any known unfixed specific exploits.

> *The vulnerability has been patched by Cisco, but some companies don't update patches regularly. In his presentation, Lynn described a now-patched flaw in the Internetwork Operating System (IOS) software used to power Cisco's routers. Although Cisco was informed of the flaw by ISS, and patched its firmware in April, users running older versions of the company's software could be at risk, according to Lynn.*[41]

Lynn claims that he previously threatened to resign when ISS proposed to reveal the specific vulnerability.[42]

Balancing Property and Propriety

After the presentation, Cisco and ISS got a restraining order against both Lynn and the conference to prevent them discussing the topic further.[43] Cisco's publicly stated rationale for the restraining order was this: "We don't want them to further discuss it," said Cisco spokesman John Noh. "This is about protecting our intellectual property."[44]

Elsewhere how intellectual property comes into this was explained as: "Cisco maintains Mr. Lynn found the flaw by reverse-engineering its product, which the San Jose, Calif., company said violates the law."[45]

Cisco's press release of 29 July on the subject noted, in part that:

> The court's order includes reference to the fact that ISS and Cisco had prepared an alternative presentation designed to discuss Internet security, including the flaw which Lynn had identified, but without revealing Cisco code or pointers which might help enable third parties to exploit the flaw, but were informed they would not be allowed to present that presentation at the conference.[46]

An ISS spokesman said the presentation shouldn't have been given because it was incomplete.[47] Cisco's PR amplified that point:

> In accordance with industry guidelines, Cisco, like other companies, generally does not release security notices until enough information exists to allow customers to make a reasonable determination as to whether or not they are at risk and how to mitigate possible risk.[48]

The Cisco PR promised a security advisory within the next day, and Cisco released one the same day as the PR.[49] One wonders why the security advisory wasn't released the same day as the conference presentation, regardless of which version of the presentation was given.

Whatever the reason for the restraining order, this probably won't be the last time companies have to decide how to balance intellectual property, fixing bugs, informing customers, getting customers to deploy the fixes, and the vendor's own reputation. The bigger the company, the higher the stakes, not only for the company but also for its customers and those affected by its software.

Restraining the Wind

News reports say that Lynn agreed to the restraining order, while reasserting that he had done a public service. Meanwhile, a PDF of Lynn's presentation was available on the Internet within two days. The URL at which it was first available switched within a day to show a copy of a letter from ISS's lawyer and of the injunction,[50] but copies of Lynn's slides are available elsewhere, for example from Germany.[51] Blog postings and news articles about the case proliferate. Restraining the mind of the Internet once it has gotten this kind of information is like restraining the wind.

A Draft, Not Yet a Hurricane

Lynn's slides spell out why such vulnerabilities could be important:

Wide Deployment

Switches

Routers

Access Points

In other words, Cisco's hardware tends to be widely deployed as the switches, routers, and access points that make up the fabric of the Internet. It is well known that many ISPs pick a single router vendor, so within a given ISP that vendor's routers could be a monoculture. The slides go on to list some motivations that people might have for taking advantage of such lack of diversity:[52]

Keys To The Kingdom (MITM)

Control the network traffic

Packet sniff in far off lands

Modify traffic

Break weakly authenticated encryption (passwords, etc.)

Routers in major ISPs would be optimal places for Man in the Middle (MITM) attacks, in which an attacker intercepts packets passing between two communicating parties and uses them to steal information or to deduce how to pretend to be one of the parties in order to gain access through one of the endpoints.

The most important claim in Lynn's presentation is that it is possible to fool Cisco's watchdog software and shell through one or more types of attacks. That is, it is possible to insert your own program onto the router to do practically anything. Anything could include shutting down network connections, which would be bad enough in itself. If a user's computer is compromised and has to be taken off the Internet, the Internet is still up. That is not necessarily so for a router, for example, a router connecting directly to an ISP's customer sites, for which there may be no alternate route. Any alternate routes could well be running the same software and be susceptible to the same attack. An attack that could modify the router software sufficiently that it wouldn't boot again even with manual intervention.

Then there are all the MITM attacks that could be staged. Just as an example, suppose the attacker decided to shut down connections to a major news server and replace content with its own. The possibilities are summarized in Lynn's slides as:

World Domination!

Such an exploit is about as close as you can get to that via the Internet.

Protection or Harassment?

Security experts could be expected to say Cisco was harassing one of their number, and they did.[53] But when even the *Wall Street Journal* (*WSJ*), usually known as a supporter of big business, weighed in with a headline "Cisco Tries to Squelch Claim About a Flaw in Its Internet Routers"[54] and continued by saying Cisco was threatening Lynn with the restraining order, it would seem that whatever the motives of the parties, the case had turned into a public relations problem for Cisco.

> *"The vulnerabilities are out there on the Net in full broadcast mode," said Gilman Louie, a tech-industry veteran who heads In-Q-Tel, a venture-capital firm backed by the Central Intelligence Agency. "The bad guys get to it faster than everybody else. I'd rather have disclosure and let everybody respond."*[55]

If Michael Lynn could disassemble Cisco's code, it is safe to assume a real black hat cracker could do the same. And while Cisco and ISS could get a restraining order on Michael Lynn and the Black Hat Conference to stop them even talking about the presentation any more, they couldn't stop the presentation from being distributed over the Internet,[56] nor could they stop everyone from Bruce Schneier[57] to the *WSJ*[58] from discussing it.

For that matter, Michael Lynn didn't have to quit his job and give the presentation to get his point across. He could have just stood up there and said he couldn't give the presentation, and it's pretty likely a copy of the PDF would have made its way to the Internet within 2 days anyway, given that no doubt various reviewers had copies.

Fear Can Cause Alarm

So, why did he do it? He says: "I wanted people to be afraid a little bit . . . because I needed people to act."[59]

As you've seen in Chapters 2 and 3, fear is often what it takes to get through denial to action. He must have been afraid himself; he thought the problem was bad enough to risk his livelihood twice.[60] He also says there's still plenty of time to act, so maybe we can have a rational reaction to fear rather than a panic reaction; maybe scared can be prepared.

After Michael Lynn's presentation became available over the Internet, there were reports that one reason he hadn't waited on Cisco before making the presentation was that Cisco had not informed its customers that there was a problem; it had made new software available to its customers, but hadn't told them why nor that it was urgent for them to upgrade to the new software. One of the customers Cisco didn't inform was the U.S. Department of Homeland Security (DHS).[61] Representatives of several federal agencies met with Lynn immediately after his talk and thanked him. One even gave him a challenge coin, used to commemorate especially challenging military missions. US-CERT invited him to DC to help formulate national cyberstrategy.[62]

PR Disaster or Public Service?

This isn't really about Cisco; the principles illustrated here are larger than that. See, for example, the section on "From Phishing to SCADA Attacks" Chapter 10 for more on how an Internet vulnerability can affect numerous other infrastructures, from nuclear plants to electric power distribution to telephone service.

Security by obscurity just doesn't work, no matter how big you are. And even if you have the law backing you up, which would you rather have—a public relations disaster brought on by not disclosing a fixed vulnerability or a reputation burnished by assisting security researchers in publishing such a vulnerability?

Kowtowing Is Not Security

The point in Mike Lynn's slides about packet sniffing in far off lands could be a coy reference to widespread allegations that Cisco has provided hooks in its routers for the Chinese government to use for packet sniffing.[63] Lest anyone think I'm picking on Cisco, similar allegations of modifying software to the specifications of the Chinese government have been heard about many other companies, including Symantec, Yahoo!, and Google.[64] (*Kowtow* is a Chinese word for bowing to the ground before the emperor.) If such router hooks really exist, they would be a gold mine for miscreants, who could sniff packets not only in far off lands but perhaps also in nearby lands, if the same software turns out to exist on routers in countries other than China. If such backdoors actually exist, they would make for much easier exploits than finding a buffer overflow.

The flip side of this is that governments in countries that pride themselves on being free should think twice about requiring information carriers to tap their own networks. Catching criminals and terrorists is necessary and laudable, but beware of collateral damage. See Chapter 10 for more about this.

To quote Warren Buffet from another context: "If we can't tolerate a possible consequence, remote though it may be, we steer clear of planting its seeds."[65]

That sounds like good advice.

If It's Broke, Don't Sue It

For some years now, Point to Point (P2P) file-sharing application networks such as Kazaa, Grokster, and BitTorrent have been spreading various kinds of information around the Internet efficiently and quickly. No one disputes that it's happening. Many people dispute what it's good for.

P2P: Piracy or Market Demand?

Some distributors of traditional content such as music via CDs or movies via theaters and DVDs claim that much P2P content is illegal stolen copyrighted material. There are also claims that P2P transmission of content is adversely affecting physical media sales. The Recording Industry Association of America (RIAA) and the Motion Picture Association of America (MPAA) have pursued this matter assiduously, most recently claiming victory in a U.S. Supreme Court case involving Grokster. Other parties claim that record and movie sales are declining because of poor quality and the recent economic slump, and furthermore that online distribution actually helps promote physical media sales. The Electronic Frontier Foundation (EFF) has assisted in defense of Grokster. Both sides claim partial victory in the Supreme Court case. I will omit details of that case in order to get to the real point.

According to some estimates, more than half of all traffic (measured in bytes) over U.S. Tier 1 Internet carriers is P2P file-sharing traffic. If that is true, it represents a huge market demand for online content distribution. Lawsuits and new laws can only delay the inevitable. For example, private encrypted P2P networks have now sprung up.[66]

Meanwhile, Apple demonstrated with the iPod that people will pay for online content, made a tidy business out of it, and ran Apple's stock up in the process. Is Steve Jobs the only captain of industry who can pull this off? Can no one come up with a workable business model for online movie distribution?

Hollywood's Origins in Piracy

This is not a new situation. One reason that Hollywood is in California is that Thomas Edison and others had formed a patent monopoly based on the East Coast:

In December 1908, the motion picture inventors and industry leaders organized the first great film trust called the Motion Picture Patents Company, designed to bring stability to the chaotic early film years characterized by patent wars and litigation. The Edison Film Manufacturing Company, the Biograph company, and the other Motion Picture Patents members ended their competitive feuding in favor of a cooperative system that provided industry domination. By pooling their interests, the member companies legally monopolized the business, and demanded licensing fees from all film producers, distributors, and exhibitors.[67]

This seemed like a good idea at the time. But not everyone thought so:

A January 1909 deadline was set for all companies to comply with the license. By February, unlicensed outlaws, who referred to themselves as independents protested the trust and carried on business without submitting to the Edison monopoly. In the summer of 1909 the independent movement was in full swing, with producers and theater owners using illegal equipment and imported film stock to create their own underground market.[68]

The MPPC, also known as the Trust, proceeded to confiscate equipment, cut off supplies to independent theaters, and otherwise obstruct independents through the Trust's subsidiary the General Film Company.

Several of the outlaw independent theater presenters moved to the orange groves of southern California and went into content production, thus forming the beginnings of the Hollywood motion picture industry.

Eventually the courts turned against the Trust and in 1915 determined the Trust and General Film were a monopoly acting in restraint of trade. Later, the courts ordered the monopoly dissolved.

Pirates or Innovators?

Edison, meanwhile, stuck to his original short film format while the rest of the industry had moved on to the longer feature film format and Hollywood had started organizing production through the studio system and turning actors into stars as a powerful marketing device. Hollywood movie sales increased, while Edison's decreased. The monopoly was too stodgy for its own good. Instead of innovating, it tried to use the law to keep others from doing so. Sometimes so-called pirates are actually good free-market capitalists. In the end, the pirate independents were the better innovators and competitors, and they even succeeded in outcompeting in the courtroom.

This could happen again.

Risk Also Means Opportunity

The word entrepreneur is often associated with small, brash startup companies, but big companies can seize the day just as well—sometimes better, because they have more resources. For more on how risk also means opportunity, read the next chapter, about Small Businesses. As Lord Levene, chairman of Lloyd's said:

> *Tomorrow's successful businesses will be those who wake up now and respond to the new era of risk. And the successful insurers will be those who invest more time in listening to businesses, to understand more about their agenda and the issues they face. Together, we must go beyond the development of products and think outside the box.*[69]

This applies as much to other businesses as to insurers. How can you turn economic externalities caused by the connectivity into a competitive advantage for your business?

Resources spent figuring out how to use Internet distribution as marketing and as a sales delivery channel are more cost-effective than resources spent suing "pirates." Lawsuits may do away with some online distribution methods, but they thereby provide unnatural selection for new ones that are even better at evading legal challenges. Better instead to see online distribution as a market opportunity and find ways to capitalize on it.

Concentrating on countries that do not require back doors for government snooping may cause some short-term sales losses yet saves inviting crooks in through the same back doors and encourages governments that have a decent respect for the civil liberties of their citizens. It's one thing to provide information to a government when presented with a proper request for specific information from a law enforcement agency; it's quite another to provide governments with access to all data that flows. Keeping most data private also limits potential legal liability for ISPs and their hardware and software vendors. Governments that know everything have many opportunities to come up with legal problems for their information sources. And perhaps most importantly, Internet customers want to know that their data is secure, which means security is a competitive advantage.

You can't restrain the ever-blowing Internet information wind of news media, mailing lists, and blogs. You can help it blow. If you find or hear of a vulnerability in your product or Internet configuration, find a fix and then announce it. This makes your company appear proactive, because it is, and you've let everybody know it. If you can't find a fix after a decent interval, consider announcing anyway; if you don't, somebody else will, and the longer you wait, the more negligent your company looks. Meanwhile, use the resources of the Internet to get others to find a fix for you; if you don't know how to do that, start with some of the companies or organizations listed in Chapter 3.

Apply basic security such as backups and encryption and don't forget to encrypt data transfers to backup and outsourcing locations and on backup tapes. Use good passwords and layers of security. Educate your people about policies and procedures, including how to avoid social engineering. Examine your Internet connectivity and that of your offsite backup storage and outsourcing locations. Examine your own computers for bugs, patches, and software diversity. Use this information to improve your security situation, keep track of such improvements, and use such records to build marketing messages to tell your customers how secure your company is compared to the competition.

Don't try to ignore, hide, or deride security information that your customers already know. For example, if you're being phished, your customers know, and they want to know that you are doing something about it.

Participate in reputation systems; see Chapter 3.

To protect yourself when all of the above fails, use financial risk transfer instruments such as insurance policies (see Chapter 11) and possibly catastrophe bonds (see Chapter 6) or, if you're an ISP, performance bonds (see Chapter 9).

As your company gets better than the competition at any of these things, it may well identify associated products that can be sold for further profit. Agility can make that possibility greater by giving individual employees, small groups, and the entire enterprise the flexibility to produce emergent behavior.

Finally, give your employees a purpose deeper than mission on which to focus their current and emergent behavior.

Notes

1. Terry Duffy, Chair of the Chicago Mercantile Exchange, "Making Uncertainty Pay," *The Economist* (April 19, 2003).

2. "Who needs firm-wide risk?," *Enterprise-Wide Risk Management*. (Risk Management, December 2000). www.financewise.com/public/edit/riskm/ewrm00/ewrm-intro.htm

3. Ibid.

4. Ibid.

5. Vladislav Surkov, "Vladislav Surkovs Secret Speech: How Russia Should Fight International Conspiracies," *MosNews.com* (MosNews, July 12, 2005) www.mosnews.com/interview/2005/07/12/surkov.shtml

6. Ibid.

7. Frederick Winslow Taylor, *The Principles of Scientific Management* (Dover Publications, January 20, 1998).

8. Robert Coram, *Boyd: The Fighter Pilot Who Changed the Art of War* (Back Bay Books, May 10, 2004).

9. John S. Quarterman, Ken Harker, and Peter H. Salus, "Combat Power and Enterprise Competitiveness," *First Monday*, Volume 8, Number 1 (January 2003). www.firstmonday.dk/issues/issue8_1/quarterman/

10. Stephen R. Covey, *The 8th Habit: From Effectiveness to Greatness* (Free Press, November 9, 2004).

11. Steven Johnson, *Emergence: The Connected Lives of Ants, Brains, Cities, and Software* (New York: Scribner, September 10, 2002).

12. Stephen R. Covey, *The 7 Habits of Highly Effective People* (Free Press, 15 September 1990).

13. "Frequently Asked Questions," *Google Code* (Google 2005). `http://code.google.com/faq.html`

14. Jim Collins and Jerry I. Porras, *Built to Last: Successful Habits of Visionary Companies (Harper Business Essentials)* (Collins, August 2002).

15. Lord Levene, "Lloyd's Chairman outlines new era of risk to World Affairs Council," Press Release, Lloyd's (April 21, 2004). `http://lloyds.com/index.asp?ItemId=7545`

16. mi2g, "Silently preparing for the $100 billion cyber-catastrophe risk," *News Alert* (February 16, 2004).

17. Nicholas Weaver and Vern Paxson, "A Worst-Case Worm," *The Third Annual Workshop on Economics and Information Security (WEIS04)* (Digital Technology Center, University of Minnesota, May 13–14, 2004).

18. Op. cit. Levene, "Lloyd's Chairman outlines new era of risk to World Affairs Council."

19. Matt Hines, "LexisNexis break-in spurs more calls for reform," *News.com* (CNET, 9 March 2005). `http://news.zdnet.com/2100-1009_22-5606911.html`

20. Ibid.

21. Ibid.

22. Ibid.

23. Caleb Silver, "Time Warner employee data missing: Information on 600,000 current, ex-workers lost by storage firm; Secret Service investigating," *CNN* (New York, May 2, 2005). `http://money.cnn.com/2005/05/02/news/fortune500/security_timewarner/`

24. Reuters, "Citigroup: UPS Lost Data on 3.9M Customers," *Fox News Business* (New York, June 7, 2005). `www.foxnews.com/story/0,2933,158727,00.html`

25. Ibid.

26. Ibid.

27. Jeanne Sahadi, "40M credit cards hacked: Breach at third party payment processor affects 22 million Visa cards and 14 million MasterCards," *CNN/Money* (CNN, New York, 27 July 2005). `http://money.cnn.com/2005/06/17/news/master_card`

28. Robert McMillan, "Court orders CardSystems to retain breach information" (IDG News Service, August 4, 2005). `www.computerworld.com/securitytopics/security/story/0,10801,103666,00.html`

29. Kevin D. Mitnick and William L. Simon, *The Art of Intrusion: The Real Stories Behind the Exploits of Hackers, Intruders & Deceivers* (John Wiley & Sons, February 25, 2005).

30. Pei-yu Chen, Gaurav Kataria, and Ramayya Krishnan, "Software Diversity for Information Security," Fourth Workshop on the Economics of Information Security, Kennedy School of Government, Harvard University (Cambridge, Massachusetts, June 2–3, 2005). `http://infosecon.net/workshop/pdf/47.pdf`

31. Steven Warren, "Encrypt Data or Invite Disaster," *eSecurity Planet* (June 27, 2005). `www.esecurityplanet.com/prevention/article.php/3515811`

32. Ephraim Schwartz, "Reality Check," *InfoWorld* (InfoWorld Media Group, San Francisco, June 28, 2005). `www.infoworld.com/article/05/06/28/27OPreality_1.html?source=NLC-STO2005-06-29`

33. Ibid.

34. Robert Lemos, "Study: Flaw disclosure hurts software maker's stock," *SecurityFocus* (June 6, 2005). `www.securityfocus.com/news/11197`

35. Rahul Telang and Sunil Wattal, "Impact of Software Vulnerability Announcements on the Market Value of Software Vendors—an Empirical Investigation," Fourth Workshop on the Economics of Information Security, Kennedy School of Government, Harvard University (Cambridge, Massachusetts, June 2–3, 2005). `http://infosecon.net/workshop/pdf/telang_wattal.pdf`

36. Bob Francis, "Security vendors enter bidding war for vulnerabilities," *InfoWorld* (July 28, 2005). `www.infoworld.com/article/05/07/28/HNzero_1.html?source=rss&url=http://www.infoworld.com/article/05/07/28/HNzero_1.html`

37. John Leyden, "Mozilla to pay bounty on bugs," *The Register* (August 3, 2004). `www.theregister.co.uk/2004/08/03/mozilla_bug_bounty/`

38. Op. cit. Francis, "Security vendors enter bidding war for vulnerabilities."

39. David Bank, "Cisco Tries to Squelch Claim About a Flaw in Its Internet Routers," *The Wall Street Journal* (July 28, 2005). `http://online.wsj.com/public/article/0,,SB112251394301198260-2zgDRmLtWgPF5vKgFn1qYJBjaG0_20050827,00.html?mod=blogs`

40. Op. cit. Francis, "Security vendors enter bidding war for vulnerabilities."

41. Ibid.

42. Kim Zetter, "Router Flaw Is a Ticking Bomb," *Wired News* (August 1, 2005). www.wired.com/news/privacy/0,1848,68365,00.html

43. Robert Lemos, "Cisco, ISS file suit against rogue researcher," *SecurityFocus* (July 27, 2005). http://online.securityfocus.com/news/11259

44. Ibid.

45. Op. cit. Bank, "Cisco Tries to Squelch Claim About a Flaw in Its Internet Routers,"

46. Cisco Systems, Inc., "Feds Grant Cisco an Injunction," *Light Reading*, PR Newswire (July 29, 2005). www.lightreading.com/document.asp?doc_id=78250&WT.svl=wire1_1

47. Op. cit. Chen, et al., *Software Diversity for Information Security*.

48. Op. cit. Cisco, "Feds Grant Cisco an Injunction."

49. *Cisco Security Advisory: IPv6 Crafted Packet Vulnerability*, Document ID: 65783, Revision 1.2 (Last Updated 2005 July 30 1300 UTC For Public Release 2005 July 29 0800 UTC). www.cisco.com/warp/public/707/cisco-sa-20050729-ipv6.shtml

50. Jeffrey White, *Stipulated Permanent Injunction*, United States District Court, Northern District of California, San Francisco Division (July 28, 2005). www.infowarrior.org/users/rforno/lynn-cisco.pdf

51. Michael Lynn, *The Holy Grail: Cisco IOS Shellcode And Exploitation Techniques*, Black Hat Conference (Las Vegas, Nevada, July 27, 2005). www.jwdt.com/~paysan/lynn-cisco.pdf

52. Ibid.

53. Bruce Schneier, "Cisco Harasses Security Researcher," *Schneier on Security* (July 29, 2005). www.schneier.com/blog/archives/2005/07/cisco_harasses.html

54. Op. cit. Bank, "Cisco Tries to Squelch Claim About a Flaw in Its Internet Routers."

55. Ibid.

56. Op. cit. Lynn, *The Holy Grail: Cisco IOS Shellcode And Exploitation Techniques*.

57. Op. cit. Schneier, "Cisco Harasses Security Researcher."

58. Op. cit. Bank, "Cisco Tries to Squelch Claim About a Flaw in Its Internet Routers."

59. Op. cit. Zetter, "Router Flaw Is a Ticking Bomb."

60. "Mike Lynn's 'exploit,' in plain (non-technical) English," *MemeStreams* (August 1, 2005). www.memestreams.net/users/dagmar/ blogid5665679

61. Justin Rood, "Cisco Failed to Alert DHS, Other Agencies About Software Security Flaw," *CQ Homeland Security* (Congressional Quarterly Inc. 2005). www.cq.com

62. Op. cit. Zetter, "Router Flaw Is a Ticking Bomb."

63. Daniel C. Lynch, "China's Great Internet Firewall," *Project Syndicate* (December 2002). www.project-syndicate.org/commentary/ lynch1/English

64. Zhang Tianliang, "Google 'Kowtows' to the Chinese Government: Internet Censorship and Monitoring 'Opens Up' the Chinese Market?," *The Epoch Times* (February 8, 2005). http://english.epochtimes .com/news/5-2-8/26332.html

65. Warren Buffett, *Chairman's Letter*, Berkshire Hathaway Inc. (February 28, 1997). www.ifa.com/Library/Buffet.html

66. Dawn C. Chmielewski, "The new threat to Hollywood: Darknets; Private, Encrypted File-Sharing Networks Set to Grow," *Mercury News* (August 4, 2005). www.mercurynews.com/mld/mercurynews/ business/12306819.htm

67. J. A. Aberdeen, "The Edison Movie Monopoly: The Motion Picture Patents Company vs. the Independent Outlaws," *The SIMPP Research Database* (Cobblestone Entertainment 2001). www.cobbles.com/ simpp_archive/edison_trust.htm

68. Ibid.

69. Op. cit. Levene, "Lloyd's Chairman outlines new era of risk to World Affairs Council."

CHAPTER 8

Small Enterprises: Surviving Risks

*... fertile conditions for starting new companies—
even new industries—and remaking old ones.*
—Michael V. Copeland and Om Malik

Small enterprises have all the same risks as big companies, but without big resources to deal with them. A private company may avoid the requirements of SOX, but it can't escape *force majeure* risks out in the Internet or possible unpatched software inside the company. A big company that loses Internet connectivity for a day or two probably has deep pockets to fall back on; it will be affected, but probably will survive, albeit with less profit. A small company that loses Internet connectivity for a day or two may not survive: unless it has insurance.

As larger companies buy insurance and the largest float catastrophe bonds, they gain even greater advantages over smaller companies, unless the smaller companies also buy insurance.

As cybercatastrophe insurance becomes standard for large companies, customers will start to expect it for all companies. Thus it will become a standard cost of doing business for all companies.

Meanwhile, a small company can turn risk management into a competitive advantage. It may even be able to turn risks into opportunities.

Small Company, Big Risk

Early fifteenth century Chinese Admiral Zheng He (Cheng Ho) explored the Indian Ocean as far as Africa with hundreds of ships carrying thousands of men and women. With that kind of redundancy he had the resiliency to be able to afford to lose some ships here and there and still accomplish his missions.

Portuguese explorers later in the same century, with only one or two ships a tenth the size of those Chinese junks, could not afford such risks. They had to take tiny new steps on each mission, around the next cape or out to the next island.

European explorers could take bigger steps when they had charts to show where they were going. Several of the earliest European Atlantic explorers, including Columbus, claimed to have seen maps of the places they planned to visit. Some people even say the early Portuguese and Spanish explorers used charts derived from Zheng He's expeditions, which had charted the entire world, from Antarctica to the Arctic, from Australia to South and North America, by 1428.[1]

Be that as it may, it is well accepted by historians that Zheng He sailed to India, the Persian Gulf, and Africa multiple times by 1421, and carried foreign dignitaries to Beijing and back among the thousands of people on his ships. This is the kind of mission only a very large enterprise or government can undertake.

Yet the Chinese retreated from the oceans by about 1430, because the emperor who supported the fleets died. His successors did not want to support such expeditions. Because China was a centrally controlled country, the emperors could and did make such things stop.

There was no emperor of Europe, so nobody could make all European states stop exploring. Tiny European states such as Portugal and Spain took longer to find routes to get anywhere by sea, and whether or not they had maps before they got there, they carefully recorded where they had been and how they got there so that later voyagers could follow them. Such rutters (logs of routes and sea, port, and weather conditions) were one form of such risk management for such voyages. They were considered so valuable that sometimes they were treated as secrets of national security, not that that stopped them from leaking rapidly to competing states. Small voyagers on the ocean sea of the Internet need rutters just as much as those early ships of the watery ocean.

Risk Management As Good Business Planning

Much of modern risk management in forms such as trip insurance and joint stock corporations was invented to enable Western merchant adventurers to increase the duration, distance, and size of their sea voyages[2] without the resources of a Chinese government to back them.

Risk management is in many ways just good business planning.

Risk Management As a Competitive Advantage

A small company can market its risk management plan as a competitive advantage. Such a plan makes the company seem responsible and dependable beyond its size, and makes it more attractive than competitors without such plans.

Prevention before Cure

Small businesses are often less stodgy than larger businesses. They may be able to be more proactive, and head off many problems that bigger companies can only try to fix after the fact.

Slim but Flexible

Small size can require small companies to be flexible. Where a major corporation would devote a department or a workgroup, a small corporation may be able to afford only a few people. Lack of resources can result in less risk management in an atmosphere of double-or-nothing high stakes gambling. Or it may result in more risk management in an effort to keep the company able to survive at all.

The cheapest risk management is prevention. Backups, redundancy, and diversity can all be achieved on a shoestring and all provide resilience in the face of attacks or failures.

Traditional Internet security such as intrusion detection and intrusion prevention boxes may cost more, but the basics such as closing unused ports and running firewalls and detectors don't cost much.

And a prudent small company may be willing to pay a few days' revenue a year for insurance to protect it against business losses from disconnects or slowdowns.

Smaller Can Mean Younger

Sometimes small businesses have younger workers, who tend to be natives of cyberspace, unlike their elders who were not raised with this technology and are more like cyberspace immigrants.

What's a Cybernative?

That younger people are mostly natives of cyberspace is self-evident to anyone under 25, or even 35, but may need explanation for older readers.

Who in your household first bought an iPod? Was it you, or a teenager? Did the teenager then buy a Mac to go with the iPod?

Who fixes grandma's computer? You, or the teenager of Generation Tech?

Can you remember a time when there was no television? Maybe, if you're old enough. How about when there were no telephones? I can't, but I can remember when many people still shouted whenever they used the telephone and they always limited their calls to less than 3 minutes because after that the rates went up, people who just knew that the telephone was only for arranging in-person meetings; certainly not for holding conversations or business meetings!

Those antique sentiments about telephones parallel exactly many older business executives' feelings today about electronic mail. These same executives now think that the telephone is a perfectly acceptable way to hear somebody's real voice. Never mind that the voice you hear on a telephone is no more a real voice than Tang is orange juice. A telephone voice has been converted to electrical waves in copper, light waves in glass, radio waves in air and space, delayed from a few milliseconds up to a few quarters of a second (depending on how many satellites it went through), and eventually emulated by a vibrating diaphragm next to your ear that in no way resembles a human mouth and throat.

If you're 25, you may be able to remember a time when there was no World Wide Web, but you probably used it in high school, and you almost certainly used the web and the Internet daily in college. You're unlikely to know what a video game arcade is, because you've always played video games on game boxes and personal computers.

Many younger folks consider electronic mail old hat because they find it easier to talk to groups of their friends all at the same time using Instant Messages (IM) or cell phone text messages.

Some older folks are cybernatives. I first used the ARPANET as an undergraduate at Harvard, and I fondly recall loading Spacewar, the first video game, off paper tape onto a PDP-1, where the controls that moved the spaceships on the screen in the gravity field were two toggle switches. I can also feel the eyes of younger readers rolling at such a primitive user interface.

To cybernatives, older folks often seem like castaways from some backward continent, washed up on the shores of cyberspace, peering under a television to see the little man below the talking head, and trying to speak into the wrong end of a telephone.

Cybernatives As a Competitive Advantage

Small businesses populated mostly by cybernatives may be better able to avoid problems not even seen by their more stodgy competitors. For example, younger workers are used to using multiple channels of communication, from IM to gaming to blogs to electronic mail, sometimes all at once while talking on the telephone and watching TV with their friends. You'll seldom find anyone under 30 who can't figure out how to do more than one thing on a PC.

Multiplexed tasks on a computer, combined with multiplexed communications through computers and other means are the air they've always breathed. Younger people are less likely to believe that only face-to-face meetings or telephone are real communications, and thus they are more likely to work well in a distributed environment, which in turn means that their companies can be more distributed. More distributed in space means more different support infrastructures and less risk due to the failure of just one of them. More distributed in time means more 24/7 coverage.

Younger workers are less afraid of different operating systems. Most of them grew up with at least two: Windows and a gaming console. Many of them installed Linux in school. Many of them bought a Mac to go with their iPod. They are perhaps less likely than their elders to believe that monoculture is the only way to have ease of use and administration. And when a company chooses diversity in OSs or other software, there are likely younger workers already familiar with the various diverse choices.

Risk Means Opportunity

Where there's danger there's opportunity for someone to come up with a less risky way, route around it, or defend against it. Small, flexible, and entrepreneurial businesses may be better able than big companies to take advantage of opportunities resulting from Internet business risk. Some such opportunities are mentioned in the next subsection.

Privatization of Research

For example, some of the research areas described in the 2004 Research and Development Exchange Workshop Proceedings[3] of the U.S. President's National Security Telecommunications Advisory Committee (NSTAC) must be nearly ripe enough to be commercialized as products that will make government, private industry, or both, safer. The Research and Development Exchange (RDX) Workshop was mostly about research in areas for which solutions are not yet known, and thus need research. But such areas are also market opportunities, and a clever company may find ways to capitalize on some of them in the near future.

For example, a recurring RDX theme is how the traditional Public Switched Telephone Network (PSTN) is converging with packet switching and the Internet. One of the consequences is that all telecommunications is becoming increasingly dependent on electric power from the public power grids. In the old days, you could pick up the telephone and get dial tone even if the power was out, because the telephone company supplied that small amount of electricity more or less independently of the electric power grid. Nowadays, a power outage can mean a telephone outage as well. This seems to add up to a great market for dependable, low-cost, readily deployable electric power generation devices and methods. Such devices should themselves be remotely sensible and controllable, of course.

Exporting Internet Security to New Industries

Meanwhile, numerous critical infrastructures increasingly depend on the Internet for their own coordination and on computers susceptible to worms, viruses, Trojans, and so on for their operation. Such infrastructures include law enforcement, emergency services, public health, the military, telecommunications, and electric power generation. Thus the market for traditional Internet security technology and for new financial risk transfer instruments expands into all these companies. While some of the financial risk transfer instruments are actually being imported from some of these industries (such as power generation) into the Internet, basic Internet security techniques such as good passwords can be exported back to those same industries. Similarly, there is a need for multi-industry reputation systems to see which industries and enterprises are up to speed on Internet security. There are many opportunities here for new products. Some of the opportunities identified by NSTAC or other government advisory or research groups may have grant opportunities to facilitate technology transfer into the private sector. Small companies can take advantage of these opportunities, with or without grants.

Riding the Fifth Wave

I used to tell a joke about a conference speaker in the 1980s who didn't see much use for millions of microcomputers, because you'd have to have one in every doorknob to use that many. Ten years later, the same conference met in the same hotel, and there was one in every doorknob.

Doorknobs are old hat now that there are a dozen in every automobile, one on its keychain, at least one in every cell phone, and so on. And with cell phones, the global reach of the Internet, and wireless Internet to fill in the gaps, not only are microprocessors everywhere, but also they can all be networked. Cheap ubiquitous networked computing can provide essentially limitless information, services, and entertainment anytime, anywhere; this is what Michael V. Copeland and Om Malik call the fifth wave of computing. The fifth wave is a threat to old ways of doing business and an opportunity for companies flexible enough to take advantage of it.

Riding the Long Tail of Content

Chris Anderson writes about the long tail of distribution. This idea applies to many forms of content, such as books, music, and movies. I'll use movies as an example.

Traditionally, there are only so many movie screens and so much shelf space in video stores. Movies that are popular enough to draw a mass audience get on the screens and on the shelves. A movie doesn't have to be as popular to get on the shelves as on the screen, but the idea is the same. If you draw a curve showing copies distributed on the vertical axis and movies along the horizontal axis, from most distributed to least, there is a short head of widely distributed movies (about 1,000 a year) followed by a long tail of movies that fewer people want to see and that don't get on the shelves.

Yet many movies in the back catalog are high quality. Some just don't happen to fit this year's fashions and may become cult favorites in later years if anybody happens to see them, some may not have gotten marketing support, and some, of course, are stinkers: just plain bad. In addition to this year's undistributed movies, the backlist includes all other movies ever made, including all the Academy Award winners and others of undisputed quality. Ted Turner has already demonstrated a market for such films with his Turner Classic Movie cable channel. Earlier, television bought up B movies such as the Frankenstein and Dracula movies and showed there was an ongoing audience for them. Both of these examples used broadcast media. The Internet permits going even deeper into the long tail. Other movies are popular with certain market subsegments, and some people would want to see them if they could get them. Any given cult movie may not be popular enough in any given geographical location for stores to stock it, but with the Internet for communications and distribution leverage, such a movie can find an audience anyway. Netflix and Amazon have demonstrated that this is the case. A movie doesn't even have to be a cult favorite to get distribution by such methods, nor does it have to depend on Netflix or Amazon. Anybody can put up a web page selling a movie, and with modern search engines an interested buyer can probably find it. The total value of the long tail is probably as high as that of the short head.

Of course, there is also a lot of junk in the long tail. Some movies really are bad, and maybe not even so bad that people will pay to watch them to laugh at them. But this leads what Chris Anderson says are the three main business opportunities in the long tail:[4]

- **Aggregators,** which include the long tail along with the short head
- **Niche** producers or suppliers whose products someone else aggregates
- **Filters,** which help people find what they consider gold among the dross

Aggregators take advantage of the unlimited shelf space of the Internet to distribute everything. They can use hits that everyone knows to lead customers to more obscure products that they may like. Example aggregators include Google, Yahoo!, Amazon, iTunes, and Netflix. Aggregators to date have tended to become big business, and tended toward becoming monopolies in the types of content they aggregate. But there is room for small businesses, too. Build a better filter and sell it to an aggregator. Or become an aggregator for a particular subsegment of content; for example, sell film noir, rather than all movies. The most lucrative example of this is probably pornography and its various subniches.

Or produce a product tightly focused on a market your company understands well and take advantage of filters and aggregators to get it to market. Many people do this already with eBay, often without even having a company. How can this be done so as to build a company?

Reach Just Your Users

Clay Shirky invented an aggregator for weblogs (blogs) called technorati (technorati.com). Technorati keeps track of which blogs reference which news articles and then ranks news articles by number of mentions, along with links to the blogs that first mentioned them. It does the same thing with books, movies, and blogs. And it permits the user to search blogs for keywords of interest.

Clay Shirky has his own blog in which he writes about Situated Software[5] for users by the dozen. He notes that software sold through the Internet has come to have what he calls the Web School virtues of scalability, generality, and completeness. Web delivery used to cost a lot for programmers, computers, redundancy, connectivity, and system administrators, so it was only worth delivering a product through the web if it could be done for enough users to get economy of scale. Selling to large numbers of users meant the product had to be general enough to interest them all and complete enough to address enough of their concerns without too many complaints. A product might have small groups of alpha or beta testers, but that was merely to see if it was general and complete enough to scale for a larger market. And even then it could fail, because users' attention is also a scarce resource, and there was no guarantee people would pay attention and pay to become customers.

Computers and connectivity and, therefore, redundancy no longer cost much, and programmers don't cost what they once did, especially if they don't have to program for scalability, generality, or completeness; such smaller systems also don't need as many system administrators. And the whole apparatus does not need as much accompanying corporate apparatus in the form of sales, marketing, and finance departments.

Software written for a small market can be seeded with specific content known to that market. The programmers may know the users, or even be some of the users. Shirky provides an example of a teacher rating service built by students where he teaches at New York University's (NYU) Interactive Telecommunications Program (ITP). In its first 24 hours of release the new service, Teachers on the Run, got five times more ratings of teachers than there were students. Most students rated all their teachers, and they did it in a day. Shirky remarked:

> *The curious thing to me about Teachers on the Run was that it worked where the Web School version failed. RateMyProfessors.com has been available for years, with a feature set that put the simplistic write/read/vote capabilities of Teachers on the Run to shame. Yet no one at ITP had ever bothered to use RateMyProfessors.com, though the weekend's orgy of rating and voting demonstrated untapped demand.[6]*

It took Shirky a while to realize that one of the most important reasons for the success of Teachers on the Run was that it used existing social networks: the programmers and testers were students, and thus knew their customers; they used an existing campus online mailing list to announce the service; and the students as customers used that and other preexisting means (class and locker-room conversation, telephone, and so on) to spread the word. The trick was to make the application useful to the community so the community would spread the word. One key way applications can do that is by letting users comment on other users' comments, thus, building community views.

For other products designed in similar ways, the designers could even use such social communication systems to implement reputation systems, announcing deadbeats who did not pay and thus simplifying collection. As Shirky notes, this makes the community useful to the application.

All this adds up to building small products fast that make their small group customers very happy, and the product vendors richer.

It seems to me that Clay Shirky is talking about building high-quality products for the long tail; high-quality products that are already filtered for their target customers. Or, in Chris Anderson's terms, niche products.

Cathedral or Bazaar?

Inexpensive hardware, software, and connectivity may mark a shift from an environment of scarcity to an environment of abundance.

An environment of scarcity tends to be characterized by rigid top-down control and power to support that control, as in governments, military, and traditional corporate hierarchies. More sophisticated societies also deal with scarce resources by developing an economy of exchange, as in a market economy in which goods are exchanged for services. Various political systems then try to assert various degrees of control over the market, ranging from Stalinist centralized 5-year plans to the sort of completely unregulated market advocated by Ayn Rand. Such mixtures of command hierarchies and market economies are what most of the world has been used to for a long time.

But if most important goods are inexpensive, there is not as much need for organization or power for competition for goods. There isn't even as much need to match values of goods exchanged. Such an environment of abundance can support a gift economy, such as that of the Kwakiutl tribe of the Pacific Northwest of North America, in which chieftains would hold *potlach* parties to compete not over how much power they had, but rather over how much they could give away. Such gift economies also exist in the modern world. Show business thrives as much on what the stars give to the fans in interviews and gossip as on income. Very wealthy people compete in philanthropy, according to how much they give away and to how deserving a charity. Academics rank by how many papers they give away and by how many people take them, as measured by citations.

The open source community lives by the contributions of thousands of volunteers who for the most part are not paid as piecework or even by how many people use their code. They aren't working primarily for money. Their salary takes care of physiological needs such as eating or shelter and basic safety needs, so they can concentrate on higher levels of Maslow's hierarchy of needs:

- **Physiological:** Thirst, hunger, bodily comforts
- **Safety:** Out of physical danger
- **Love and belonging:** Affiliation, acceptance
- **Esteem:** Achievement, competence, approval, recognition
- **Cognitive:** Understanding, knowledge, exploration
- **Aesthetic:** Beauty and patterns
- **Actualization:** Self-fulfillment
- **Transcendence:** To help others or a higher cause

The first four levels are sometimes called deficiency needs; if those needs are not met, a person is likely to concentrate on meeting them. Once those four are met, a person is more likely to explore higher level needs, which are sometimes called being needs or growth needs.[7] Such hackers' reward is not a bigger house or a faster car, but rather it is knowing that they have written something that they find pleasing and that is acknowledged as good by their peers. Such creative production is the traditional role of the open source hacker community, which should not be confused with the crackers that perpetrate phishing and other scams. As Eric S. Raymond has remarked:

For examined in this way, it is quite clear that the society of open-source hackers is in fact a gift culture. Within it, there is no serious shortage of the "survival necessities" disk space, network bandwidth, computing power. Software is freely shared. This abundance creates a situation in which the only available measure of competitive success is reputation among one's peers.

This observation is not in itself entirely sufficient to explain the observed features of hacker culture, however. The crackers and warez d00dz have a gift culture that thrives in the same (electronic) media as that of the hackers, but their behavior is very different. The group mentality in their culture is much stronger and more exclusive than among hackers. They hoard secrets rather than sharing them; one is much more likely to find cracker groups distributing sourceless executables that crack software than tips that give away how they did it.[8]

Since Raymond wrote the above in 2000, the crackers and warez d00dz culture has mostly mutated into an illegal money economy. Meanwhile, the open source community remains a gift culture.

Open source programmers don't all work for free; many of them are supported by large and small corporations that pay them salaries to be creative. And not all open source software is sold for free; Red Hat and others have made tidy businesses out of packaging or supporting open source software. A small company that wants to ride the fifth wave doesn't have to make open source software. But it is useful for such a company to know how open source works, because it may want to adopt certain features of the open source method.

Finally, some of the basic tools of the fifth wave are open source software: the Apache web server, the Perl programming language, and the mySQL database server have an open source version. The gift economy has helped make the fifth wave possible.

Companies that take advantage of some open source features have a competitive advantage over those that don't. This doesn't mean a fifth wave company has to abandon capitalism; money is still the best way to facilitate most of the global economy. It does mean that a company that wants to introduce a new product in a fifth wave environment, such as the world has become needs to use the advantages of creativity and quality control that open source provides.[9]

The Fifth Wave: Everywhere, All the Time

So what is the fifth wave? As indicated earlier in the chapter, according to Michael V. Copeland and Om Malik, who have popularized the term: "The fifth wave puts computing everywhere. It offers access to limitless amounts of information, services, and entertainment. All the time. Everywhere."[10]

They quote Rick Rashid of Microsoft as realizing that like steam engines were the solution to every problem, large or small, in the Victorian era, computers (hardware and software) have finally become cheap enough to be applied to every problem today, combined with communication networks. Of course, this realization had already been exploited for many years by science fiction writers Bill Gibson and Bruce Sterling[11] and Neal Stephenson,[12] among others; Stephenson starts his *The System of the World* with an epigraph from James Watt and ends it with Thomas Newcomen standing atop a boiler. Rashid himself helped bring on the modern computing era in the 1980s and early 1990s at Carnegie-Mellon University (CMU) when he headed development of the Mach operating system, which was based on Berkeley Unix and has since formed one of the origins of Apple's Mac OS X operating system for its Macintosh computers.

The five waves of computing are:

1. Mainframes, in the 1960s, saw the rise of IBM.

2. Minicomputers, in the 1970s, saw the rise of DEC.

3. Personal computers, in the 1980s, saw the rise of Intel and Microsoft.

4. The Internet and distributed computing, in the 1990s, saw the rise of Cisco, Sun, Yahoo!, Amazon, Google, and others.

5. Inexpensive and ubiquitous computing and networking, with open standards.

The fifth wave sounds a lot like the convergence of telephony and the Internet that has been predicted for some years now. But it goes beyond that, in shifting control from big corporations to more varied players. This is where open standards (such as Internet protocols) and open software (such as Linux and FreeBSD) come in:

> *A less understood but equally critical development is the spread of technological openness. The open-source movement has created a global tinkerer's workshop, where thousands of creative minds are constantly cobbling together code that entrepreneurs and even established businesses can cannibalize, free of charge, for parts to build new software systems. But fifth-wave pioneers grasp another dimension of technological openness: Many have begun to open up their own databases and software protocols, allowing the tinkerers to create related applications or sell symbiotic products and services.*[13]

When users demand a product, companies can quickly spring up to provide it, partly because they don't have to write everything from scratch. Most of the infrastructure is already in place, and even some of the additional software needed can be based on existing open source software.

Examples of fifth wave companies Copeland and Malik mention include Salesforce.com, Skype, and Ambient. Although the two authors don't emphasize the point, it seems all their examples are companies that sell group communication products. In other words, products that exploit Reed's law (see Chapter 1). It appears another way to explain the fifth wave is as the shift of the

Internet all the way from content (Sarnoff's Law) through two-way communication (Metcalfe's Law) to group communications (Reed's Law). Remember these laws are not mathematical predictions of network traffic; they are rules of thumb of network value, more like Black-Merton-Scholes option pricing.

Everyone can play, from Cisco with Internet telephone hardware to Ambient with its wireless bit-trickle. Walled gardens such as AOL aren't adapting very well, but established players such as Amazon, Google, IBM, and Intel are handling the transition well. Sun already played the fifth wave card with Java; it will be interesting to see if it has another such card up its sleeve. Big companies can continue to do well, while small companies can exploit new niches.

The emergence of the fifth wave is like what happened when steam engines got small and cheap enough that there no longer needed to be one huge one for a factory. There could be many small ones, and they could go in houses, even horseless carriages. They even led to other types of small engines, producing explosive growth of automobiles and airplanes, together with all their attendant industries. The fifth wave represents that kind of opportunity again.

In a Glass World, Obscurity Is Not Security

Information sharing has always been important in risk management. If you have a forum in which you and your peers can discuss risks and solutions, you have a better chance of finding and applying appropriate solutions than if you try to go it alone. Consider, for example, the FBI's InfraGard program, which enables sharing information about break-ins among companies that would not want to release such information in public.

In a fifth wave world, information sharing is even more important, and with your customers and the public, not just with your executive or technology peers. If your company is being phished, your customers know about it because they're the ones receiving the phishing mail messages. Taking the traditional corporate route and trying to pretend nothing happened won't work; it will just make your company look like it is ether inept or it has something to hide.

More generally, in a world with Yahoo!, Ask Jeeves, Google, and bloggers, it's not a safe bet that you can keep any corporate secret for very long. Certainly, some things corporations are required by law to keep secret: HIPAA requires privacy of user information, public corporations have to be concerned about SEC disclosure rules, and nobody except criminals wants user passwords revealed. But if your product has a bug that you know about, don't bet that your users won't find out about it and tell each other. If you don't tell them first, you get a black mark; enough of those and your customers may go to the competition.

Security through obscurity just doesn't work. Information sharing reduces risks rather than increases them.

Open Software for Better Software

As software is produced, more eyes looking at it mean more bugs fixed and more design flaws found. Perhaps counterintuitively, releasing many versions as early as possible also leads to better software. This is because even though early releases have many bugs, those bugs can be found quickly if many eyes are looking for them. Most of those eyes should belong to active users, who will also make suggestions about what they really want the software to do, suggestions that, if listened to, will usually improve the software. Frequent early releases also attract some users who can actually fix many of the bugs, in addition to finding them.

Even the biggest corporations can hire only so many programmers and testers. The open source community has more of those than does Microsoft or IBM. Open source software is not immune from bugs or miscreant exploits, but it is often less prone to design flaws than closed proprietary software, and open source developers take it as a point of personal pride to fix bugs when found. The most famous open source software project is probably Linux, the fastest-growing operating system in the world. There are many others: I've already mentioned the Apache web server and the Perl programming language, but the Netscape and Firefox web browsers and the mySQL database server come immediately to mind as well.

Firefox is a good example: it came into being when an Internet Explorer (IE) user got tired of having to clean up his computer from all the spyware that came in through IE. He took Netscape open source code and streamlined its user interface, producing one of the fastest spreading web browsers around. One guy, quickly drawing in a few collaborative developers, rolled his own software that is successfully going head to head with the most-used web browser in the world, made by the biggest software company in the world. That's the power of open software: He could stand on the shoulders of giants and get help from legions of colleagues.

Software was traditionally built with top-down formal project management, with everything planned out before a line of code is written, and there are places where that is still the right method, such as NASA mission software that deals with life-and-death decisions or probes that have to last for years with no hands to modify them. Such software is architected and built like a cathedral. For many other purposes, it is better to use a looser construction method, more like a bazaar in which many people and groups make different pieces and check each other's work; this is the open source method, in which community is more important than command and control. Eric Raymond wrote a paper and then a book, both called *The Cathedral and the Bazaar*, about how open source works.[14]

Open source is actually not new; it goes back at least as far as IBM Share. The Berkeley Unix project that produced the Berkeley Software Distribution (BSD) that included the reference implementation of TCP/IP spurred the early growth of the Internet in the 1980s, including both the rocketing growth of Sun Microsystems and various other versions of BSD, two of which form the basis for Apple's current Mac OS X operating system. The Computer Systems Research Group (CSRG) at the University of California at Berkeley (UCB) that developed BSD never had more than about five actual members. While they did a lot of the coding, they also served in equally important roles as coordinators, moderators, and filters, choosing what developments to accept for inclusion into product releases. Much of the work of programming and testing was done by an array of alpha and beta testers in universities and companies all over the world, from Utah to Texas to Boston to Australia to Japan to Germany, coordinated through the networks ARPANET, UUCP, USENET, and the early Internet, with the occasional workshop and conference. Releases tended to alternate between stable and development, so different user communities could choose whether to ride the latest shaky release or stick with what they had until the next stable release came along. Funding for CSRG was continued by Defense Advanced Research Projects Agency (DARPA) for years beyond what some people expected, partly because DARPA wanted to continue support for the community of researchers, developers, and users that BSD represented. The BSD development process is documented in the book about it,[15] now in its fourth edition.[16]

Richard Stallman has been promoting what he calls free software[17] for many years from his ivory tower near MIT. His GNU (Gnu's Not Unix) project has produced much useful software, most famously his Emacs text editor. Emacs itself apparently was built in a cathedral style, but the underlying Lisp library was developed in a bazaar style.

Linus Torvalds, a young hacker in Finland, took the BSD and GNU development methods and cranked them up an order of magnitude, taking advantage of the greater reach of the Internet 10 years on from the original BSD project, and the greater number of competent programmers. He also reused much BSD and GNU code in applications. While sticking to labeling releases as stable or not so that users would have a choice, Linus even cranked up the speed of releases: He was known to release a new kernel once a day. Thus was born the Linux operating system, and Linus's Law: "Given enough eyeballs, all bugs are shallow."

This doesn't mean that the same person has to both find and fix a bug. Often one person finds it (this can be a user who doesn't program), somebody else understands it (maybe a programmer, but not necessarily even one who writes in the same language as the program), and somebody else fixes it (a programmer, but not necessarily one who would have ever used the feature without it being tagged as having a bug). That requires a lot of eyeballs, but popular open source projects can easily have thousands of people using every release as soon as it comes out. How exactly this works is detailed in Eric Raymond's book.[18]

Open Your Software without Giving Away the Store

You don't have to give away everything to take advantage of the resources of the open source method and community. You can, for instance, have parallel proprietary and open source releases of your product, as, for example, Sendmail, Inc. (`sendmail.com`) has a free version (`sendmail.org`) of its mail delivery product. Or you can provide an interface to your product on which people can build open source applications. And you can simply use open source principles in your software production: involve users at every step, release early and often, delegate everything you can, and involve the community![19]

Any of these approaches should get you a better product, more users, and a better reputation with those users, thus attracting still more customers.

Early Release and Stock Price

Releasing early and often may seem to contradict the point at the end of Chapter 7 that vulnerability disclosure can hurt share prices. Small companies mostly are not traded on public stock exchanges, but that is not the main point. This is where marking releases as development and stable helps: only customers willing to risk bugs should be using development versions, and they are thus effectively beta testers. Customers using stable versions should experience fewer bugs, and fixes for any that do turn up should be at least as fast as in a closed source model.

Go Global

Even though the fifth wave facilitates small, quick, inexpensive projects, it also facilitates building on them to produce products with global reach. It is increasingly easy to go global.

This leads to the question of where to base a global product. India and China may be cheaper for programming or call centers or other outsourcing, but coordination may best be done from the United States or a G7 country or other country that has discarded protectionism as a major instrument of economic and scientific policy.

For example, the 2004 Indian Ocean tsunami revealed that there were seismometers and hydrophones that could have provided warning, but they weren't connected in such a way that enabled them to actually do it. There has long been a Pacific Ocean tsunami warning system involving such instruments, and now such a system for the Indian Ocean is being prepared. There is also a bigger project in process, called The Global Earth Observation System of Systems (GEOSS) that intends to connect such instruments plus satellites and other ground, air, and ship-based sensors into a worldwide real-time sensing system. Such a system would not only provide warning of tsunamis, but it would also facilitate agricultural planning, track disease conditions, deforestation and dust storms, reforestation and increased rainfall, impending famines, and have many other uses.

Resistance has been encountered:

> *India, which has a strong telecommunications and scientific infrastructure, has been reluctant to share data from its network of seismometers. Because the information is considered vital to national security, the government prevents it from being sent out in real time—a serious potential problem for the fledgling Indian Ocean tsunami warning system. Some data are held indefinitely as they may pertain to nuclear testing. And economic considerations also come into play: satellite images and other kinds of high-resolution data are sometimes reserved for sale.*[20]

Of course, the United States isn't perfect in those regards, but it is the United States that has provided most of the funding for GOESS to date, and many other countries are much more protectionist.

If there is resistance to sharing information for such a system with obvious benefits to the world and to the countries providing the information, there is likely to be resistance to sharing other kinds of information. One reason some countries are resistant to providing the requested information is that there is fear there that other countries might be able to process weather information more quickly or completely and feed the results back, thus outcompeting domestic weather services.[21] In other words, developing countries have their own fears of outsourcing. Such a fear can easily carry over to commercial projects.

So, the best place for projects with global reach may not be in countries with the least expenses but rather in countries with the least impediments to communications, which may mean the most developed countries, in which information sharing can more readily be implemented and used as a competitive advantage.

Small As Competitive

A small business also needs to implement diverse and redundant backups with encryption; fortunately, the Internet makes that easy. A small company should still apply standard Internet security measures such as firewalls, intrusion detection, and spyware scanning. And a small company should, if it hasn't already, check its insurance policies for appropriate coverage and see about buying cyberinsurance. A small company that does those things should have fewer exploits and anomalies and should be able to react more readily when they do happen. Such a company looks good to its customers, which makes such Internet business risk management a competitive advantage.

Numerous small companies have been named in this chapter as ones that have done well in the current networked world, including Salesforce.com, Skype, Ambient, Sendmail, and Red Hat. Others started small and leveraged the Internet to become big, such as Yahoo!, Google, eBay, and Cisco. Big companies such as IBM and Intel are successfully adapting, but small companies may in general have an advantage of flexibility. On one hand, the global reach of the Internet brings perils from worldwide, yet on the other hand that global reach brings business opportunities, in sales, contacts, and publicity. Global reach facilitates open source, and open source methods can provide still more leverage for a business. Open source projects such as Apache and mySQL provide high-quality web and database servers to companies no matter how small, leveling the playing field with big companies. Small companies can also adapt some open source methods directly to get more eyeballs finding and fixing their bugs and producing more features. A big business is more likely to try to do things in the old way, as if information could still be readily hidden. A small business that pursues such opportunities without trying to hide problems has a competitive advantage over a small or even a large business. Small businesses can more readily ride the long tail of the fifth wave.

Individuals also have numerous opportunities to exploit. eBay is a bigger economy in itself than many countries put together, and that economy is largely composed of individuals selling things that otherwise never would have found a market. eBay handles much of the risk management for the seller and for the buyer, with detailed instructions for sellers of what is expected of them, followed by feedback from buyers, which feeds into ratings for sellers. eBay and Amazon and an increasing number of other e-tailers provide such reputation systems for their customers that prevent many perils that might otherwise arise. In doing so, they enable business opportunities for small businesses that did not previously exist. Through these and other applications, the Internet is enabling numerous ways for businesses from the smallest up to do more business with more risk management.

Notes

1. Gavin Menzies, *1421: The Year China Discovered America* (New York: Harper Perennial, January 1, 2004).
2. Peter L. Bernstein, *Against the Gods* (Wiley Publishing, Inc., August 31, 1998).

3. *2004 Research and Development Exchange Workshop Proceedings*, National Security Telecommunications Advisory Committee (NSTAC) (Monterey, California, October 28–29, 2004). www.ncs.gov/nstac/reports/2005/2004 RDX Workshop Proceedings.pdf

4. Chris Anderson, "How Finely Can You Slice Aggregation?," *The Long Tail* (Typepad, July 22, 2005). http://longtail.typepad.com/the_long_tail/2005/07/how_finely_can_.html

5. Clay Shirky, "Situated Software," *Clay Shirky's Writings About the Internet* (March 30, 2004). www.shirky.com/writings/situated_software.html

6. Ibid.

7. William G. Huitt, "Maslow's Hierarchy of Needs," Educational Psychology Interactive (Valdosta State University, Valdosta, Georgia, 2004). http://chiron.valdosta.edu/whuitt/col/regsys/maslow.html

8. Eric Steven Raymond, "Gift Outcompetes Exchange," *Homesteading the Noosphere* (Thyrsus Enterprises, 2000). www.catb.org/~esr/writings/cathedral-bazaar/homesteading/ar01s19.html

9. Ibid.

10. Michael V. Copeland and Om Malik, "How to Ride the Fifth Wave," *Business 2.0* (July 2005). www.ambientdevices.com/cat/press/fifth-wave-business-20-ambient.html

11. William Gibson and Bruce Sterling, *The Difference Engine* (Spectra, January 1, 1992).

12. Neal Stephenson, *The System of the World (The Baroque Cycle, Vol. 3)* (New York: William Morrow & Company, October 1, 2004).

13. Op. cit. Copeland and Malik, "How to Ride the Fifth Wave."

14. Eric S. Raymond, *The Cathedral and the Bazaar: Musings on Linux and Open Source by an Accidental Revolutionary* (O'Reilly, October 1999). www.catb.org/~esr/writings/cathedral-bazaar/cathedral-bazaar/

15. Samuel J. Leffler, Marshall Kirk McKusick, Michael J. Karels, and John S. Quarterman, *The Design and Implementation of the 4.3 BSD UNIX Operating System* (Reading, MA: Addison-Wesley, 1989).

16. Marshall Kirk McKusick and George Neville-Neil, *The Design and Implementation of the FreeBSD Operating System* (Reading, MA: Addison-Wesley, 2004).

17. Joshua Gay, Richard M. Stallman, and Lawrence Lessig, *Free Software, Free Society: Selected Essays of Richard M. Stallman* (Free Software Foundation, October, 2002).

18. Op. cit. Raymond, *The Cathedral and the Bazaar*.

19. Ibid.

20. Naomi Lubick, "Something to Watch Over Us," *Nature*. (July 14, 2005). www.scidev.net/pdffiles/nature/436168a.pdf

21. Jamais Cascio, "The Struggle to Go Global," *Worldchanging.com* (July 20, 2005). www.worldchanging.com/archives/003158.html

Internet Service Providers: Bonded and Insured

Big Internet Service Providers (ISPs) currently pay out too much for Service Level Agreement (SLA) violations. Many of these payments are goodwill payouts for violations that didn't actually happen in order to retain customer goodwill when the customer does not believe the ISP's validation of its own performance. Performance bonds and third-party adjustment can help with this problem. The bond issuer gets a new line of business, the ISP pays out less overall, and the ISP customer is happier even if there is no payout, because the SLA is independently verified. There may even be fewer requests for payouts, because there is less suspicion on the part of the customer. The enterprise customer of an ISP with a performance bond should have less to worry about regarding SOX and other legislative requirements because the bond will help control one major source of Internet business risk. While most ISP outages or performance events are small, a performance bond should give quite a bit of comfort regarding the rare big ones.

Catastrophe Bonds for *Force Majeure* Events

Cyber risks are taking on the characteristics of natural disasters such as earthquakes in California and Japan. Those natural disasters are going to happen sooner or later, and their future locations are known. Similar *force majeure* Internet risks go beyond crime and targeted distributed denial-of-service

(DDoS) attacks. They can be too big for ordinary insurers, and governments don't want to be left holding the liability.

Catastrophe bonds, commonly known as *cat bonds*, are an as yet unexplored solution to cyberhurricane risk management. A cat bond is like a treasury bond or a municipal bond floated to raise money for a new school or highway, except that the catastrophe bond may be issued by financial houses, insurance companies, and some hedge funds. Bonds are also in use for packages of automobile loans, mortgages, and credit card debts.

If the catastrophe happens and trigger requirements are met, the bond is liquidated to pay off a third party and interest stops. But that can happen with stocks (any company can fail and the market can crash) or even municipal bonds (municipalities can go bankrupt).

Retrocessional SCOR

Goldman Sachs and Marsh-McLennan Securities co-managed the placement of a $200 million catastrophe bond offering on behalf of SCOR, France's largest reinsurer. This bond provides retrocessional capacity, that is, reinsurance of reinsurance. In particular, it provides 3 years of protection for SCOR's property and construction portfolio against Japanese and United States earthquakes and European windstorms. It is sold in several parts, or *tranches*.

Bond tranches can be rated by rating agencies such as Standard & Poor's. This is common practice for other bonds such as, for example, a completion bond, which guarantees a mortgagee that a mortgaged building will be completed on time so the building can be used as collateral on the loan. Different tranches can be stripped at different ratings, for example, AAA at x%, AA at y%.

Stripped in this case refers to separating the bonds into several pieces, or *strips*, each of which represents part of the principal and has its own interest payment, or coupon. In the case of a catastrophe bond, strips are also ordered according to which ones go first to fund a catastrophe when it happens.

Ratings of cat bond strips depend on what priority of loss each tranche has. For example, the first loss piece, or the tranche that goes first to fund the loss, could be either first or last tranche, and traditionally is retained by the issuer. Not all bonds are floated on open markets; some are sold directly to investors.

At least one of the SCOR cat bond tranches has an investment-grade rating.

Cat Bonds As New Money

For SCOR, the issue effectively created a new pool of capital for monetizing risk that had heretofore been unavailable even to this sophisticated and well-resourced industrial leader.

The catastrophe bond placement provided it with a new source of capacity, at a competitive price, and with almost no credit risk. This credit quality is important

when the protection being purchased is against very large losses, which is pre-
cisely when—if it were to happen—reinsurers would be likely to be strained.
With catastrophe bonds, money is raised through the placement of notes with
investors. This money is put into a trust account, where it is held in the first
instance to pay any claim that results under the reinsurance contract. Because
the money is secured in advance, credit risk is virtually eliminated. This is an
important advantage that catastrophe bonds have over traditional reinsurance
contracts, where credit risk exists to varying degrees depending on the credit
quality of the reinsurer and the sufficiency of collateral, when posted.[1]

Investors in the SCOR cat bond included reinsurers, insurers, commercial
banks, hedge funds, and investment advisors.

ISPs may already use cat bonds indirectly, through insurance policies that are
backed by cat bonds. More direct applications are described in the next section.

Performance Bonds As Risk Backbone

Catastrophe bonds can provide a risk management backbone for industry by
creating an investment instrument of wide distribution and known risks. Such
bonds can be developed further for other deployment scenarios to hedge and
monetize Internet risks.

In addition to denial of service, perils in the Internet can cause degradation
of service, which also can have severe economic consequences. If a backhoe
cuts a cable that carries Internet traffic, some nodes may become unreachable,
and there may be congestion that affects many other nodes. A delay of 8 seconds is enough to make the typical Web user stop trying, causing delayed
transactions. A customer who encounters such delays often may not come
back another day. Some IT personnel may still believe that technology for
encryption, detection, authentication, and authorization is enough to establish
trust and, therefore, to provide adequate security. Yet when denial of service
shades into degradation of service, security merges into performance.

The Experience of Electric Utilities

Electric utilities have long experience that indicates that any technology can
fail, and technology is used by people who can misuse it. Not every hurricane
causes complete destruction, and not every outage turns off the lights in every
house. There are blackouts, and there are brownouts. Even the power outage
of August 2003 left lights on in many houses in Buffalo, New York. Risk management must involve calculations of the probabilities of such failures, including both partial failures and catastrophic failures.

Adequate coverage would best include events or consequences that were
not completely foreseen in probability calculations.[2] For example, there has

already been one case in which an electric utility customer sued and won (including on appeal) physical damages because of loss of business due to a power outage. The U.S. District Court of Arizona remarked in its decision that:

> *The Court finds that "physical damage" is not restricted to the physical destruction or harm of computer circuitry, but includes loss of access, loss of use and loss of functionality.*[3]

For more discussion of this issue of whether loss of access can constitute physical damage, and if so who is liable, see Chapter 11.

Figure 9-1 illustrates a solution used by electric utilities.

One financial instrument electric utilities use for risk management is performance bonds, which hedge basic risks such as energy availability. These kinds of policies are derivatives of bonding instruments. Instead of providing cover for catastrophic events, they ensure levels of performance that pay off in the event that the principal party cannot deliver at the level of service being guaranteed.

ISP SLAs Inside and Out

Internet Service Providers (ISPs) guarantee a high degree of connectivity to their enterprise customers through Service Level Agreements (SLAs) but in turn often find the service they provide degraded by events at peering points or on other provider networks beyond their control. While the SLA may guarantee connectivity only between the customer premises and the local access point, or from one point on the provider network to another on the same provider network, the enterprise customer will blame the Internet Service Provider for any degradation of service. After all, it is the local ISP the customer is paying for access to the Internet.

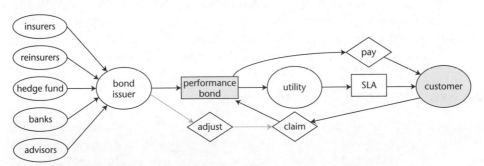

Figure 9-1:   Utility performance bond

Increasingly Specific Inside

In the past, performance guarantees in the form of SLAs were introduced more often as a differentiator in the sales process, with vague language and minimal consistency between providers in what was promised, how it was measured, and how it was enforced. But as commerce becomes more dependent on the Internet, the cost of outages has also increased, and the guarantees of SLAs have become more specific. They usually refer to uptime of the basic Internet connection between a customer site and provider's access point, and to packet loss and latency across the provider network.

Still, Most of the Internet Is Outside

However, the challenge to Internet Service Providers is that they control only their own network region of the network of networks that is the global Internet, yet their customers will hold them responsible for outages that affect them even though they may be caused by events beyond the operational control of their provider. And while an Internet Service Provider may have a well-designed network and significant ability to monitor its own network, it may be interconnected with networks that are less reliable, with networks into which the ISP has no visibility, and with networks through other networks that they know nothing about. The result is that they may not even be able to identify the causes of outages, let alone design contingency plans or perform rapid disaster recovery; they may first hear about outages from outraged customers.

Self-Verification Leads to Goodwill Payouts

A financial problem with current ISP SLAs is illustrated in Figure 9-2.

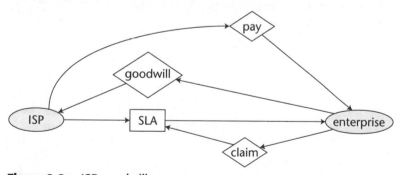

Figure 9-2:   ISP goodwill payouts

ISPs currently pay out too much in SLA payments because they pay out mostly for goodwill, not for actual SLA violations. This is because ISPs currently verify their own SLAs. ISP customers are naturally suspicious of such self-verification and will often refuse to believe that an ISP has not violated its SLA when the customer thinks it has. Faced with such customer suspicion, ISPs often decide to pay anyway rather than risk losing the customer.

ISP Performance Bonds

If instead an ISP could buy a performance bond and get verification from an independent third party associated with the insurance company, everyone would be happier. The ISP customer would have a way to get independent verification. With third-party verification, questions of whether an event was inside the ISP, at its peering points, or elsewhere, might get better answers, because a third party could examine the rest of the Internet beyond the ISP better than ISPs typically do. ISP performance bonds are illustrated by Figure 9-3.

If the claim is not verified, the ISP customer is probably still happy, because the verification is more credible than that from the ISP, simply because the ISP is not verifying itself. If the claim is verified, the insurance company would pay and the customer would be happy. The ISP would be happier because the customer would be happier, plus the total payouts should be less, so the cost of the performance bond should be less than the former goodwill payouts. The insurance company would be happy because of a new line of business. InternetPerils is an example of an organization that can catalyze this process by helping examine claims for SLA compliance.

The Bonded Marketing Advantage

There is also a marketing advantage to the ISP. With a performance bond, the ISP can market its connectivity as utility grade. This could be a big advantage in a market where the players typically compete primarily on price. A performance bond could be a significant differentiator. If this catches on, expect to see *Bonded and Insured* on every ISP's business card and web site.

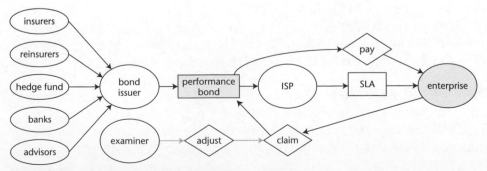

Figure 9-3: Performance bond claims

Better SLAs for Product Differentiation

The use of third-party verification could also enable more sophisticated SLAs. Most SLAs are about performance within the ISP's network. But most ISP customers buy access to the ISP to get access to the Internet, not just that ISP. There are a few examples of SLAs that involve measurements of peering points between ISPs. That tells more of the story, but does not address performance through other ISPs and the last mile to the customer's customers. Third-party verification could do that, as well. So third-party verification could enable a range of SLAs beyond the rudimentary SLAs that are currently available.

An SLA for the ISP customer's performance all the way through the Internet to the customer's customers would be a different beast than a single-ISP SLA. An all-Internet SLA would be a major differentiator for the ISPs that had it, especially for those ISPs that first offer it.

Such an SLA would be beyond the core competence of any single ISP. Each ISP knows a great deal about its own network but knows very little about any other ISP's network. While an ISP could develop Internet-wide measurement techniques, that would be beyond the core competence of an ISP. It could also be difficult to implement, since other ISPs will be unlikely to let a competitor place measurement nodes on their networks or be pleased by many probes into their networks. An independent third-party verifier can do such measurements with less controversy, and by doing so can enable new SLAs beyond a single ISP.

Each such SLA could be covered by a performance bond. Calculation of coverage and pricing will be very interesting, because the bonded ISP does not control all the paths involved. Yet ISPs do control their peering, which strongly affects paths through them to the rest of the Internet. So, the better the off-Net SLA an ISP has bonded, the better the ISP should look competitively.

In other words, performance bonding for ISP SLAs requires third-party verification of the SLAs, which in turn can enable new and more extensive types of SLAs, which can also be bonded. And each level of bonded SLA can become a market differentiator for the bonded ISP.

Turning an Economic Externality into a Competitive Advantage

All this should be good for the Internet in general. Because performance bonds and third-party verification of SLAs will better-quantify Internet service, they will give ISPs incentive to produce better service individually and collectively, providing better service for ISP customers, and more profits for the ISPs with the best bonds.

In other words, performance bonds can help turn an economic externality into an accountable competitive advantage.[4] One ISP's performance traditionally affects another ISP's customer's experience without direct economic consequences for the first ISP. If the second ISP uses off-Net SLAs to manage the effects of the first ISP's performance for the second ISP's customers, those SLAs become a competitive feature for the second ISP. ISPs that use such SLAs will thus have a good chance of outcompeting ones that don't. SLAs enabled by performance bonds and third-party verification can thus provide incentive for ISPs to improve the Internet as a whole.

Bond Issuers

Catastrophe and performance bonds are a good idea, but they require large amounts of money. Who will issue them?

Insurance Companies

As Internet connectivity approaches expectations of utility-quality levels of service, service level requirements will drive the carriers to seek out the kinds of performance guarantee policies that their cohorts in the energy industry now write with their carriers. It is an attractive market, limited to a number of large players, among them AIG, Chubb, Marsh, Lloyd's, and the largest European players, often on a manuscript basis.

While only a few Internet carriers may be large enough to need bonds to cover their risk, the number of enterprises that could use similar financial instruments to cover their risks is larger. Thus there is a sizable market for Internet catastrophe and performance bonds.

It may seem that telephone carriers would already have SLAs and performance bonds to cover them. They do not, because they are regulated in such a way that their risks are limited.

In the context of contemporary cyber risk insurance policies, the coverage has extended to the depth of house fires, or factory fires, in commercial analogues. Now, that is enough to make a market for a certain amount of risk on the consumer side, but it does not fully instrument the risk to the extent that it can be monetized and managed by the underwriters. An individual business may be covered for an outage that lasts a week. If only your business is covered and only you are struck by a covered outage that triggers the policy, then the underwriter has succeeded in covering his risks.

If, however, your company and another 100,000 businesses that share a given Internet topology or inhabit some common risk vector, then the underwriter is in grave trouble.

Though the policies of AIG, Chubb, CNA, and others cover risks to commercial networks and computer systems such as worms and viruses and denial-of-service attacks, the risks that taunt and discomfit the underwriters are those that will catastrophically interrupt service on the Internet causing wide-spread closing down of data carriage across industries, regions, and common Internet topologies.

Bond Markets

Few insurance companies are large enough to play in the performance bond space, but there may be other players. Municipalities have long floated bond issues on open markets when they want to raise money. Large ISPs could do the same.

Government

Governments sometimes act as insurers of last resort. However, natural disasters already strain the resources of governments and the willingness of taxpayers to fund emergency relief for people who build houses on beaches or next to earthquake faults. The Northridge Earthquake in Los Angeles in 1994 was one of the incentives for the development of catastrophe bonds. Governments would do well to encourage the development of a thriving catastrophe and performance bond market, rather than ending up having to deal directly with Internet catastrophes that affect not just one or two industries such as automobiles or airlines, rather every industry, because every enterprise uses the Internet.

The time has come to apply financial instruments to Internet business risk, including insurance, catastrophe bonds, and performance bonds.

Pricing

For performance bonds, a maximum price may be set by what an ISP is currently paying out in goodwill SLA payments. However, there may be sufficient additional advantages to performance bonds, such as even more goodwill due to, for example, claim adjustments using real third-party data, so that a still higher price could be charged.

The more sophisticated off-Net SLAs enabled by third-party verification may have more complicated pricing because they may include carve-outs to avoid covering problematic areas of the Internet. However, such pricing can provide another means of ISP differentiation and thus more choice for the customers.

Beyond Performance

ISP customers are increasingly concerned with aspects of ISP services beyond performance. Already some ISPs make antispam measures a selling point. Some carry user protection farther, into spyware prevention and other measures, building walled gardens to keep wildlife of the Internet out and their users in.

Newer problems customers care about include phishing and pharming; see Chapter 2 for definitions of these terms. Pharming is perhaps the more obvious of these problems. An ISP that has its domain name servers hijacked loses service to its customers until it gets them back, and also loses reputation.

An ISP that is discovered to be a hotbed of phishing web servers or phishing mail sending is also likely to lose customers. To date, ISPs haven't had to deal with phishing as directly as spam because it is often unclear where phishing mail originates or where phishing servers are located. This is changing, especially with the phishing repository of the Anti-Phishing Working Group (APWG), `www.antiphishing.org`, which incorporates reports of phishing web servers from many APWG members into a database. Such a database has potential for revealing which ISPs are compromised in which ways. Reports could be sent directly to the ISP. Or they could be made public, in a reputation system. An ISP known to harbor phishing servers, knowingly or unknowingly, could be less competitive. An ISP that proactively addresses the problem could be more competitive.

Phishing and pharming also have potential for insurance and bonds. SLAs could be extended to cover these new threats. Bonds could cover them. And insurers would probably require proactive measures on the part of the ISPs. Such insurance and bonds would provide further differentiation for ISPs.

Bonded and insured: this is a way to provide product differentiation and value added services for ISPs, thus helping them compete beyond price. Such financial risk transfer instruments could produce a viable business model for ISPs.

Notes

1. Christopher McGhee, "Catastrophe Bonds Come of Age," *MMC Views*, 2 (2000). Article accessed at `www.mmc.com/views/00winter mcghee.shtml`

2. Walter S. Baer, "Rewarding IT Security in the Marketplace." (The RAND Corp., September 2003). `http://intel.si.umich.edu/ tprc/papers/2003/190/BaerITSecurity.pdf`

3. U.S. District Court, Arizona, American Guarantee & Liability Insurance Co. v. Ingram Micro, Inc. Civ. 99-185 TUC ACM, 2000 U.S. Dist. LEXIS 7299 (D. Ariz., April 19, 2000). `www.phillipsnizer.com/library/ cases/lib_case155.cfm`

4. Op. cit. McGhee, "Catastrophe Bonds Come of Age."

CHAPTER 10

Governments: Guarantors of Last Resort

a holistic and synoptic view
—U.S. National Strategy to Secure Cyberspace

Government traditionally serves as insurer of last resort when all other means fail. The recent growth in cyberhurricanes plus electronic crime and terrorism gives government great incentive to plan ahead, not only to protect its own agencies but also to protect whole industries. While sometimes a government can afford to bail out an industry directly as guarantor of last resort, that gets expensive quickly both in money and in political capital. It is better if government can, through a variety of financial, legal, and regulatory incentives and sanctions, encourage private industry to handle most of its own risk management.

As society becomes ever more dependent upon the Internet, global communications are more vulnerable to natural and man-made disasters. As a result, it is important to have an ongoing, sustainable, accurate, complete view of the Internet, its pieces, its strengths and weaknesses, that reveals its many layers of complexity. The Internet is one of the most interdependent and interconnected communication systems ever built. A terrorist attack on a data center in Hong Kong could affect traffic in New York, or a back hoe cutting a cable in Canada could slow down traffic in Seattle. Many groups, agencies, and companies monitor specific pieces or try to simulate the interaction of larger parts; however, looking at the big picture, looking at the Internet in a comprehensive, complete and timely way, is done by few, if any, of these organizations. Governments cannot do this adequately, at least not alone, but they can assist private industry in doing it. Even better, they can assist in promoting a private cyberinsurance industry, which will then require better overall Internet security.

Encouragement and oversight may not be enough; laws and military force may be necessary in some cases. Yet there are limits to what government can and should do, and in some cases it has already tried too hard to do too much.

Alerting Businesses

Government can play a role in alerting businesses, but to date has not been very active. The U.S. National Strategy to Secure Cyberspace of February 2002[1] was interesting, particularly in its recommendation for a holistic and synoptic view of the Internet and its problems.

Such an aggregate and detailed view over space and time is exactly what was missing when the boll weevil took decades to mosey up from Mexico to Texas and across the southern United States in the early twentieth century, eating the monoculture cotton crop as it came. There was no national crop epidemic watch. Several years after the bug started eating crops in Oklahoma, that state had to ask Texas A&M for advice. Farmers had not prepared for the worst by diversifying crops. Bankers had not arranged to handle massive loan defaults. Crop failure led to farm bankruptcies, which led to bank failures and whole towns being deserted. Deserted topsoil blew away and contributed to the dust bowl and the Great Depression; see Chapter 2 for more about monoculture.[2]

A holistic and synoptic view of the Internet would reveal problems as they occurred, permitting both reactive and preventive action. The market could see more clearly which enterprises had adequately managed their risks by running secure software and applying patches in a timely manner and which enterprises had not. Such a fine-resolution big picture could be useful to insurers and also in any resulting legal liability cases.

Preventive Advice for Enterprises and Insurers

Unfortunately, the U.S. National Strategy to Secure Cyberspace[3] was somewhat lacking in specifics regarding the roles of enterprises and insurers. It did not use the word "should," and it did not even hint at potential liability. Yet the scale of the potential risk is at least on the scale of airline failure, large enough that government will not want to try to bail out the affected enterprises, even if it has the resources to do so. Some preventive advice now could help avert major problems not very far down the road.

The federal government could mandate cyber-insurance for its contractors. However, that would not have much effect before there is a market for such insurance so contractors could buy it. Defining liabilities more clearly while encouraging insurers and enterprises to deal with them seems a better course. For example, a law or perhaps a presidential directive could state:

All government contractors are required to have CI (cyber insurance) equal to 25% of the value of the contract within 4 years or passage, and 50% of the value within 6 years of passage, if any portion of the contract development, deliverable, operations, maintenance, or support is provided over or through the Internet.[4]

Such a requirement would not make it a crime not to have such insurance; it would simply make it increasingly difficult for contractors to sell to the federal government if they didn't have it. Contractors would no doubt raise their prices to the government accordingly, which means the taxpayers would end up paying for this, but the result should be a healthy Internet insurance market.

Anything government can do to raise the profile of Internet business risk management in government and industry, including insurance and catastrophe bonds, should help. Possible methods might include:

- Participating in or organizing conferences
- Congressional subcommittee hearings
- Commissioning studies on the subject that could be published
- Funding ongoing observations of the Internet
- Funding research into detection, characterization, and amelioration

The Information Sharing and Analysis Centers (ISACs) are a step in the right direction. Perhaps they can be leveraged more, both by sending information through them and by using contacts with people involved in them to emphasize that it is time to do something about Internet business risk.

Coercive and Ameliorative Action

Governments sometimes play more draconian roles, many of which will be discussed in this chapter:

- Making standards such as FISMA or ISO 17799
- Legislatures passing laws
- District attorneys prosecuting perpetrators
- Courts convicting and sentencing
- Prisons incarcerating
- Military intervening
- Political negotiating
- Acting as insurer of last resort
- Repealing laws
- Reforming tax codes
- Reforming subsidies

Many of these latter roles are best avoided if there are other ways to deal with a situation: Keeping someone in prison for life can cost more than sending them to Harvard, and military interventions have casualties, collateral damages, and political and economic repercussions for many years. However, sometimes a law is the most effective way to set a societal norm, and sometimes repealing or at least modifying a law is the best way to fix a failed attempt at legislation.

Governments sometimes act as insurers of last resort. However, natural disasters already strain the resources of governments and the willingness of taxpayers to fund emergency relief for people who build houses on beaches or next to earthquake faults. The Northridge Earthquake in Los Angeles in 1994 was one of the incentives for the development of catastrophe bonds. Governments would do well encouraging the development of a thriving catastrophe and performance bond market, rather than ending up having to deal directly with Internet catastrophes that affect not just one or two industries such as automobiles or airlines, rather every industry, because every enterprise uses the Internet.

Government Departments and Agencies As Large Enterprises

Government departments and agencies range from small to as large as large businesses, not even counting the Pentagon (see the section later in the chapter about the military). While the government may be self-insuring, government agencies have all the same vulnerabilities as corporations and other nongovernmental organizations. As of this writing, no major government department or agency has been seriously damaged by Internet security attacks or crime, so far as we know. However, that is only a matter of time. Preparing in advance would be prudent. And preparing in advance by buying appropriate security measures and requiring private contractors selling to the government to do the same and by buying Internet business connectivity insurance would promote better security and risk management on the Internet both inside and outside the government.

Law Enforcement

Not every Internet business risk is an act of God or an accident. Some risks are crimes knowingly perpetrated by gangs or individuals for illegal profit. While there are measures enterprises can take to protect themselves, in some of these cases having the long, although slow-moving, arm of the law in reserve may be necessary. In addition to deceptive practices such as spam, phishing, and pharming, there are also unfair practices perpetrated by manufacturers and vendors of computer hardware, software, and services.

Deceptive Practices

Commerce continues to embrace the Internet and to become dependent upon it. In banking in particular, deposits, withdrawals, balances, statements, lines of credit, and other financial transactions and instruments are increasingly available via and used over the Internet. Financial institutions that are based on the Internet are even more dependent on it. Any enterprise that does commerce through the Internet is at risk of financial or identity theft involving the Internet.

Spam

Some surveys indicate that the great majority of spam is perpetrated by a few hundred people, mostly located in the United States.[5] This presents an opportunity for legal solutions to spam.

On one hand, it is possible to sue a spammer and win using nothing but existing laws; I and others did this back in 1997.[6]

Most attempts to pass antispam laws have been seriously flawed in at least two major ways.

1. They confuse spam, which is unsolicited bulk electronic mail, with commercial electronic mail. Politicians would, of course, like such a bogus definition of spam, since they could themselves then spam voters. Yet mail sent in large quantities to people who didn't ask for it is spam, regardless of whether it is political, religious, or commercial in content. And involving content in a definition of spam risks serious U.S. First Amendment and freedom of expression problems with any laws against spam.

2. The second major flaw of most attempts to pass antispam laws is that spammers almost always get involved in the legislative process, masquerading as legitimate businesses, and legislators almost always try to compromise between the spammers and the antispammers and end up drafting laws that legitimize spam rather than prevent it.

On the other hand, it may be easier for law enforcement to prosecute cases if they have laws tailored to the problem. The CAN-SPAM Act of 2003[7] is one attempt at antispam legislation. It has many problems, among them that it actually limits spam liability under a previous anti-junk-fax law. Nonetheless, it has been used to convict at least one big spammer, including a sentence of jail time.[8] It is not clear that spam has decreased in volume since that conviction, but at least it doesn't seem to be increasing like it was.

Phishing

Law enforcement cannot be expected to deal with phishing alone, because a single phishing case usually involves relatively small sums of money, and it takes thousands of dollars just to put a detective on a case. Even worse, phishers usually deliberately stage their attacks through multiple countries both to make phishing harder to trace and harder to prosecute, because it then involves multiple legal regimes in multiple countries. However, with some assistance in finding local legal leverage points, such as Internet Service Providers that are (knowingly or unknowingly) harboring multiple phishing servers, private industry may be able to demonstrate sufficient aggregation for the law to deal with phishing using existing laws.

In such cases, laws may not even be needed. For example, if there is sufficient evidence that phishers are using nodes set up for phishing at a specific Internet Service Provider (ISP), often that ISP will take down the phishing node. Or if there is sufficient evidence that a legitimate node has been compromised for phishing, the node's owners, supplied with such evidence via the ISP, can take action. Most ISPs are honest and do not knowingly harbor phishers or customers who do so. While ISPs may not want to act as police for their own customers, they may nonetheless welcome evidence gathered and presented by external entities. An honest ISP will want to take action. Even a complicit ISP will probably want to take action when faced with such evidence, because it wants to appear to be honest. Such an ISP may even turn honest because it fears future complicity will be revealed, and a chronic pattern of compromise becomes harder to explain away over time.

New laws have recently been passed against phishing, and there are as of this writing bills in progress against spyware. Both the direct and indirect approaches of these bills have pros and cons.

Pharming

Government can play only limited roles in dealing with pharming, because the main defenses are technical and operational. It is not clear that new laws are needed, because fraud is already illegal. Pharming is sometimes facilitated by spyware.

Spyware

There are already laws and bills in progress for spyware.[9] Legislating against spyware is perhaps even more of a minefield than legislating against spam, because it is difficult to avoid confusion between unauthorized monitoring of a computer system and implicitly authorized monitoring, such as performance monitoring by service providers. Yet such a bill should not exempt ISPs or hosting centers whose facilities are being used to host multiple instances of spyware-based phishing or pharming or other attacks if the service provider has been informed that is the case and has not taken basic steps to deal with it. Third-party monitoring by Internet performance or security monitoring firms that do not intrude past security barriers such as firewalls also should not be outlawed, but it is easy for a bill to do so inadvertently. Some parties may applaud a spyware bill that outlaws espionage by government agencies, but intelligence agencies probably wouldn't take the same view.

Most spyware these days is installed through the Internet, yet no anti-spyware bill should outlaw installing software through the Internet, since so much legitimate software is installed that way these days. Such a bill should take care not to outlaw anti-spyware software, as well, and probably even should include limitations on liability of such software and its vendors.

Then there are enforcement questions. Some bills currently in progress authorize the Federal Trade Commission (FTC) to regulate spyware, but according to the press, the FTC has said it does not want such further authorization, since it already has the power to deal with deceptive or unfair practices.

Sometimes the best course of legislative action is no legislation; this may be such a case.

Adware

Some spyware bills currently in progress also attempt to outlaw *adware*, which is software that imposes advertisements on the user that the user did not request. Many of the same problems of clarity and enforcement exist for adware as for spyware.

Unfair Practices

Much press has covered Internet fraud such as spam, phishing, pharming, and spyware and adware that occur through the Internet after computers have been purchased and are deployed. But why should a software or hardware vendor or OEM or retailer be immune if it preinstalls software that is deceptive or otherwise engages in unfair acts?

Vendor Liability As a Driver for Insurance

In addition to attempting to directly reduce deceptive or unfair practices, legal liability for software or hardware manufacturers or OEMs or retailers could help drive a market for insurance. A vendor that faces possible fines is more likely to buy insurance to cover losses. This topic is covered in more detail in Chapter 11.

Security Vulnerabilities: Unforeseen, Chronic, and Unfixed

Some security vulnerabilities are unforeseen; a vendor cannot be expected to see the future or to preempt every potential flaw. However, once a vulnerability is discovered, a vendor should have some responsibility to provide a patch or upgrade to fix it. The longer the time the vendor takes to patch after the vulnerability after discovery, the more a vendor becomes negligent. Such negligence should increase if the vulnerability was first discovered by an exploit.

Beyond patching, perhaps a vendor should have some responsibility to distribute a new release after numerous patches accumulate or after a long time has elapsed since a patch has been released for a major exploit. It is well known that many software users do not patch their software. Perhaps they should bear some liability for not doing so. Perhaps the more copies of the software an organization is running, the more liability it should accrue for not patching. But if aggregation increases with number of users, shouldn't the vendors, who have the most users, have the most liability? And shouldn't the vendors, who have the best ability to fix vulnerabilities at their source, have a different kind of liability than any of their customers or users?

This is an example of what Hal Varian, professor of business and economics at the University of California at Berkeley and number nine on Accenture's list of top 50 business intellectuals, wrote about in 2000 in the *New York Times*: ". . . one of the fundamental principles of the economic analysis of liability: it should be assigned to the party that can do the best job of managing risk."[10]

And what of software that has well-known design flaws that lead to numerous and chronic exploits, design flaws that make it very likely that there will be another vulnerability discovered, even though the exact nature of it cannot be predicted? Only the vendor of closed-source software can fix such flaws. Should not such software bring liability upon its vendor?

These remarks about software liability are, thus, by far mostly just opinions. Perhaps some of them should become laws. The law is a blunt instrument that often has unforeseen side effects, but so is some of the software currently out there on the Internet.

The Biggest Offenders Have the Most Lobbyists

There will be some difficulty getting software liability laws passed. According to the *Washington Post*:

> The number of registered lobbyists in Washington has more than doubled since 2000 to more than 34,750 while the amount that lobbyists charge their new clients has increased by as much as 100 percent.[11]

The most hazardous software is that with the most aggregation of damages, which is usually the most widely used, which often means sold by the biggest or most profitable companies. Such companies can afford to lobby for exclusions from liability bills. This makes passage of such bills unlikely unless the public demands them and Congress and perhaps the Executive branch decide to do something about it.

The closest thing to software liability that seems to be occurring in 2005 is California SB96, which is about liability for P2P software that does not prevent transmission of copyrighted software.[12] This is more an example of proactive corporate lobbying to get laws passed that limit corporate liability. The kind of software liability that would promote general Internet security would be liability for selling software that has bugs or design flaws that make it easy to break. As of this writing, there appear to be no such bills.

The Bigger They Are, the Harder They Fall

Yet difficult does not mean impossible. Establishing liability for selling tobacco products to minors and for knowingly selling cancer-causing products was also difficult. It took an internal whistleblower and a major effort on the part of state and federal governments, but eventually it was done.

Automobile manufacturers used to take little responsibility for dangerous flaws in their vehicles. Nothing much happened to change that until one person, Ralph Nader, took it upon himself to expose those flaws and those manufacturers' reluctance to spend money on even elementary safety features such as seat belts.[13] The initial response of the manufacturers was to counterattack against Nader, while making minimal safety improvements. Nonetheless, the president of General Motors (GM), one of the largest and richest companies in the world, was forced to appear (March 22, 1966) before a Senate subcommittee, to apologize to Nader for GM's campaign of harassment against him.[14] Unsafe vehicles have not completely vanished from the roads, but the average vehicle sold today is far safer than in the early 1960s, and when a hazard is discovered, manufacturers frequently recall vehicles to fix them. No one today assumes that automobile manufacturers should be free from all liability for the cars and trucks they manufacture. One of the major roles of government in this case was to call attention to the problem via the Senate subcommittee hearings.

Aircraft manufacturers are also held to a high standard of safety. The Federal Aviation Administration (FAA) gets involved every time an airplane crashes. The FAA, the airlines, air travelers, and the public expect crashes to be few, defects that caused crashes to be fixed quickly, and aircraft vendors that knowingly sell defective airplanes or that don't fix them quickly to be liable.

Why should software companies be immune from liability for their products? In other industries, not even the biggest and richest companies and tycoons have been immune. It may be that the most successful companies are the ones least suited to make safe products.

It may be that the very qualities that help people get ahead are the ones that make them ill-suited for managing crises. It's hard to prepare for the worst when you think you're the best.[15]

Yet eventually even the customers of companies that think they're the best will conclude, after enough times patching and reinstalling and running spyware detectors, that such a company's self-image is inaccurate. If the company also turns out to be legally liable, customers are likely to reach such a conclusion more quickly. Such disillusioned customers can vote with their pocketbooks by buying from competitors. Not even the biggest companies are immune to that. The bigger they are, the harder they fall.

Let the Punishment Fit the Crime

Not every crime should be a felony, and not every vulnerability or even exploit should be a crime. If we are to use the blunt instrument of the law, we should at least try to use it carefully.

Probably no one wants the average cable modem or DSL or wireless Internet user liable for criminal charges for not installing enough security measures.

The average user is essentially clueless about how to prevent his computer from being taken over, so assigning liability to him would be pointless. Assigning liability to the network operator would make more sense.[16]

One might want to have unpatched machines or ones that spew malicious traffic shut off the Internet by their local ISP, but even that is problematical. The computers most likely to be unpatched are those owned by mom and pop in their homes, that is, by the people least likely to be malicious and also least likely to know how to patch. In addition, given the recent track record of cable companies in mistaking even simple standard protocols, such as traceroute, for malicious traffic, it would not be prudent to depend on ISPs for policing; there is more on that in Chapter 9.

On the other hand, a company that knowingly sells software with numerous security holes enabled right out of the box perhaps should face criminal or at least civil liability. Laws could make such a distinction by taking aggregation into account. For example, a vendor that knowingly sold software with a vulnerability that is then exploited on more than 1000 computers could face legal liability.

Any such laws need to take into account due process and also some phenomena that may be new to the Internet or at least to computer software, such as open software. Open software projects tend to be diffuse and do not have deep pockets. Establishing who is liable could be difficult, and a punishment that would be appropriate for a large commercial software vendor, maybe even a slap on the wrist, could wipe out an open source distributor.

Another outcome of such laws should be to set a social norm that distributing hazardous software is not socially acceptable, thus encouraging active self-policing.

Levels of Government Trying Different Legal Regimes

A popular reaction to annoyances is: "There oughta be a law!"

This is especially true for major inconveniences with large economic and reputational risks, as phishing, pharming, spyware, and other online exploits have done. Sometimes a law may be the best way to establish that society won't tolerate something anymore. But how do you get the right law, especially when legislators are being pushed by their constituents to do something quickly, and therefore with little time for research or input from affected parties?

A national law may seem like the most effective reaction, but a federal law that preempts state or provincial or metropolitan law also preempts multiple attempts to fix the problem in different ways. Some of those different ways may turn out to be better than a federal law, especially a rushed federal law. While problems that take advantage of the Internet's ability to reach anywhere quickly often don't have better local fixes, that is still possible, especially if a local area adopts something else that works better with its local law. The something else could be an improved detection mechanism or a different local Internet connection such as municipal wireless with effective filters. Such a combination may be a long shot, but the more different solutions that are tried, the more likely some locality will come up with one that works.

Are There Too Many Crimes?

Sometimes laws go too far and should be amended to do less.

SOX Considered Nitpicking

In the wake of corporate financial scandals involving Enron, Anderson, World-com, and others, the U.S. Congress passed Sarbanes-Oxley (SOX). The intention was good, but the actual law may have overshot the target, doing too little to actually fix the problem, while costing too much in requiring extraneous detail.[17] "The trouble with Sarbanes-Oxley is that it was designed in a panic and rushed through in a blinding fervour of moral indignation."[18] While CEOs will complain about any constraints on their ability to act, sometimes their complaints are valid.

The accounting, auditing and lawyering clearly have gone too far. The partners of outside auditing firms have become more conservative than ever, refusing to sign off on many transactions and practices that have been allowed for years due to worries about what the Public Company Accounting Oversight Board might do or say. That auditor must get the opinion of a "concurring" partner for every serious decision and a third partner may get involved if there is a filing to be made to the Securities and Exchange Commission (SEC). If those partners can't reach consensus on a subject such as "revenue recognition," the issue gets kicked upstairs to a national review process inside the audit firm and possibly reaches the point of arbitration. At each stage, the auditors are worried that the PCAOB will exercise its "peek-a-boo" privilege and demand to see an avalanche of paper that illuminates how they've done their jobs.[19]

Not all of this is due to SOX, but SOX is an example of the problem.

The reason this is so crippling is that there are many gray zones in Generally Accepted Accounting Principles that require judgments to be made. If accountants and auditors can't make decisions, CEOs have to devote enormous resources to resolving what are often petty issues. They can't concentrate on growing their businesses, which has serious consequences for job creation, the financial markets and U.S. competitiveness in the world.[20]

The real problems with Enron, Worldcom, and the other high-profile corporate flameouts weren't that their executives didn't follow the letter of accounting procedures. The real problem was not even that they came up with creative new methods of using financial and legal procedures, in addition to old hacks they hid. The real problem was a lack of communication within those corporations, lack of proper board oversight, and lack of a culture of ethics. Everyone knew that every corporation did it, so the ones that did it best should make the most out of their unethical scams!

. . . it would be difficult to argue that mere book-keeping was the main thing. Yes, it is outrageous that the true state of those companies was disguised. But when firms collapse that way, it is usually because they have borrowed too much and squandered the money. Accounting impropriety may conceal those errors, for a time, but is hardly ever the main cause. Bad business judgment, with or without criminal intent, is far more often to blame.[21]

The Basel II attempt to build an ethical culture within and among corporations may be better than the SOX approach of trying to nail down picky details. Basel II also takes into account that the biggest corporations are so international and tightly coupled with the financial and political elites of numerous countries that no single country can effectively supervise them. See Chapter 5 for more about Basel II.

The CEOs have a point. Requiring them (and others) to spend too much of their time on what should be routine details detracts from job creation and harms the economy, thus making the country less competitive and creating more risks.

Maybe it's time for Congress to try more ethics and less nitpicking. It will help if Congress sets an example first, which may require the voters, courts, and the Executive branch to require Congress to do so. The same holds for other countries.

Not Every Citizen Is a Terrorist

In the wake of 9/11, the U.S. Congress passed some laws, such as the PATRIOT Act. It is no longer possible to open a bank account without supplying a physical address. Nail clippers are confiscated at airports yet flight attendants serve drinks in metal cans and glass containers that can easily be made into sharp pointed objects. Well meaning as such measures may be, they can go too far. Treating citizens as if they were all terrorists may make some of them feel more comfortable. It is also making business travelers avoid commercial air travel and making many of us wonder whether the United States is the best country in which to keep our money. Thus, such measures have two costs: the direct costs of funding them, which comes out of taxpayers' pockets, and the indirect costs of adverse effects on the economy. Less tangible costs include increasing concern over what use government may make of all the new information it requires, and what other entities may obtain access to that information.

Similarly, government's ability to demand personal information from ISPs and libraries (which are many people's primary Internet access points) has a chilling effect on Internet use and commerce. At what point do security measures cause more harm than good? Governments would do well to consider that question, and consider repealing some of the more draconian security measures passed in recent years.

Not Every Foreigner Is a Terrorist

Tightening immigration procedures after 9/11 was probably prudent. However, there can be too much of a good thing. According to Steve Forbes:

Despite the weak dollar, the number of visitors from overseas during the past three years is down 23%. International conventions and seminars are not taking place in the U.S. because organizers can't be sure their delegates will be allowed into the country.[22]

Overinspecting every incoming person and refusing too many people, thus, has immediate economic effects. It also has longer-term effects:

More alarmingly, foreign students are increasingly turning to non-U.S. universities. Australia, Canada and other nations have been effectively luring these students by assuring them that if they qualify, they won't have to undergo repeated, humiliating hassles at their borders. By contrast, foreign students now

in the U.S. know that when they go home for summer vacation or holidays, their
probability of returning to school is no sure thing.[23]

Many educated professions in the United States these days depend upon
people from other countries, as do universities; especially university research
departments.

The Internet by its nature has always been a worldwide endeavor, as is the
research that supports it and that it supports. Attempting to criminalize a hard
line at national borders is not an effective way of dealing with the Internet
community. Rather, laws should encourage ethical behavior and more
research and commerce.

Economy Is Security

Why can the United States project military power sufficient to take over two
countries in two years? Because it has the largest economy in the world. What
has kept the U.S. economy ahead of all others? A continent's resources got it
started, and a revolutionary political system let it continue. But what has consistently kept the United States ahead has been the next big thing: having the
next big technical innovation first.

Innovation Drives Productivity

As Deborah Wince-Smith, president of the Council on Competitiveness, said:
"There is a direct correlation between productivity and innovation and this is
a first-tier economic priority for the country."[24]

Or at least it should be a priority. U.S. automobile manufacturers are behind
again, having to play catch-up on hybrid fuel vehicles, which Japanese manufacturers introduced and U.S. customers want. Outsourcing of jobs has moved
on from manual labor and blue collar jobs to call centers, computer programming, tax accounting, and x-ray interpretation. China and India are now moving beyond copying and outsourcing into innovation, while U.S. corporations
increasingly emphasize the next quarter's profits and the federal government
cuts research spending. As William Brody, president of Johns Hopkins University and co-chair of the Council on Competitiveness's National Innovations
Institute says, "I'm worried that the U.S. is moving away from risk-taking."
He also says this trend will ". . . eventually drive America into second-class
status."[25]

This problem is widely perceived in the United States and beyond. A recent
article in *Chief Executive* Magazine says:

Left to languish are issues of equal or greater economic importance, such as
America's eroding competitiveness, a decline in R&D and work force education,

and a slowdown in high technology efforts aimed at promoting broadband and the Internet. ... other serious issues [exist] such as the ballooning federal budget deficit, health cost burdens on companies and soaring energy prices.[26]

There are too many examples to examine in this book, so a selection will have to do.

Economic Policy and Business Judgment

The problems that SOX was supposed to solve don't all begin within corporations. ". . . bad economic policy can sometimes contribute to bad business judgment."[27]

Governmental legal and financial policies can encourage corporations to cheat, lie, and steal, in which case band-aids such as SOX won't solve the problem. *The Economist* recommends four major agenda points that could help government encourage good business: ". . . genuine, as opposed to phoney, corporate-governance reform, tort reform, tax reform, and corporate-welfare reform."[28]

By corporate-government reform they don't mean more regulation and oversight; they mean encouraging the market for corporate control, even including encouraging takeover attempts. Tort reform could reduce windfall trial settlements against corporations. Tax reform could do away with writing off corporate debts against taxes, and thus reduce corporate borrowing. Corporate taxes could even be reduced (every CEO should like that), and the resulting government revenue shortfall paid for by eliminating the reputed $100 billion per year in subsidies the government pays to various industries.

All of these proposals are debatable. Encouraging takeover attempts could make corporate management pay even more attention to the bottom line and less to the basic vision, mission, and goals of the corporation. Tort reform would best be accompanied by better defined liability, especially software liability, and so forth. But the main point remains clear: fiddling with accounting rules won't fix the problems SOX was meant to solve, and some of those problems originate with government policies, which only government can change.

Funding Research As Economic Policy

The United States does not traditionally go in for Soviet-style 5-year plans nor even Japanese-style directed economic policy, but ever since Thomas Jefferson established the Patent Office, the United States has promoted innovation. U.S. agencies such as the National Institute for Standards and Technology (NIST), the National Science Foundation (NSF), the Defense Advanced Research Projects Agency (DARPA), the Defense Information Systems Agency (DISA), and others have for many years supported basic and applied research through grants and purchases of equipment, software, and services.

In recent years, the budget for NIST's Advanced Technology Program (ATP) has been zeroed out, DARPA has shifted its emphasis to the very near term, and other agencies such as NSF have not been given additional funding. There is the new Homeland Security Advanced Research Projects Agency (HSARPA), but it seems to be underfunded. In addition, education has not improved, oil prices are up, and the federal budget deficit, once under control, is now inflating rapidly.

The voters wanted an emphasis on security and fighting terrorism. However, it seems increasingly less prudent to try to achieve those goals by trading long-term security in the form of R&D and the economy.

This is not a partisan issue. In one poll, "the majority of chief executives polled are Republicans who support Bush overall," yet those 593 CEOs are the ones who expressed the just-quoted concerns about R&D and other issues.[29] Nor is this solely a U.S. issue. Some other countries may have some of the same problems.

What Not to Fund: Specific Technical Requirements

The White House has recently issued a common ID mandate for federal employees and contractors.[30] Some have said this is similar to how the federal government funding of the ARPANET eventually changed how business operates.

Indeed, ARPA (now DARPA) funded the early ARPANET, which led to the Internet, and DCA (now DISA), among other agencies, promoted it by buying equipment from fledgling Internet vendors. This is one of the most famous examples of a small amount of government research funding resulting in a huge economic payoff.

However, let's not forget that the federal government also promulgated GOSIP,[31] which was a requirement that computer systems sold to the federal government had to support the ISO-OSI protocol suite, which was similar to TCP/IP but different. Different in that while TCP/IP was the result of a process of multiple implementations interacting with standardization, ISO-OSI was a product of standards committees, and lacked not only many implementations, but even many more users. GOSIP was a waste of time and money. Fortunately, the U.S. government wasn't as serious about ISO-OSI as were many European governments and the EU. In Europe, OSI implementation was farmed out to individual countries, separating implementation artificially across national boundaries. That and the backwards OSI standardization method held back internetworking in Europe until the rapid deployment of the Internet in the United States and elsewhere eventually made it clear that OSI was going nowhere. Users in Europe suddenly voted with their feet starting about 1991, abandoning OSI for TCP/IP. The U.S. National Institute for Standards and Technology (NIST) repealed the procurement mandate for GOSIP in 1995.[32]

Where the U.S. government succeeded in networking was in promoting research, development, implementation, and deployment. Support by the National Science Foundation (NSF) for NSFNET, an early Internet backbone network that was faster than the ARPANET, is another good example.

Where it failed was when it tried to mandate a technical choice, as for example with GOSIP.

Other governments have no better track records at mandating technical choices, as for example with OSI, and it's not clear they have as good track records at promoting innovation. Japan, for example, was impeded in using the Internet until 1994, when the Japanese government loosened regulations on who could do international communications. I still remember the line of people snaking across the floor of the huge Makuhari Messe convention center near Tokyo at the 1994 Interop trade show, a line of users waiting to get a CD of software so they could get on the Internet. However, both Japan and Korea have done much better than the United States at deploying universally available broadband Internet access, and at getting many people to use it; see the next section of the chapter for more information on this.

This particular White House directive about a common ID gives the Department of Commerce 6 months to consult with other government agencies and come up with a standard. If there's a requirement to consult with industry or academia, I don't see it. I hope this comes out better than, for example, key escrow, a previous government attempt to mandate authentication methods.

And just to stress the point again, government is not good at mandating specific technical choices. The reasons for that include how technology changes more quickly than laws and that legislators cannot all be experts on technical subjects. Governments should stick to promoting research, development, implementation, and deployment in technical areas.

Security Management Standards

It is possible to standardize requirements without standardizing specific technical solutions to them. Examples of this approach appear to include the U.S. Federal Information Security Management Act (FISMA) and related standards and the international standard ISO 17799. The purpose of both of these is to promote enterprise-wide security management, with support from the top of the organization and buy-in at all levels.

FISMA is elaborated in NIST's FIPS 199 on Security Categorization, in a series of NIST Special Publications 800-nnn, and in FIPS publication 200 on minimum security standards. There is some coordination between these FISMA standards and guidelines and requirements for SOX, GLBA, and other laws. Apparently an organization that complies with FISMA will also comply with those laws. Dr. Ron Ross of NIST tells me that NIST remembers GOSIP and is taking a different approach this time; his presentation at the 2005 Texas Regional Infrastructure Security Conference (TRISC) was most informative.

ISO 17799 has been around in one form or another for many years and has in recent years seen a surge of interest. I would attribute this interest to the increased use of the Internet in commerce. The current version of ISO 17799 is quite extensive and detailed. It and FISMA cover many of the same topics, albeit organized differently. There is apparently some effort to harmonize the two.

Standards have their pitfalls: they are slow, they can get mired in detail, and there always seems to be more than one. Nonetheless, standards such as FISMA and ISO 17799 involve voluntary cooperation with a minimum of coercion, and are thus preferable to, for example, criminal sanctions. And this time perhaps these standards can avoid legislating technology.

Internet Broadband for Economic Security

The United States does appear to be a country with a prominent case of lack of emphasis on a number of economic problems. One of the more glaring examples is Internet broadband access. Japan and Korea saw in the 1990s that the United States was likely to forge ahead in broadband access and chose to remain competitive by promoting broadband in their own countries. Today, Japan and Korea have broadband up to 10 or even 40 megabits per second available to 95 percent of their populations at prices similar to what U.S. residents pay for basic telephone service. In Korea, online culture fostered by widespread use of fast broadband has become sufficiently influential that fictional objects in online games now sell for hundreds of dollars and online organizers are said by some to have tipped the result of the most recent Korean presidential election. The United States has nowhere near that high availability or uptake of broadband.

Just funding broadband access projects is not enough, as the state of Texas demonstrated with its Telecommunications Infrastructure Fund (TIF). Deriving $200 million a year from a 1 percent tax on revenues of telephone and cable companies in Texas, TIF spent that money for several years funding local broadband projects throughout Texas, especially in rural areas. While some good did come of it, such as schools with broadband connections, to my knowledge not a single one of the funded projects produced a sustainable business model.

TIF did also have the inadvertent effect of producing the Texas Internet Service Provider Association (TISPA), which formed in reaction to the original interpretation by the Texas state comptroller that the TIF tax was to apply to ISPs as well as to telephone and cable companies. TISPA hired a lobbyist who spoke to the comptroller who decided it did not so apply. TISPA since has taken an interest in both state and national telecommunications policy, and some say that it was the model for the Canadian ISP association.

To my knowledge, none of the successful rural or urban wireless Internet companies in Texas ever took any TIF money. They also never got taxed for

TIF, thanks to TISPA. Sometimes one of the principle roles of government is not to overregulate and not to tax. The United States and some state governments have been relatively good about those things. However, apparently those things alone are not good enough, given how far ahead Japan and Korea are in broadband.

TIF indicates that completely subsidizing broadband access does not work, and Japan and Korea have the advantage of being more compact and more urbanized countries than the United States. Nonetheless, some of the methods Japan and Korea used may be adaptable to the United States. Newer methods such as wireless Internet access may provide further technical means. What the U.S. government lacks is the will to try things until it finds something that works.

China and India are as big and as distributed as the United States. We shall see whether they solve the broadband access problem before the United States does. If so, that will be a big win for China and India, while the United States will slide further behind. Private sector initiative seems like the best hope at this point for U.S. competitiveness. The U.S. government would do well to encourage that initiative, while encouraging ethical behavior and avoiding ill-considered security laws.

Terrorism and Economics

A lunch companion at the 2005, U.S. Homeland Security Partnering Conference asked me why Internet security was represented at all at the conference, given that it is very hard to kill anyone through the Internet. This comment misses the point of terrorism, because terrorism isn't really about killing; it is about terror.

Terrorism: A Means to Political Ends

The purpose of terrorism is to achieve political goals, which usually involve withdrawal of what the terrorists regard as occupying powers, the destruction of governments the terrorists consider oppressive and illegitimate, and the establishment of a new government along the lines of an ideology the terrorists support. Terrorists use terror because it provides them leverage so that they can fight their enemies who are vastly superior in economic means and military power, and because terrorists consider their cause just and their enemies evil.

> *Terrorism has become for its perpetrators, supporters and sponsors, the most attractive low-cost, low-risk, but potentially high yield method of attacking a regime or a rival faction.*[33]

But wouldn't an even lower-cost, lower-risk, and higher-yield method be more attractive?

Terrorism, Crime, and Sabotage

People who won't stop at using terror won't stop at using more ordinary criminal means. The Irish Republican Army (IRA) has been accused of staging bank robberies, most recently one on December 20, 2004 that netted 26.5 million pounds.[34] Terrorists in Iraq sabotaged oil deliveries by holding up delivery trucks and taking their papers while they were in line to pick up their cargo. Chechen nationalists appear to have persuaded President Putin of Russia to approve a referendum on Chechen independence by punching holes in oil pipelines, thus threatening Russia's major source of foreign exchange. In none of these cases were any lives lost.

Attacking Systems Provides Leverage

In the Chechen case, a bloodless tactic appears to have made more progress than many years of warfare and conventional terrorism. The key to the success of the Chechen tactic is that it attacked a system on which its enemy regime depends.

Attacking systems provides the kind of leverage terrorists exploit to fight a vastly superior enemy. The Internet provides the means to attack systems worldwide, which means that the Internet provides huge leverage. Sooner or later terrorists will use it for that purpose.

From Phishing to SCADA Attacks

To date, terrorists may have been held back from attacking through the Internet because of a lack of expertise in the Internet and in systems supported by it. But they no longer have to learn how to do it themselves. The rise of criminal gangs profiting from spamming, phishing, pharming, and other crimes provides a market from which terrorists may simply buy what they need.

The U.S. Department of Homeland Security's budget allocates somewhat over 1 percent to cybersecurity and about the same to critical infrastructure protection. At the 2005 Homeland Security Partnering Conference the speakers and attendees were in proportion with the funding; national laboratories and major research universities were heavily represented, as one would expect given the budget emphasis on nuclear, biological, and chemical threats.

Yet the SCADA systems that control electrical grids and other critical infrastructures increasingly run over the Internet. And they do so without much security. The same kinds of exploits that permit miscreants to build herds of bots by breaking into home and corporate computers could easily be adapted to compromise SCADA systems. The criminal gangs behind phishing and pharming and the like have no direct economic incentive to do this, unless someone provides them with funding.

What Is Critical Infrastructure, Anyway?

For that matter, systems disruption does not have to involve traditional critical infrastructure. On a blog someone asked rhetorically, "What are they going to do, take down eBay?"

Well, if a terrorist wanted to get maximal publicity while affecting an infrastructure used by more people than the entire populations of several major countries, what more effective way than to take down eBay or Google or Yahoo!?

> *In order to create the wide spread sense of fear he seeks, the terrorist deliberately uses the weapons of surprise and disproportionate violence in order to create a sense of outrage and insecurity. As Raymond Aron observes: 'an action of violence is labelled "terrorist" when its psychological effects are out of all proportion to its purely physical result. . . .'*[35]

Taking down a major Internet service on which tens of millions depend fits that bill exactly, except that no physical violence has to be involved.

Effects, Not Damage

Effects are the purpose of terrorist operations, not damage. The U.S. military has developed a doctrine of Effects Based Operations (EBO)[36] that explains why the first Gulf War was so quick and why the initial military part of the second Gulf war was so successful.

Unfortunately, the opposition in Iraq, currently consisting of hundreds or thousands of small groups, not even necessarily coordinated with one another, has adopted its own version of EBO.[37] The key to EBO is that your opponent has to depend upon sophisticated systems such as an electrical grid, a water system, petroleum distribution, or the like. EBO doesn't work very well against jungle or desert tribesman. It can work well to destroy a state, but it's not clear that it works well on the resistance after a state is destroyed. However, it does work well against a larger and more powerful enemy, because such an enemy is likely to depend upon many sophisticated systems.

Leveraging Opinion Is More Effective Than Leveraging Violence

A major disadvantage of traditional terrorist tactics such as car bombing or suicide bombing is exactly that they kill people, which can easily turn public opinion against the terrorists, even public opinion on the part of their own people. If instead they can get similar publicity and leverage by attacks on systems without killing anyone, terrorists have every reason to adopt such new tactics. After all, as John Robb, veteran counterterrorism operative, Internet market analyst, entrepeneur, and executive, and author of the Global Guerrillas blog on which he posts very perceptive insights about open source warfare and the bazaar of violence, reminds us, "war is a conflict of minds."

The U.S. EBO doctrine emphasizes minimal collateral damage so as to avoid adverse public opinion. The opposition may be catching onto that point. The public may become numb to dead and wounded in a war zone, and most of the combatants in Iraq may think of themselves as military or as acting in self-defense. But those who use tactics such as beheadings bring on themselves the name of terrorist. And any who choose to strike beyond the seas will also be labeled as terrorists if they kill when they strike.

That may be what they want if their goal is still to provoke a worldwide war of civilizations. However, some years after 9/11, traditional terrorist tactics don't really seem to be bringing that goal much closer. In fact, traditional terrorist tactics almost never attain their perpetrators' political goals. As the director of the Center for the Study of Terrorism and Political Violence at St. Andrews University in Scotland, Paul Wilkinson, has said:

> *Even taking into account the influence of terrorism as an auxiliary tactic in revolutionary and independence struggles and in the rise of fascism between the First and Second World Wars, the overall track record of terrorism in attaining major political objectives is abysmal.*[38]

Terrorists may be unaware that even major historical figures who used terrorism advised against depending on it:

> *Most of the key modern theorists and leaders of revolutionary insurgency, such as Mao Tse Tung and Che Guevara, have recognised the dangers of depending on terrorism and have come down against giving it a major role in the struggle for revolution. The few cases where terrorism played a major part in bringing about sweeping political change arose in a limited number of colonial independence struggles against foreign rule.*[39]

Terrorists may continue to ignore history or to pretend that the problems of their region are solely colonial or postcolonial. Or they may decide to face facts: traditional terrorism just doesn't work very well.

A clever terrorist may realize that nonlethal actions against systems may be the best way to mobilize global public opinion for their ends, or at least against the ends of their enemies. And there are few more wide-reaching means of global nonlethal action than the Internet.

Keeping Terrorists from Using the Internet

If the Internet has such potential for use by terrorists, what can be done about it? Part of the answer is to continue with the same things that are needed to defeat any terrorists, including tried-and-true principles such as these five:[40]

- Determination to defeat the terrorists within the rule of law and democratic process
- No deals and no concessions, no matter how bad it gets
- Apprehension, prosecution, and conviction before courts of law
- Penalization of state sponsors of terrorism as if they were harboring pirates
- Continued diplomatic efforts to resolve political conflicts

At least since Thomas Jefferson sent the Marines to the Shores of Tripoli, the apprehension and penalization principles have often involved military force. However, force alone won't stop terrorism; diplomatic efforts are also needed, as demonstrated in Northern Ireland, where the IRA finally disavowed violence in 2005, and Sri Lanka, where force didn't succeed in 500 years.

But what about the Internet in particular? Some people have called for cutting off the Internet at the borders of the continental United States upon terrorist attack. This makes no more sense than saying that we'll cut off the electricity and telephone systems in cities if they're attacked. The Internet is information, and economic applications of the Internet use information from the entire world.

Besides, one of the main purposes of EBO is to deny the enemy information so as to isolate him and make him less able to respond, less able to function normally, and less acceptable to the outside world. Such goals, once achieved, are very near winning. Who would want to grant an enemy such an advantage?

Perhaps the best course, then, is to isolate the terrorists. That's a laudable goal, and one that should be pursued. Unfortunately, it is easier said than done. There is more discussion on this in the next section about military networks.

What else can be done, then? Pursue all the already discussed measures of diversification and security, including a holistic and synoptic view of the Internet, plus promote a robust economy, including a cyber-insurance market. In the end, living well is not only the best revenge; it is the best defense.

Military Networks Aren't Immune

While the military services and their research agencies such as DARPA would like to build military networks that are self-healing and immune from outside attack, actually even military networks are not perfect, nor are military personnel immune from social engineering. Most military networking hardware and software is actually bought off the civilian market. Given that lives are directly at stake, one can hope that military security policies, procedures, and training are more robust than their civilian counterparts. Nonetheless, the vast majority of military personnel work in noncombat roles and even combat soldiers can be credulous when a civilian contractor shows up with the latest upgrade. An upgrade that could contain more software than the soldier expected.

Self-Healing Networks

A popular topic of industrial and government-sponsored research these days is autonomic computing, or self-healing computing systems and networks, which attempt to self-regulate and to heal themselves like living systems do. Autonomic systems could be very useful in military use, especially in the field, because they could recover from lost nodes or other damage.

But even self-healing networks can be compromised.

Well-placed Trojan horse software in military networks could wreak havoc during a battle, and spyware could relay important intelligence to the enemy. Self-healing networks are a wonderful idea but also one that will never be implemented perfectly. There will always be new combinations of exploits that the authors of the self-healing algorithms didn't think to detect, much less heal.

For example, what if the self-healing software itself is compromised? When will a military network's immune system be compromised, effectively giving the network AIDS?

Enemy action may be the cause, or it could be a commercial upgrade inadvertently interfering with some other part of the system.

And slowdowns could be as bad as outages. An outage during a battlefield situation, or even during a tricky deployment, could be fatal or at least very expensive. Sneakier and perhaps more effective because harder to detect could be a network or server slowdown. While getting through the cycle of observation, orientation, decision, and action (OODA) quickly in general always provides an advantage over one's opponent, it's even more important with tighter OODA loops. The tighter the OODA loop, the more infrastructure performance matters.

Performance is also security. This is a point that is frequently overlooked. One of the most basic performance features of the TCP/IP protocols, the Van Jacobson slow start algorithm that causes TCP to notice packet loss and to transmit more slowly, was added in 1988, 5 years after widespread deployment of TCP/IP in 1983. The slow start algorithm helps keep TCP from overloading a congested network and helps keep a slow network from appearing to the user to be unresponsive. Back then, it may not have been practical to expect performance algorithms to be part of the basic design, because experience and performance experiments were necessary to demonstrate the need.

Further performance modifications to TCP/IP were proposed but were resisted. Explicit congestion notification and rate based flow control were available but were never adopted. Part of the resistance was apparently due to the end-to-end principle, which states that intelligence should be at the edges of the network, not in the middle. However, only recently have end user corporations started to take quality of service seriously. One recent development is the popularity of the Application Performance Index (APDEX) and related consortium organized by NetForecast.[41]

Experiments will still be necessary for self-healing military networks, but the basic need for performance algorithms and monitoring should by now be obvious.

How Can the Military Protect Itself?

What can government and the military do to protect against such problems?

Watch the Watchers

Adding external performance and security monitoring to military networks, even to supposedly self-healing networks, would be an important step. Even a self-healing network that has multiple built-in detection and healing mechanisms may benefit from external detection systems, if only because external systems may have developed in a different environment and may have encountered threats that the built-ins were not designed to handle. Where can the military get such external detection systems?

Encourage the Economy

The best place to get external detection systems is from a commercial market in such systems. Some kinds of detection systems may not yet exist. But the military has many means of encouraging a robust civilian market, the most obvious being procurement. Some people at the old Defense Communications Agency (DCA, now DISA) were justifiably proud of the role they played in promoting the early Internet by buying early commercial networked workstations and routers. DARPA has long been a source of funding for new development that the military wants. With technology transfer, DARPA grants can lead to commercial products.

Unfortunately, the U.S. Department of Defense (DoD) has in recent years de-emphasized research unless it is likely to lead to practical military applications within a few years. In addition, DARPA has placed increasing restrictions on the researchers it does fund, limiting exploration, often requiring researchers to be U.S. citizens, and controlling dissemination of results. The U.S. citizen restriction is particularly onerous, since most U.S. university departments these days, especially those working in computer science or information technology, have many foreign graduate students.

Many academic researchers now avoid DARPA and apply for grants from other agencies, especially the National Science Foundation (NSF). In NSF's Directorate for Computer and Information Science and Engineering, research proposals more than tripled from 1999 to 2004. However, NSF has not received additional funding to compensate for this shift, and the result is the percentage of grants accepted by NSF has fallen and the total amount of research funded by NSF has not increased.

DARPA is a military research agency, so its current emphasis on practical military applications is understandable. However, if DARPA is not to fund basic research, what agency will do so? Government could increase research funding for DARPA, NSF, or some other agency or agencies to regain the former lead of the United States in research. After all, DARPA was originally established (as ARPA) shortly after the Soviet Union launched Sputnik, the first orbital satellite, with a purpose of making sure the United States did not fall behind again in applied science. Put another way, if the United States won't fund research, perhaps some other country will, maybe China, maybe India.

Encouraging a network business continuity insurance market would help, because insurers would then require more robust security in their customers, and insurance customers would require better security from their hardware and software vendors. For more about this, see the Chapter 11.

The Modern Military Eats from the Internet

Government can further encourage civilian security through all the means already discussed, including education, hearings, R&D grants and contracts, partnering, agency policies and procedures, agency purchasing, regulations, and even laws, especially liability laws. In other words, many of the best ways government can improve military risk management are precisely the same ways government can improve civilian risk management, because the military draws so much from the civilian sector. In addition, better civilian risk management should produce a more robust economy, which means more resources available for everything, including the military.

Napoleon said, "An army marches on its stomach." The modern military eats from the Internet, whether it is connected to it or not. Napoleon held a contest to find a better way of preserving food and got canning in glass jars, which permitted him to feed his 600,000-man army going to Russia. The modern military could help promote better civilian risk management and, thus, produce the resources to better be able to take action when action is necessary.

Of course, better food preservation didn't keep Napoleon from disastrously misjudging the risks of invading Russia. He knew Russian winters were much more severe than those in France, that his supply lines and retreat paths would be very long, and that Russia had long experience of using such factors to defeat invaders. Yet he invaded anyway. After many months, the huge and costly battle of Borodino, famine, disease, Cossack raids, and an early and severe winter, only 10,000 men of Napoleon's invading army left Russia alive.

Napoleon also said, "In war, three-quarters turns on personal character and relations; the balance of manpower and materials counts only for the remaining quarter."

Better network monitoring won't prevent today's military from making similar strategic mistakes. Nonetheless, better network monitoring, forensics, and risk management in general will make good strategy easier to implement, and it will make the economy and thus the country and the world healthier in the process.

The Ancient Anasazi: An Archaeological Cautionary Tale

Smithsonian Magazine published an interesting story ("Riddles of the Anasazi," by David Roberts[42]) about the ancient Anasazi of the Four Corners region of the U.S. southwest, where present-day New Mexico, Colorado, Utah, and Arizona meet. For centuries, since perhaps 1500 B.C., the Anasazi built buildings and roads and practiced agriculture and pottery. Then around the year 1200 A.D. they started suffering depredations by parties as yet unidentified who attacked them, killed them, and ate them. The evidence of cannibalism was quite controversial when it was originally published, but so much more evidence of it has come to light that it has become hard to refute.[43]

Cliff Forts versus Coordinated Mesas

At first the Anasazi reacted by building fortified residences in increasingly hard-to-reach niches in cliffs. One of the last things they built on the cliffs was a wooden platform wedged into a rock face.

Eventually, at the end of the thirteenth century, the Anasazi abandoned their cliff faces and moved to mesa tops to the southeast—at least three mesas, each of which could see at least one of the others.

It was not difficulty of access that protected the settlements (none of the scrambles we performed here began to compare with the climbs we made in the Utah canyons), but an alliance based on visibility. If one village was under attack, it could send signals to its allies on the other mesas.[44]

The mesas did have perimeter defenses: they were 500 to 1000 feet tall, and they each had only one way in. But their individual perimeter defenses were not as extreme as back on the cliffs, and perimeters were only part of the new mesa defense system. Their descendants, the Hopis, still live on mesa tops.

In this case, ever more restricted fort perimeters did not work. What apparently did work was coordinated observations and cooperation.

In the Internet, adding more firewalls, intrusion detection, and spyware scanners won't solve the problem in the end, because you're just building higher walls around individual fortified organizations. The attackers and the *force majeure* events that affect those organizations are not limited to affecting a single organization. Aggregate damage cannot be defeated by individual action, no matter how heroic. Too much reliance on every organization for itself can even lead to additional havoc because of laws restricting access across artificial-to-the-Internet national boundaries, or chilling effects on commerce because of too much government intrusion inside a single country.

Aggregate damage demands collective action. Organizations such as APWG help organize collective action against phishing. The FBI's InfraGard helps organize more general collective security actions. SANS has long been doing the same specifically for the Internet. See Chapter 3 for more examples of such organizations. Some of them are government-sponsored, and this is an area where government can be very useful: sponsoring collective action against aggregate damage. Sometimes such action has to include passing laws or even using military force. Far more often such government action is better spent as encouragement via conferences and hearings and standards and research funding for the private sector to do the right thing.

Fear Is Not Security

James Seng points out Bruce Schneier's essay, "How Long Can the Country Stay Scared?", in which Bruce remarks:[45]

> *There are two basic ways to terrorize people. The first is to do something spectacularly horrible, like flying airplanes into skyscrapers and killing thousands of people. The second is to keep people living in fear.*

The ancient Anasazi tried to deal with a terrible enemy by retreating to fortified residences on increasingly hard to reach cliffs. Who was this enemy that attacked the Anasazi, killing them and eating them? Apparently, there was no large external invading force; it would have left traces that would have been found by now. The best theory as to who the attackers were appears to be the Anasazi themselves. The Anasazi society apparently fragmented and warred with itself, producing a state of fear that continued for decades. That society with a chronic state of fear and fortification failed. It eventually abandoned the cliff dwellings.

The survivors mutated into a society of mesa dwellers who protected themselves via superior observation and cooperation. Their mesa dwellings were fortified in the sense that each one was about a thousand feet above the surrounding territory and had only one way up, but that wasn't their main feature. The mesa dwellers apparently kept watchers on the mesa tops who could see real perils approaching and alert people on the same and neighboring mesas in time to do something specific, rather than keeping everyone in fear all the time.

Ongoing observations of neighbors and landscape sounds like a holistic and synoptic view of the nearby network and the surrounding territory. Living alert sounds better than living in fear, and in at least the case of the ancient Anasazi, fear and fortifications almost killed them, while living alert helped them survive.

Alert to All Risks

Living alert is better than living in fear. There are limits to how much governments can do and sometimes they have already done too much. GOSIP and OSI in general were good historical examples of government going too far, and I think parts of the PATRIOT Act and of SOX are examples of having gone too far.

Regarding terrorists, it is worth remembering, as the *Economist* reminds us,[46] that at the turn of the nineteenth to the twentieth century many governments overreacted to anarchists in many of the same ways they are currently overreacting to terrorists (torture, repressive laws for their own people, restrictions on foreigners, and the like). In between you can find many other examples, ranging from the Barbary Pirates of the early nineteenth century to the Red Brigade of the middle twentieth century. For that matter, one of the main reasons for the U.S. Bill of Rights was historical memory of the English Civil War and living memory of arbitrary arrests, dispersals, and the like by the colonizers during the then recent War of Independence. The U.N. Declaration of the Rights of Man has similar roots in the atrocities of the Second World War. Benjamin Franklin was right: "They that can give up essential liberty to obtain a little temporary safety deserve neither liberty nor safety."[47]

Opponents of the state come and go. If the state reacts with repression whenever they come, the result is a continual ratcheting down of liberty.

Sarbanes-Oxley is an overreaction for a different reason. It attempts to treat symptoms rather than causes. Encouraging ethical corporate culture is much harder than attempting to legislate accounting details but also more necessary. Perhaps the London Stock Exchange has a useful approach in requiring a risk management plan for a company to be listed. The banking industry's Basel II has a great deal of detail, but does attempt to deal with corporate culture, and with a minimum of governmental intervention.

Nonetheless, as Hurricane Katrina has reminded us, there are some things that governments are uniquely required to handle, such as large-scale flood control and emergency evacuations and relief. The Great Mississippi River Flood of 1927 affected nine states and displaced 700,000 people, very few of whom received public assistance. Public reaction to that disaster and the failure of state and local governments to prevent or address it caused the passage of the 1928 Flood Control Act that gave the U.S. federal government responsibility for the system of levees and barriers that keeps the Mississippi River from changing course or flooding towns and countryside along its current course. This responsibility seems to have been lax in the years before the Great New Orleans Flood of 2005, and even more lax during and after it. The consequences of government failing in its most basic responsibility of protecting its own people are disastrous.

Not all government agencies failed, of course. The National Weather Service distributed the most apocalyptic weather warning I've ever seen; the mayor of New Orleans did order an evacuation (even if he couldn't get a fleet of schoolbuses in action to help evacuate), the Coast Guard went into action at once, and there were other good examples, plus numerous cases of private and individual action. But in its most basic responsibilities of prevention and amelioration, government in general, and especially the federal government, which was responsible for the levees that failed and flooded the city of New Orleans and for large-scale relief efforts that came too late to save many who drowned there and elsewhere on the Gulf Coast, failed.

Even in that horrible case, private resources could have been drawn on more, if there had been coordination to do so. Several airlines did help evacuate people, when asked by various private parties. Numerous individuals and companies offered boats and food and water. Communications were also sorely lacking. I would have thought somebody would have been ready with boats and loudspeakers, at least, but nobody was.

There are many opportunities for private entrepeneurship in better communications and coordination, for everything from ensuring adequate emergency food and water storage in large public buildings to communications during an emergency. Many of these opportunities should produce products and services that will be equally useful in developing countries, and some of them will be applicable to developed countries. Imagine if you could network a rural area by dropping solar-powered Internet relay stations off the back of a pickup truck (or a helicopter) every quarter mile or so. Suppose that they were cheap enough that you could afford for half of them to fail, robust enough that most of them would work even if dropped in water, and flexible enough to find their neighbors automatically.

Government can help get such applications developed and deployed by sponsoring research. In addition to the obvious public good, government will no doubt be interested in such things for battlefield applications. The coordination techniques that would permit such cheap drop-off network nodes to automatically configure could also be applied in urban neighborhoods to produce robust mesh networking.

I heard a television news anchor assert that we have no CIA looking into hurricanes like we do for terrorists. Actually, we probably have much better intelligence on weather than we have for terrorists. Many observation methods are operational, after many years of gradual addition of more techniques, as described in Chapter 3. Weather prediction may not be as good as we would like, but even 24-hour notice of a hurricane's landfall is much better than none.

Do we have the same kind of data fusion of multiple sources of information for Internet perils? Bits and pieces of it exist, but major pieces are still missing. Government can help in the same ways it did for the ARPANET and NSFNET: by sponsoring research, operational prototypes, public portals, and technology transfer. Encouraging Internet and cyber-insurance will also help.

Nevertheless, governments will pass some laws mandating specific technical solutions because of pressure from constituents to do something, we all would be better off if government would rather encourage research, implementation, standardization, deployment, and commercialization of new techniques.

Similarly, government intervention in details of corporate operations through laws such as SOX has its limits. Encouraging ethical and flexible corporate operations is harder than dashing off a compliance law in haste but better in the long run.

Notes

1. *National Strategy to Secure Cyberspace,* U.S. Department of Homeland Security (February 2003). www.whitehouse.gov/pcipb

2. John S. Quarterman, "Monoculture Considered Harmful," *First Monday* (February 2002).

3. Op. cit. *National Strategy to Secure Cyberspace.*

4. Ibid.

5. Gregg Keizer, "Spam: Born in the USA," *TechWeb News, InformationWeek* (August 12, 2004). www.informationweek.com/story/showArticle.jhtml?articleID=28700163

6. "Judgement Against Spammer for Immediate Release," *Press Release,* Tracy LaQuey Parker, Patrick Parker, Zilker Internet Park, TISPA, EFF-Austin, (Austin, Texas, November 11, 1997). www.tigerden.com/junkmail/cases/flowerspressrelease.html

7. 108th U.S. Congress, *CAN-SPAM Act of 2003* (Washington, DC, 2003). www.spamlaws.com/federal/can-spam.shtml

8. Linda Rosencrance, "Spammer Sentenced to Nine Years in Jail," *Computerworld* (November 5, 2004). www.pcworld.com/news/article/0,aid,118493,00.asp

9. A senior policy official within the administration. "Spyware," Personal communications (May 2005).

10. Hal R. Varian, "Managing Online Security Risks," *New York Times* (June 1, 2000).

11. Jeffrey H. Birnbaum, "The Road to Riches Is Called K Street: Lobbying Firms Hire More, Pay More, Charge More to Influence Government," *Washington Post,* p. A01 (June 22, 2005).

12. Introduced by Senator Murray, *Bill Number: SB 96 Amended Bill Text: Peer-to-peer networks: file sharing* (Sacramento, California, Amended in Senate March 1, 2005). www.leginfo.ca.gov/pub/bill/sen/sb_0051-0100/sb_96_bill_20050301_amended_sen.html

13. Ralph Nader, *Unsafe at Any Speed* (Knightsbridge Pub. Co., 1965).

14. "Unsafe at Any Speed," *Wikipedia* (May 9, 2005). http://en.wikipedia.org/wiki/Unsafe_at_Any_Speed

15. James Surowiecki, "Crisis Management," *New Yorker* (June 13, 2005).

16. Rosencrance, "Spammer Sentenced to Nine Years in Jail."

17. "Sarbanes-Oxley: A price worth paying?," *Economist* (Economist Newspaper Limited, London, May 21, 2005), pp. 71–73. www.economist.com/printedition/displaystory.cfm?story_id=3984019

18. "American capitalism: Damaged goods," *Economist* (Economist Newspaper Limited, London, May 21, 2005), p. 11. www.economist.com/printedition/displaystory.cfm?Story_ID=3984578

19. Op. cit. Editor, "Editorial: Accounting Lunacy, Indeed," *Chief Executive* (Montvale, New Jersey, June 2005), p. 72.

20. Ibid.

21. Op. cit. "American capitalism: Damaged goods."

22. Rosencrance, "Spammer Sentenced to Nine Years in Jail."

23. Steve Forbes, "Asinine Way to Treat Ultimate Asset: People," *Forbes Magazine* (July 4, 2005). www.forbes.com/columnists/business/forbes/2005/0704/031.html?_requestid=23764

24. Rebecca Fannin, "Unlocking Innovation," *Chief Executive* (Montvale, New Jersey, June 2005), pp. 38–42.

25. Ibid.

26. Peter Galuszka, "Where is Our Economic Policy?," *Chief Executive* (Montvale, New Jersey, June 2005): pp. 30–37.

27. "American capitalism: Damaged goods."

28. Ibid.

29. Op. cit. Galuszka, "Where Is Our Economic Policy?"

30. George W. Bush, *Policy for a Common Identification Standard for Federal Employees and Contractors* (White House, Washington, DC, August 27, 2004). www.whitehouse.gov/news/releases/2004/08/20040827-8.html

31. V. Cerf and K. Mills, "Explaining the Role of GOSIP," *Request for Comments*, RFC 1169, Network Working Group (August 1990). http://asg.web.cmu.edu/rfc/rfc1169.html

32. *Profiles for Open Systems Internetworking Technologies (POSIT)*, National Institute for Standards and Technology (May 15, 1995). www.itl.nist.gov/fipspubs/fip146-2.htm

33. Paul Wilkinson, "Terrorism: Motivations and Causes," *Commentary*, No. 53 (Canadian Security Intelligence Service (January 1995). www.csis-scrs.gc.ca/eng/comment/com53_e.html

34. BBC, "Police say IRA behind bank raid," *BBC News* (London, January 7, 2005). http://news.bbc.co.uk/1/hi/northern_ireland/4154657.stm

35. Paul Wilkinson, "Terrorism: Implications for World Peace," *Preparing for Peace* (Westmoreland General Meeting, November 2003). www.preparingforpeace.org/wilkinson.htm

36. Brigadier General David A. Deptula, "Effects Based Operations: Changing the Nature of Warfare," *Defense and Airpower Series* (Aerospace Education Foundation, Arlington, Virginia 2001).

37. John Robb, "Massively Parallel Operations," *Global Guerillas*, 21 June 2005. http://globalguerrillas.typepad.com/globalguerrillas/2005/06/massively_paral.html

38. Op. cit. Wilkinson, "Terrorism: Implications for World Peace."

39. Ibid.

40. Op. cit. Wilkinson, "Terrorism: Motivations and Causes."

41. Peter Sevcik, *Application Performance Index (APDEX)* (apedex.org, 2004). www.apdex.org

42. David Roberts, "Riddles of the Anasazi, *Smithsonian Magazine* (Smithsonian Institution, July 2003). www.smithsonianmag.com/smithsonian/issues03/jul03/anasazi.html

43. Richard A. Marlar, Banks L. Leonard, Brian R. Billman, Patricia M. Lambert, and Jennifer E. Marlar, "Biochemical evidence of cannibalism at a prehistoric Puebloan site in southwestern Colorado," *Nature*, 407 (September 7, 2000), pp. 74–78. `www.nature.com/cgi-taf/ Dynapage.taf?file=/nature/journal/v407/n6800/abs/4070 74a0_fs.html`

44. Ibid.

45. Bruce Schneier, "How Long Can the Country Stay Scared?," *Minneapolis Star-Tribune* (August 27, 2004). `www.schneier.com/essay-055 .html`

46. "For jihadist, read anarchist," *Economist* (London, August 18, 2005). `www.economist.com/displaystory.cfm?story_id=4292760`

47. Benjamin Franklin in *Historical Review of Pennsylvania* (1759).

CHAPTER 11

Insurers and Reinsurers

The impact of Moore's Law on the financial world is inestimable—computing . . . has enabled risk packaging to grow ever more precise, ever more real-time, ever more differentiated, ever more manageable.[1]

—Dr. Dan Geer

A single Internet event may affect multiple enterprises simultaneously; this is what insurance companies call *aggregation*. And even if one enterprise has patches, firewalls, and intrusion detection and is not infected by the latest worm, if its neighbors on the Internet are infected, excess traffic from them may cause congestion that may affect the patched enterprise's connectivity anyway. Enterprises cannot fix all such problems.

SOX, GLBA, HIPAA, PIPEDA, DPD, and other laws require ever-higher standards of diligence that at some point become so costly that an enterprise finds it more cost-effective to buy insurance rather than to spend still more on diligence.

Enterprises need to shift some of the risks of using the Internet and even some of the risks of noncompliance with regulations onto other entities using financial risk transfer instruments, starting with insurance policies. Insurance, catastrophe bonds, performance bonds, and capital withholding are tried and true in other industries and can be imported to the Internet.

Because many of these new (to the Internet) risk management strategies involve insurance, insurers and reinsurers will be involved with many of them. Some strategies, such as bonds, may nonetheless be issued by other parties.

To minimize gaps and maximize protection, evaluate all types of risks, including content, for an enterprise and structure a comprehensive insurance program, involving both traditional and emerging coverage products. Some such risks can be transferred to others by means of contracts. Other risks need to be covered by insurance. Some insurance coverage can be added to existing policies. Other coverage needs new policies, and even new instruments. And some risks an enterprise will want to or need to retain; for those a risk management plan is needed.

Policies: How to Make It Easy

Internet business continuity insurance needs to become as easy as fire insurance.

Assessments: Sprinkler Systems

A fire insurer first does an assessment to determine whether the enterprise has a sprinkler system and posted evacuation routes. An enterprise that wants Internet business continuity insurance will be assessed for firewalls and patches, for password and other policies, and for nonredundant routing and performance beyond the firewall. This will be like checking a map of fireplugs.

Adjustments: Internet Forensics

Claims adjustment should include rechecking many of the same things as for the original assessment, plus forensics to determine what was going on in the Internet at the time of the claimed incident.

The Risks: First and Third Party

Insurable cyberloss is composed of two broad categories: first-party digital or electronic asset damage and third-party liability.

First-Party Loss: Your Company Is Harmed

First-party loss includes damage, loss, or corruption of data and software arising out of nontangible events such as virus, cracking, power surges, or programming error. Insurance is provided to cover third-party costs to research, reconstruct, or recreate the lost or damaged data. Insurance coverage is also available for any loss of income arising from the preceding damage. This is not just for loss of income generated directly by online sales but also includes subsequent offline business loss such as the loss of billable hours at a law firm. Another loss is additional operating expense, such as additional cost of temporary manual work-arounds, setting up hot sites, and other expenses associated with maintaining routine operations.

Third-Party Loss: Someone Else Is Harmed

Third-party liability loss includes injury arising out of *content* or information publicly visible through the web, or secured deep in a corporate database, or distributed through e-mail. Typical infringement claims arising out of web site content include libel, defamation, and trademark or copyright infringement. An even greater source of cyberliability is unauthorized access of confidential information, whether client data, trade secrets, personal health records, or financial information such as credit card information. Every Internet-using company has potential for liabilities arising out of intentional or unintentional network harm to a third party due to worm or virus transmission, or malicious use such as (even inadvertently) hosting a denial-of-service (DoS) attack. Recently passed state and federal statutes such as HIPAA, SOX, and GLBA contain requirements that are heightening the awareness of potential plaintiffs and in some cases creating a standard duty of care against which a civil suit could be based.

Brief History: Claims Drive New Insurance

Standard insurance policy language was developed long before the Information Technology (IT) revolution. In the late 1990s increasing reliance by companies on their information infrastructure produced a wave of new claim activity arising from unanticipated sources. Manufacturers and retailers were being sued for torts that were originally associated with advertisers, such as trademark, copyright, and libel, arising out of things like deep linking, framing, and metatags. Companies began to file claims against property policies for first-party data loss and software damage. Underwriters either paid the claims because the policy language was indefensible or litigated the intent.

What Is Physical Damage?

Is loss of use of property physical damage? If it is, various existing insurance policies may apply. If it isn't, new coverage is needed.

Ingram Micro: Maybe It Is

In 2000, in *American Guaranty v. Ingram Micro*,[2] Ingram Micro successfully argued that physical damage covered by a property policy included harm to circuitry and subsequent loss of use of that property. However, that decision was not as broad as it might seem.

Ingram Micro does not precisely answer the question whether damage to computer data is "physical loss or damage." Instead, Ingram Micro appears to stand for the proposition that when the computer data stored in a computer is altered, the computer itself has suffered "physical loss or damage."[3]

And that decision was not final.

Also, the federal district court's decision in Ingram Micro may not be the last word on this subject. The case settled after the Ninth Circuit Court of Appeals refused to hear an early appeal before trial. The federal district court's decision may be highly persuasive, but it is not binding on other courts. So, at least technically speaking, the matter is open to further debate if an insurer wants to test the issue in a different court against a different policyholder.[4]

There has been at least one more significant case since Ingram Micro.

AOL v. St. Paul: Maybe It Isn't

In 2002, *AOL v. St. Paul Mercury Insurance*,[5] St. Paul successfully argued that the programming damage AOL caused to computer owners using AOL 5.0 was not tangible property damage and therefore not eligible for coverage under a general liability program. That decision was upheld on appeal in 2003.[6]

Moral: Don't Depend on Property and Liability Insurance

The issue of whether or not data damage is tangible physical damage or not has been at the core of coverage disputes regarding data and software damage.

Since about 2000 the courts and the insurance community have started to accept that standard property and liability insurance programs are *not* designed to respond to typical cyberclaims. The addition of specific cyberexclusions on standard package programs and the offering of express coverage through endorsements or standalone policies have strengthened the insurers' arguments against coverage in core insurance programs.

Early Cyber-Insurance Programs

Around 2000 about half a dozen insurers aggressively marketed distinct cyber-insurance programs, expecting quick development of a new marketplace similarly to those for employment practices in the early 1990s and pollution liability in the 1980s. Standalone employment practice and pollution policies became very popular when express exclusions were added to standard general liability programs.

Meanwhile, the economic downturn caused buyers to try to cut their insurance costs, even dropping core insurance programs.

The main reason for the cyber-liability market falling short of the original predic-
tions is simple—it has fallen foul of the hard market that has been experienced
since 2001. Spiraling insurance premiums during the past three years have made
it difficult for the majority of UK businesses to source appropriate cover at a price
they can afford. It is not surprising that most have been reluctant to move new
insurance coverages, such as cyber-cover, up the agenda. Faced with dramatic
hikes in premiums, there is usually little or no budget available for anything other
than core insurance coverage.[7]

Awareness and Observation

Also, unlike pollution and employment practices liability, cyber risk seems
more ephemeral, and its probability and costs are not well understood. When
a building burns or people die from pollution or government officials are sued
for harassment, the public is well aware, and the cases are sensational
(although it is worth remembering that there were times not so long ago when
fire insurance and environmental insurance were unknown, and it was not so
obvious that they were needed).

When a company has its security breached and suffers financial loss, the last
thing it wants to do is to augment the harm with a lot of publicity. Better to keep
quiet than alert the competition and open the company to further litigation—or
so many companies seem to believe (see also the material on vulnerability disclosure in Chapter 7). It remains to be seen how SOX and other statutory disclosure requirements will affect both the awareness of first-party loss and
litigation trends. And some recent security threats such as phishing are very
visible to the target's customers. Trying to act as if the problem does not exist
can backfire: Customers want to know their bank, vendor, or other enterprise is
proactively doing something about the problem, not trying to hide it.

A general lack of understanding by both the buyer and the seller has also
hampered market growth. Many companies still expect firewalls and other
traditional security measures to solve all security problems. Corporate IT managers generally do not have a background encompassing economics or
finance. As Ty Sagalow of AIG has said:

There are technologists who don't understand the notion of risk management.
Their view is that you list all the things that can go wrong and you eliminate
them one by one and then, when you run out of money, you give up.[8]

This problem works the other way around, as well. Corporate risk managers
and insurance brokers generally do not have the technical understanding to
access the value of risk transfer. They may understand financial risk transfer
instruments, but they don't know how to apply them to Internet technology.

All these types of people need to be shown, preferably literally shown using graphical visualizations, that aggregate damage requires collective action: what the risks are, how they aggregate outside any single enterprise's firewalls, their probabilities, and how new insurance policies and other risk transfer instruments will help.

Quantification and Aggregation

One reason insurers have not been quick to offer appropriate and appropriately priced coverage is that they do not have the data they need to build actuarial tables and probabilistic models. In addition to denial-of-service, perils in the Internet can cause degradation of service, which also can have severe economic consequences. If a backhoe cuts a cable that carries Internet traffic, some nodes may become unreachable, and there may be congestion that affects many other nodes. A delay of 8 seconds is enough to make the typical web user stop trying, causing delayed transactions. A customer who encounters such delays often may not come back another day. Some IT personnel may still believe that technology for encryption, detection, authentication, and authorization is enough to establish trust and, therefore, to provide adequate security. Yet when denial-of-service shades into degradation of service, security merges into performance.

Insurers don't know how probable various events are, nor their probable effects or duration, nor who or what they are most likely to affect. For any kind of risk management solution, there needs to be a database of historical events on which to base the actuarial calculations, plus ongoing data collection, event detection and characterization, value assignment, and risk assignment, to keep the solution up to date as Internet risks change. Quantification of the risk has proven difficult, especially on the first-party side. This is partly because insurers, enterprises, and even ISPs tend to believe that such quantification is not possible.

In fact, while difficult, quantification is possible, but it takes a broader view than just looking at the periphery of one's own company. Insurers are used to a broader view, encompassing entire industries, but the degree of potential aggregation facilitated by the Internet is unprecedented. Traditional theft and fraud tend to be limited to a single company at a time. Even financial problems tend to be limited to single industries. Most *force majeure* events such as power outages and natural disasters such as hurricanes, tornados, earthquakes, and wildfires tend to be geographically limited. Internet risk is not so limited; cyberhurricanes such as a worst-case worm can affect many companies in multiple industries all over the world at the same time.[9] That could be an insurance company's worst nightmare: all the policyholders of a class of insurance making claims simultaneously. (Of course, that's why reinsurance and catastrophe bonds are also needed.) Insurers do not know how to measure such risks.

Meanwhile, AIG has deliberately gone ahead without quantification, as Ty Sagalow explained:

AIG has been taking on these types of risk for 75 years. We were one of the first companies to offer directors and officers insurance in the case of shareholder suits, and employment practices liability insurance in cases of class-action discrimination suits, and we were among the first to create environmental liability insurance. For these types of insurance in the beginning, there wasn't enough actuarial data, but we just began. You gather the information as quickly as you can and you adjust terms, conditions, and rates. These programs are now mature, multi-billion dollar premium industries. They didn't start out that way, but this is where cyber-insurance is today.[10]

Insurance will be the capstone in the new security architecture, but meanwhile quantification for holistic and synoptic detection, reaction, and reputation systems can begin that will provide collective leverage against aggregate attackers and *force majeure* events while waiting for the insurance companies to get up to speed.

Policy Language: Still in Process

Policy language, especially on the first-party side, is new and requires much more time and effort for both the insurance broker and buyer to complete a thorough analysis and understand the coverage options. Few companies have yet successfully integrated IT into the corporate insurance decision process.

The express cybercoverage market is reviving, specifically in the areas of healthcare and banking, due in large part to the sensitivity of the information and the increasing reliance on information technology. SOX and HIPAA already make some enterprises wonder if insurance might be less expensive than ever-higher standards of diligence. With the economy turning up, enterprises can now afford such insurance, and insurance companies can sell it if they try. Many executives today do agree that intangible information assets are more important than their physical assets, so we will see.

Shortcomings of Traditional Products

Traditional property policies are designed to protect tangible property against tangible property perils such as fire, flood, and earthquake. Typical property policies also require a tangible property loss before they will pay any business interruption or extra expense loss. To ensure that intangible data claims are not paid, many insurers have also added explicit exclusions pertaining to intangible assets such as data information stored in electronic format. Traditional crime policies, also built around insurance for tangible property, often exclude the theft of information such as trade secrets.

General liability programs are typically drafted to respond only to tangible property damage. Many general liability programs also have a narrow scope of coverage for *advertising and personal injury*, but it is now common to see language designed to specifically exclude cyber-related activities such as chat rooms and banner ads.

Errors and Omissions (E&O) or professional liability programs may provide coverage for some third-party cyber liabilities, but are unlikely to protect against all of the liabilities previously discussed. Common exclusions include claims arising out of security breaches, the release of confidential information, and acts by rogue employees. E&O coverage is also generally limited to claims arising out of the delivery of a specific service, excluding claims arising out of a network unrelated to the delivery of a product or a service such as the spread of a virus to an affiliate or supplier.

Directors and Officers (D&O) insurance may provide some protection against third-party cyberliabilities, but as you will see later in this chapter, some other types are probably not covered.

Collective Action through Financial Instruments

Cyber- and especially Internet use entails risks that no single enterprise can fix directly. Such aggregate risks need collective action. Insurance has been a traditional form of collective action for such risks ever since Names first gathered at Lloyd's coffeehouse in seventeenth century London to examine port logs and weather records to determine prices for underwriting ocean voyages. Insurance and more recent financial risk transfer instruments can be adapted to the Internet, and such adaptation will involve designing further financial risk transfer instruments for the Internet.

Financial Liability Can Help Drive Insurance

If the New York Stock Exchange and NASDAQ followed the example of the London Stock Exchange[11] and required listed companies to describe their risk management plans, more companies would probably form such plans. And as part of those plans, U.S. companies would have more incentive to buy insurance and bonds.

Potential financial liability in the form of perhaps not being listed on a stock exchange is one form of what Dr. Hal Varian of Berkeley meant when he wrote in the *New York Times* in June 2000 the following: ". . . one of the fundamental principles of the economic analysis of liability: it should be assigned to the party that can do the best job of managing risk."[12]

The chairman of Lloyd's, Lord Levene, in April 2004 recommended that enterprises themselves can do a better job of managing risk by doing what they do best: give it higher priority.

The first relates to business interruption. It's estimated that 90% of medium to large companies which can't resume near-normal operations within 5 days of an emergency are out of business within a year [17]. And in today's so-called global village, the impact of an emergency in one place can be felt, like a tidal wave, across the world.

Chairman Levene continued:

The hi-tech age is also bringing the problem into sharp focus. So called "cyber risks" are emerging which did not exist even a few years ago.... And in a frightening combination of cyber and terrorism risks, over half of companies anticipate a major cyber attack by a terrorist organisation within the next twelve months [27]. Demand for cyber insurance was accordingly up 75% in 2003 [28], and the market is forecast to reach $2 to $3 billion over the next few years [29].[13]

He recommended board level priority for risk awareness, "including, but not limited to, business interruption costs, corporate fraud, and increased liability claims."

Legal Liability Can Help Drive Insurance

Software vendors that produce poorly designed and buggy software that is readily exploitable for use in spreading worms, viruses, Trojans, spam, and other problems throughout the Internet should perhaps bear more liability than others. Enterprises that use software that is known to be particularly susceptible to compromise might also bear some liability, especially if they fail to apply known patches. See Chapter 10.

Insurance Can Help Drive Security

Financial or legal liability would incent enterprises to buy insurance and bonds. And then, as Hal Varian has pointed out, another force comes into play:

. . . the incentives of the insurers: they only want to insure clients who use good security practices, giving them every incentive to instruct their clients in how to improve their Internet security. Just as an insurer of an office building will give you a reduced rate if you have sprinklers every 12 feet, an insurer against computer crime will give you a reduced rate if you install security patches within two weeks of their posting, provide continuing education for security staff and engage in other good risk management practices.[14]

So, insurance will improve the security of the Internet, and legal liability can help produce a market for Internet insurance.

Bonds for Financial Depth and Stability

Because the Internet is worldwide and increasingly it seems every business uses it, the potential for aggregation is high. Reputable researchers reported in May 2004 that a single worst-case worm could cause $50 billion in economic damages in the U.S. alone.[15] That is more than Hurricane Andrew, which was the most economically destructive hurricane ever recorded, plus all the hurricanes of 2004.

Catastrophe Bonds: Financial Capacity

Insurers thus may need extra financial capacity to cover such risks. Catastrophe bonds (see Figure 11-1) can provide a risk management backbone for industry by creating an investment instrument of wide distribution and known risks. Such bonds can be developed further for other deployment scenarios to hedge and monetize Internet risks.

Catastrophe bonds are commonly used by reinsurers to cover earthquakes, hurricanes, floods, and other large natural disasters. They are like other bonds, except their coupons pay at a higher rate, and when the catastrophe happens, the principal goes away to cover the damage. Yet the likelihood of the principal of a cat bond (as they are called) vanishing is not correlated with similar risks for stocks or other bonds or investments, so hedge funds, reinsurers, pension funds, and so on, invest in them for diversification.

Performance Bonds: Beyond Outages

Performance bonds are used by electric utilities to cover brownouts. Internet Service Providers (ISP) can use performance bonds to cover Service Level Agreement (SLA) violations. This will introduce ISP certification, ISP competition on a factor other than price, and reduced ISP expenses. For more information see the Chapter 9.

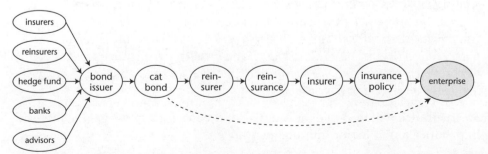

Figure 11-1: Catastrophe bonds

Capital Withholding: Banks as Self-Insurers

Banks commonly keep a certain amount of capital in reserve to deal with risks (see Chapter 5). Such capital withholding is a form of self-insurance and can be used for some Internet risks. Aggregated Internet anomalies may still require cat bonds for sufficient capital.

Options for Internet Business Risk

At some point in the not so distant future, we will probably see a market develop in put and call futures options for Internet business risk. The same scale-free structure of the Internet that makes loose connections produce value beyond traffic also produces risks with no limit on their size.

Such a market could use some comparison indexes. The Application Performance Index (APDEX) organized by NetForecast could perhaps be adapted to such a purpose. APDEX provides a single small integer number to rate application performance, boiling down various input variables. See Chapter 10.

Similar indexes are needed for Internet performance, including ISP performance taking into account interconnectivity beyond peering, and Internet connectivity, reach, and performance of enterprises by industry.

Insurance Strategies

Virtually every company uses the Internet for some type of business process and is, therefore, exposed to network risk. Network risk can and is often categorized by underwriters into the following three categories—Technology Risk, Media Risk, and eBusiness Risk. These categories are not only helpful for taking inventory of enterprise risk areas but are also useful when considering insurance as underwriters typically have designed insurance product around these risk groups.

Technology Risk by Technology Companies

Technology risk is that faced by companies that deliver a technology product or service. Companies within this group include computer programmers, application developers, network security administrators, and so forth. Essentially, these companies are providing some type of *technology* service to others for a fee. Typically, these companies will carry some type of errors and omissions insurance that is designed to protect against liability arising out of the failure of a product (prepacked software) or service. However, as the development and use of Application Software Provider (ASP)–driven services has come a blurring of technology and typical nontechnology services. Many consulting or information-related services are now providing applications over the Internet for client customization and use. For example, in the past companies may have provided salary and benefit review consulting through traditional face-to-face meetings and static written reports. Now, companies are offering online access to real-time data that can be customized to a client's specific needs. Direct and instant access to individualized custom reports provides valuable real-time *consulting* services. The application may be customized and directly integrated into a customer's intranet. Is the customer paying for a technology product or consulting services? Underwriters have traditionally organized themselves around *Miscellaneous Professional Services* and *Technology Services*. While a particular underwriter may be comfortable with the technology risk, they may not have the policy forms or inclination to underwrite the nontechnology- or traditional consulting-related risk.

If your firm provides any type of service to others it should consider errors and omissions insurance. However, close consideration should be given to the level of *technology* risk in the operation. If the company is a network consultant, it is clearly a technology risk and underwriters would typically provide coverage for many network-related perils. However, if the enterprise is providing some type of consulting service and simply relies heavily on technology to deliver the service, the standard *miscellaneous* errors and omissions coverage may not address network related liability risks.

Media Risk from Content Distribution

Prior to the widespread use of the Internet, if a company wanted to reach a broad audience for advertising, promotion, or publication, there was a controlled process that required a certain level of scrutiny and consideration. With the advent of the Internet, any individual is empowered with instant access to a universal audience. *Media risk* refers to all of the potential liabilities arising out of the distribution of content, including but not limited to the disclosure of confidential personal or corporate information, libel, and copyright and trademark infringement. In addition, content risk can include the liabilities resulting from persons acting on the posted information. For example, someone could suffer a loss if he or she acted on false or misleading financial information or physical loss if he or she takes dietary advice.

Historically, advertisers, publishers, and others in the media business protected themselves against the risks mentioned above with a specialized *publishers liability* policy. A standard General Liability program purchased by a brick-and-mortar company may carry limited protection for *advertising* liability but coverage will not apply to companies in the business of advertising. Some newer general liability policies will extend limited coverage to a web site used to promote a company's services but even these newer policies exclude liability arising out of chat rooms and the like. Standalone eBusiness policies have been designed to expressly cover network-distributed content such as AIG's netAdvantage and CAN's NetProtect product.

If the enterprise is in fact an online publisher or advertiser, close attention should be given to the protection afforded for network-related liabilities. For example, if the company is an online newspaper, would coverage exist if the network was hacked and published articles were altered?

EBusiness Risk by Users of Networks

Arguably, the most misunderstood and pervasive of network liability–related risk is general eBusiness risk. Typically, the term *eBusiness liability risk* is used to define any liability arising out of a corporate network. Included in this category of risk are the following:

- Transfer of virus.
- Malicious use of the corporate network to perpetrate some type of crime or other disruption such as a distributed denial-of-service (DDoS) attack.
- A security breach resulting in the release of confidential information such as clients', customers', or suppliers' trade secrets, the personal information of employees.
- Disruption of a customer's, supplier's, or partner's operation due to the failure of a networked process. For example, a customer is unable to access the inventory and ordering system that you have provided for them and subsequently suffers financial loss.

A technology provider may buy an E&O policy, but it will protect only against claims arising out of professional (often defined) services provided to others. So, a company providing network security services may have coverage for network liability arising out of its work; it may not have coverage for all of its eBusiness risk. For example, if a technology company were hacked and confidential employee information were released, their E&O policy may not respond. If an employee of a technology company transferred a virus via an e-mail to a friend at another company in personal correspondence, there may be no coverage. General liability coverage is primarily designed to protect against third-party claims arising out of bodily injury or tangible property damage. Since the type of liabilities arising out of eBusiness activities do not involve tangible bodily injury or property damage, traditional general liability coverage is unlikely to respond. General liability policies will typically include a narrow scope of coverage for *personal injury*, which is often defined to include *oral or written publication that violates a person's right to privacy*. However, in order to avoid paying eBusiness claims, some underwriters are excluding this coverage or redefining the coverage to exclude electronic distribution. In any event, underwriters are likely to use the definition of *oral or written publication* to argue that a hack or stolen information is not *publication*.

The insurance industry has created specific policies to address network liability risks. Network liability coverage is typically offered as a separate and distinct insurance policy. The coverage may also be included with errors and omissions in a *package* policy. Some underwriters will also offer *first-party* network damage bundled with network liability insurance. (First-party damage applies to financial loss suffered directly by the company following a network-related event.) Because the coverage is new and varies significantly from insurer to insurer, it is critical that the policy terms are closely reviewed. There are, for example, insurers offering network liability insurance, but the *covered network* is defined to include only that part of the network under the insured's direct control. Under this particular program, any hosted environment may be excluded from coverage.

First-Party Loss

Up to this point, the insurance discussion has centered on liability issues. However, network failure may also cause direct financial harm to the enterprise. First-party cyber-insurance is a form of property damage insurance. What makes first-party cyber-insurance unique is the fact that the loss is intangible. Traditional property insurance is designed to cover tangible property damage resulting from perils such as fire, flood, and earthquake. First-party cybercoverage is designed to cover electronic damage to information assets caused by specified perils such as a breach of network security or malicious code. Traditional insurance was not designed to cover the loss of, damage to, or destruction of intangible data and code. Over the years, creative plaintiff attorneys have argued for property damage coverage under traditional insurance policies, but the courts have increasingly ruled in favor of the underwriters, who argue this is not the intent. Underwriters have strengthened their position by expressly excluding electronic data or expressly including electronic data subject to a very low limit. In addition, underwriters point to the fact that specific programs have been designed for first-party cybercoverage.

When considering first-party cybercoverage, you should look closely at the terms of the policy. As with network liability coverage, there is no standard policy language and the quality of coverage varies significantly from carrier to carrier. Property insurance for tangible assets is typically written on an *all risk* approach, which means that the insurance applies to all risk except those excluded in the policy. (Common exclusions include war and nuclear perils.) The all risk approach commonly used for tangible property insurance is much broader than the *named peril* approach used by first-party cyber-insurance. The specific perils covered under first-party cyber-insurance often include unauthorized access, unauthorized use, and malicious code. All electronic perils are not covered. For example, if an in-house IT professional accidentally deletes every customer record, there is no coverage. On the other hand, if a maintenance employee were to accidentally cause a fire and burn a building, traditional property insurance would likely respond.

When assessing the value of a first-party cyberprogram, companies should look closely at the *named perils* or specific coverage triggers. Consider whether the unauthorized access coverage trigger includes or excludes the acts of employees. Also, look closely at how the claim will be adjusted. Damages are typically defined as the cost to reconstruct, replace, or reprogram lost, damaged, or destructed data but may include only the cost associated with third-party reconstruction and not necessarily the hours your company spends. If the information and network can only be reconstructed using your employees, coverage may be less meaningful.

First-party cyber-insurance will also typically include coverage for *business interruption*. Business interruption insurance is designed to pay for extra expense and profit that is lost following a covered event. Look closely at the definition of business interruption and how the damages are calculated following a loss. Business interruption claims are notorious to adjust under traditional brick-and-mortar insurance policies. It may be very difficult for many companies to put a value on lost profits following a cyberloss. However, some cyber-underwriters have simplified the insurance by agreeing in advance to some hourly loss amount.

Also, note whether or not the business interruption insurance includes *Contingent* business interruption. Contingent business interruption applies to a loss following a covered event that happens to a business you rely on. For example, if your ISP suffers an attack, your first-party cyberprogram will not cover it but may cover your resulting loss of income if the program includes *Contingent* business interruption.

Pricing: Internet Insurance As a Profitable Business

But is Internet insurance good business for insurers? Can insurers or bond issuers make money this way? Dollar values for prices cannot be set a priority now, but methods of setting prices can be outlined. Let's look first at the general case.[16]

Value of Outages to Insurance Customers

One basis of pricing is what an outage is worth to the insurance customer. There are at least two main ways to determine that: disaster accounting and letting the customer choose.

Disaster Accounting

After a hurricane or flood or earthquake, government agencies and private companies take account of what was lost in order to determine how much assistance is needed: This is called disaster accounting. This is done partly by examining the situation on the ground, for example, by counting flattened houses and comparing them to the tax rolls. It is done partly by comparing estimates of the severity of the current incident to previous disaster accounting of previous incidents. And it sometimes involves asking insurers the value of the claims they are receiving. Insurers should have some information on even Internet disasters from previous claims, if any, perhaps including claims on insurance that did not actually cover an Internet outage. So for Internet business continuity insurance, all these methods can be used. In addition, data about the Internet itself can be used to determine not only the probability and time distribution of an outage, but also its likely space distribution and likely effects on certain classes of businesses; I'll come back to such data later.

Let the Customer Choose

Another way to determine the value of an outage to the insurance customer is to let the insurance customer supply that information when buying a policy, by choosing insurance from several price levels, just as with life insurance. This method is straightforward and quite attractive. It does bring along with it some traditional insurance problems that have to be taken into account, such as adverse selection and moral hazard.

Skewed Populations

The availability of insurance can produce an insurance buying population that is different from the general population (*adverse selection*) and policyholders can be more likely to do the things they're insured against (*moral hazard*).

Adverse Selection

Customers who buy insurance can tend to be more likely to suffer harm than the general population. That is, a customer may buy insurance because the customer knows the insured event is likely to occur. In the case of Internet business continuity insurance, a business using a cut-rate Internet provider may figure that buying insurance is cheaper than switching to an ISP with better redundancy or capacity. The insurer will need to protect against such Internet moral hazard by assessing the policy buyer's security state before selling the insurance (and pegging the policy's price to that state).

Moral Hazard

Insurance may actually give the policy buyer incentive to bring on the misfortune insured against. This is why insurance usually has a deductible amount. In the case of Internet business continuity insurance, moral hazard could take the form of the policy buyer becoming lax about traditional security measures, for example, by not patching software or keeping intrusion prevention signatures up to date. The insured could also switch to a lower-cost Internet provider, not worrying about redundancy or capacity in the expectation that insurance would cover any losses thus incurred. The insurer will need to recheck the insured's security state when adjusting any claim. Insurance customers may even seek out insurers who do more checking at assessment and claims adjustment, because a savvy customer will know that such checking will help prevent moral hazard.

Perception and Price

It may seem obvious that better insurance costs more, but that isn't necessarily the case.

Quality of Service Can Determine Price

The cost of an outage to the insurance customer is not the only criterion for pricing. For example, in automobile insurance, the insurers are all selling more or less the same thing, and quality of service determines price. In some cases, price may even be determined by perception of quality of service due to marketing. An insurer or bond issuer that takes into account the historical and actual state of the Internet in assessments and adjustments should have an edge in quality of service, and the vendor that plays up that edge in marketing should be able to charge premium prices.

Price Can Determine Quality of Service

Conversely, sometimes price determines quality, that is, customers won't buy an inexpensive product because they think it can't be worth much. Thus, the simplest pricing criterion for Internet risk securities is: start high, then justify the price with real data. Customers and reinsurers are starting to demand such real data.

Underwriting, Assessments, and Tailoring

Guarding against adverse selection and moral hazard requires assessments and reassessment at claims adjustment. Such interaction between the insurer and insured can have further effects. Underwriting can improve the insured's security through assessments, and assessments can affect the policies written.

Underwriting and Premium Rates

Underwriters will look at many different factors when assessing the risk and rates used for determining the premium. First, underwriters will look closely at the business and the manner in which it uses the network. Companies that handle a high level of confidential information such as medical or financial records will start in a much higher rated classification. At a minimum, underwriters will require a questionnaire asking about basic network security measures. Underwriters may also require conference calls or if the risk warrants, on-site security assessments. Many underwriters employ in-house technologists who can help with a technical assessment. Some underwriters may require a third-party security assessment. The level of information is based on the use of the network and the limits being quoted. It is important to note that there is a high degree of judgment when pricing these risks because the coverage is relative new and underwriters are just beginning to quantify these risks.

Tailored Policies

Maybe one way of dealing with risks outside the firewall is to tailor an enterprise's (or customer's) Internet connection for maximal utility and least risk for that particular customer, perhaps by selecting the best-fitting connection, and perhaps by constructing an insurance policy to cover problems that are likely to occur, especially where a standard policy doesn't fit so well. Maybe the best way to build Internet insurance isn't to make a few big policies; maybe it's better to tailor a policy for each customer's Internet situation.

The Internet provides the means for insurers to write and deliver such policies; see Chapter 8 and the discussion of riding the fifth wave.

Tailoring has connotations of something being handmade, and there probably would be a professional services aspect to this. But what if that aspect consisted largely of presenting a few automatically generated tailored policies for the customer to choose from? The customer could then choose the one that fits best, thus selecting coverage for the customer's own valuation of the possible loss at a price acceptable to the customer. This is similar to the way automobile insurance works. Given sufficient data about Internet connectivity and performance, Internet insurance policies can be just as flexible.

Case Studies

A few concrete examples offered in the next subsections may help to clarify the principles discussed so far.

BJ's Warehouse: The Poster Child for Network Liability Insurance

In June 2005, BJ's Wholesale Club entered into a tentative settlement with the FTC regarding its release of credit card information in early 2004.[17] The FTC did not assess any fines, but the company has agreed to submit to 20 years of third-party security assessments.

According to the FTC, BJ's problem was in not applying basic security measures when transferring or storing data:

> *The FTC alleges BJ's failed to adequately protect customer information by failing to encrypt data when it was transmitted or stored on computers in BJ's stores.[18]*

And, according to the FTC, even when BJ's did apply security measures, it did not do so correctly:

> *BJ's also stored customer information longer than necessary—up to 30 days, in violation of bank security rules—and stored data in files that could be accessed using commonly known default user identity codes and passwords, the FTC said.[19]*

BJ's admitted no fault.

General liability insurance typically would not cover actions of this nature brought by the FTC, but what about the $13,000,000 in damages alleged in multiple civil suits brought by banks, thrifts, and others who incurred bad debt, lost transactional revenue and incurred additional expense to reissue credit cards?

BJ's 10Q of April 30, 2005, makes no mention of insurance recoveries for either the pending damages or the more than $3M set aside for legal defense. While special *network liability* insurance for an event just like this is available, many companies still do not secure the coverage. Underwriters of traditional general liability insurance programs will tell you that they never intended to cover claims like BJ's but that new *network liability* policies will.

Arguments for coverage under traditional general liability programs have been made but, depending on the policy version, at best there will be a fight for coverage. Here is why:

- Some underwriters are simply excluding personal injury from general liability coverage.
- Newer general liability programs often contain specific Internet related exclusions.
- If there are no other applicable exclusions, personal injury in a general liability policy typically requires an *oral or written publication of material that violates a person's right of privacy*. Underwriters have argued that a hack or information leak is not *publication*.

This is a good illustration of the limits of general liability insurance and the need for network liability insurance. Almost every company faces network risks and should at a minimum consider the cost and benefit of network security liability coverage. In a case like this, the insurer would probably assess the basic security measures in place by the company and insist on them being robust before issuing the insurance, so buying insurance could actually help prevent the problem the insurance is for.

System Administration As a Criminal Activity

In 1995 Randal L. Schwartz was convicted of three felony counts,[20] one for altering without authorization two computer systems, and the other two for accessing a computer with intent to commit theft. Randal thought he was doing his job as a contractor at Intel by running the standard system administration program crack to look for bad passwords, and by forwarding his mail so he could read it while on the road giving talks. Intel took a different view.[21] The specific law used by the prosecutor is an Oregon law, but similar laws exist in other states, laws so vague that modifying your account to forward your mail can be considered unauthorized alteration of the computer system.

Randal was not a malicious cracker like Kevin Mitnick,[22] nor was he a teenage script kiddie.[23] Randal was and is a well-known computer professional, an expert in his field, author by then of two books about the Perl programming language, and a frequent speaker at conferences and tutorials. He is, in fact, a pillar of the Unix and Internet communities. The World Wide Web would not have grown as quickly and as easily as it did without Perl, nor without Randal's efforts to promulgate Perl. Does being a pillar of the community make one immune from criminal activity? No (just ask Ivan Boesky). However, simple timing mistakes while attempting to do one's job in the generally accepted manner should not constitute felonious behavior. But they can, so beware.

Read up on codes of online ethics, such as that of the Association for Computing Machinery (ACM)[24] and familiarize yourself with your employer's guidelines and local laws. And encourage your employer to insure the enterprise, its officers, and you from external lawsuits that might end up with you as the fall guy.

Targeting the C-Class

Legal liability can also result from less obvious factors. Carter Schoenberg wrote a case study called *Information Security & Negligence: Targeting the C-Class*.[25] Carter is a former homicide detective, and he takes a concrete case-study approach:

Rather than analyzing a hypothetical situation where a company is hacked by one of several means or subjected to the involuntary mass-propagation of a virus or worm, let's focus on a real-life incident, dissect each component supported by fact and effectively diagram a blueprint for how you cannot only be targeted for a lawsuit or criminal prosecution, but demonstrate how you will lose. This loss will inflict a financial casualty, which may dramatically impact an organization's fiscal health.[26]

His example is of a financial institution that had a web page defaced, apparently because the company hadn't applied a patch to its IIS 5 (Microsoft's Internet Information Server version 5). No customer or financial data was compromised as a result of the attack. Nonetheless, the financial institution had a responsibility to provide access to financial information and transactions to its customers, and according to news reports, customers had limited or no access during the attack. So, was the financial institution negligent? If so, how would you prove it?

Laws for negligence vary per state, but in the United States there are now a number of national laws that take precedence, such as SOX, HIPAA, and GLBA. These permit discussing this case in specific terms, including quantifiable harm, opportunity, and motive. Carter goes so far as to say:

This scenario will ultimately lead to shareholders targeting corporate executives as being personally liable seeking seizure of personal wealth and even criminal sanctions.[27]

Technical IT and security personnel probably won't avoid involvement, either; at the least they may be deposed in a lawsuit.

In such a situation I think I'd be for all four of the following:

- A high standard of diligence
- Robust Directors and Officers (D&O) insurance
- Relevant Errors and Omissions (E&O) insurance
- Internet business continuity insurance

And if I were a system administrator, I'd want specific internal operational policies that I could follow to the letter, so as to avoid being the target of a lawsuit.

Carter Schoenberg's example case did involve an external attack. However, it did not involve a cracker specifically targeting that particular financial services institution for any reason other than that it happened to be running an unpatched copy of IIS, along with a number of other organizations that were attacked. So, this was a *force majeure* event in the sense that it was not specifically targeted and had aggregate effect. However, there were things the financial institution could have done, but didn't, of which patching the software was only the first.

Carter includes an interesting timeline showing patching shortly after point of discovery as manageable risk, developing over time still not patched into negligence and eventually gross negligence. And he compares typical cost for a system administrator to apply a patch versus fines and fees in a court case: the latter can cost a hundred times more than patching.

Carter also mentions settlement of a lawsuit as being preferable to litigation partly because of risk of public exposure and resulting loss of reputation and perhaps financial consequences. I wonder if we shouldn't turn that around and establish reputation systems that discover unapplied patches, nonredundant routes, congestion, and so on; inform the affected enterprise first; and after a decent interval make remaining problems public. Such a reputation system would be tricky to implement, because it would not want to invite crackers to attack. However, it might be possible to do it in such a way as to encourage enterprises to patch and deploy so as to avoid security problems. And while I'm not a lawyer or a police detective, I would guess that companies that patched when warned would be less likely to be held liable in legal cases.

Carter's article is a very interesting nuts and bolts examination of just what legal liability might mean for a specific case. There are a number of points in there that I suspect many enterprises have not considered.

Leveraging Technology with Financial Risk-Transfer Instruments

Insurance and related financial risk transfer instruments permit leveraging technology with nontechnical risk instruments. Such instruments, in turn, promote use of security technology via assessments and adjustments. Such assessments and adjustments by their nature compare the state of the insured company against that of others, thus broadening the outlook of technical security measures from building forts for individual enterprises to improving the general state of Internet security. Insurance itself consists of pooling risk, and thus directly and indirectly promotes collective action against aggregate Internet risk.

Notes

1. Daniel E. Geer, Jr., "Risk Management Is Where the Money Is," *Digital Commerce Society of Boston* (November 3, 1998).

2. Marquez, Senior District Judge and U.S. District Court, Arizona, *American Guarantee & Liability Insurance Co. v. Ingram Micro, Inc. 2000*, No. 99-185 TUC ACM. (April 18, 2000). www.2001law.com/article_445.htm

3. Catherine L. Rivard and Michael A. Rossi, "Is Computer Data 'Tangible Property' or Subject to 'Physical Loss or Damage'? Part 1," International Risk Management Institute (August 2001). www.irmi.com/Expert/Articles/2001/Rossi08.aspx

4. Ibid.

5. Gerald Bruce Lee, District Judge, *America Online, Inc. v. St. Paul Mercury Ins. Co.,* United States District Court for the District of Virginia, (Alexandria, Virginia, June 20, 2002). www.phillipsnizer.com/library/cases/lib_case288.cfm

6. Wilkinson, Circuit Judge and Niemeyer, Circuit Judge, *America Online, Inc. v. St. Paul Mercury Ins. Co.,* United States Court of Appeals for the Fourth Circuit (October 15, 2003). http://laws.lp.findlaw.com/4th/022018p.html

7. David Walsh, "Cyber-Liability; Down the Wire," *Post Magazine,* (April 29, 2004). www.internetperils.com/risk/walsh.php

8. Rebecca Wetzel, "Market Drivers for E-Business Defense Technology," *Business Communications Review* (January 2003). www.wetzel consultingllc.com/BCR.SecurityArticle2003.pdf

9. Nicholas Weaver and Vern Paxson, "A Worst-Case Worm," *The Third Annual Workshop on Economics and Information Security (WEIS04),* Digital Technology Center, University of Minnesota (May 13–14, 2004).

10. Op. cit. Wetzel, "Market Drivers for E-Business Defense Technology."

11. Op. cit. Walsh, "Cyber-Liability; Down the Wire."

12. Hal R. Varian, "Managing Online Security Risks," *New York Times* (June 1, 2000).

13. Lord Levene, "Lloyd's Chairman outlines new era of risk to World Affairs Council," Press Release, Lloyd's (April 21, 2004). www.lloyds.com/index.asp?ItemId=7545

14. Op. cit. Varian, "Managing Online Security Risks."

15. Op. cit. Wetzel, "Market Drivers for E-Business Defense Technology."

16. John S. Quarterman, Peter F. Cassidy, and Gretchen K. Phillips, *Internet Risk Bonds: Essential Reinsurance Proxy for CyberHurricane Risk Management,* InternetPerils, Inc. (July 2004).

17. Mark Jewell, "Massachusetts Retailer Agrees to Audits, Security Measures in ID Theft Case," Associated Press (June 17, 2005). www.securityinfowatch.com/article/article.jsp?site Section=379&id=4506

18. Ibid.

19. Ibid.

20. John S. Quarterman, "System Administration as a Criminal Activity, or, the Strange Case of Randal Schwartz," *Matrix News*, Volume 5, Number 9 (September 1995).

21. Steve Pacenka, "Computer Crime? *State of Oregon v. Randal Schwartz*," Washington County Circuit Court C94-0322CR (April 8, 2001). `www.lightlink.com/spacenka/fors`

22. Tsutomu Shimomura and John Markoff, *Takedown: The Pursuit and Capture of Kevin Mitnick, America's Most Wanted Computer Outlaw—By the Man Who Did It*, New York: Hyperion Books (January 1, 1996).

23. Charles C. Mann, "Brave New Web," *Boston Magazine*, Volume 88, Number 4, pp. 32–36 (April 1996). `www.lightlink.com/spacenka/fors/press/bosapr96.html`

24. R. E. Anderson, D. G. Johnson, D. Gotterbam, and J. Perrolle, "Association of Computer Machinery (ACM) Code of Conduct," *Communications of the ACM*, Volume 36, Number 2, pp. 98–107 (1993). `http://onlineethics.org/codes/ACMcode.html`

25. Carter Schoenberg, *Information Security & Negligence: Targeting the C-Class*, InfosecWriters (February 2004). `www.infosecwriters.com/text_resources/pdf/InformationSecurityCClass.pdf`

26. Ibid.

27. Ibid.

CHAPTER 12

Summary: Managing Internet Risk in a Scale-Free World

Growth in new kinds of networks creates new situations that present new forms of risk and new forms of opportunity. Businesses have actively explored the content and financial reward opportunities of the Internet, but have not done as good a job in foreseeing and handling the new risks this infrastructure brings. Government has stepped in with laws such as SOX, GLBA, HIPAA, FERPA, PIPEDA, and DPD, which can help somewhat. However, those laws are all too focused on detail to completely manage the big picture. Standards such as FISMA and ISO 17799 can help in structuring security management. Although compliance with such laws and standards may actually increase expenses, overall Internet business risk management can actually reduce expenses both in the event of a risk and in the meantime while awaiting such an event. Plus risk management may reveal new opportunities for profit.

The Pain: Storms, Pirates, and Outages

Organizations that use the Internet are increasingly at risk of outages, slow-downs, lost transactions, lost customers, reputational damage, lost profits, increased competition, and even going out of business. Reputable researchers estimate a single worst-case worm could cause $50 billion in economic damage in the United States alone,[1] more than that caused by all the hurricanes of 2004, the worst hurricane year to date in the United States, and even more than

Hurricane Katrina of 2005. Some big-company CEOs think that they face a $100 billion worldwide risk.[2] There are plenty of smaller risks, as well, including cable cuts, phishing, pharming, and blackmail, and an average of $2 million per company in lost business from each major worm or virus.[3]

Yet the global reach and convenience of the Internet continues to be attractive because it provides cost savings, access to customers, suppliers, and outsourcers that might otherwise be inaccessible. It offers capabilities, especially types of group communications that would otherwise not be available. A company in an industry that uses the Internet can't afford to be the one that doesn't.

How can this pain of Internet business risk be managed?

The Problem: We're All Neighbors on the Internet Sea

A computer connected to the Internet is different from an unnetworked PC. When floppy disks were the usual means of transferring data and programs, viruses spread slowly, worms weren't possible, and few people used PCs as communications devices. Nowadays, few people use floppies anymore, and online communications range from blogs to financial transactions.

A company connected to the Internet is different from a bricks-and-mortar company. Profits, competition, and reputation can be affected by more people and more means, both external from and internal to the company.

A world connected by the Internet is different. Just as jet airplanes have every major city on the planet within one day's travel, the Internet has placed every networked computer on the planet within a second's communications. Communicating with your own colleagues is easier; reaching new customers, suppliers, and colleagues is easier; and everyone communicates more, in more ways, and in more groups than before.

Can't Ignore It; Can't Fix It; Need to Manage It

The Internet is a loosely coupled non-hierarchical distributed network. No single organization can control it. Any organization that wants to use it would do well to accept that the Internet introduces sizeable elements that cannot be controlled and therefore risks that must be managed without direct control.

With this local and global reach and convenience come opportunities. Unfortunately, opportunities exist for illicit as well as legitimate commerce. Closing the doors and windows to keep the crooks out won't work. We can't go backward anymore than we can all stop flying or driving. As Professor David Farber put it: "It is part of the business fabric. It's like your telephone, it may annoy you but you can't get rid of it because you'll be out of business."[4]

I can remember when some people were still having difficulty getting used to the telephone. Now, an entire generation of people has grown up as natives of cyberspace. Any old timers still having trouble immigrating into that place need to get on with it if they want to stay in business.

Not Just Another Infrastructure

The Internet is not just another homeland infrastructure that needs securing. Part of the U.S. government has acknowledged that fact:

> *The information infrastructure is unique among the critical infrastructures because it is owned primarily by the private sector, it changes at the rapid pace of the information technology market, and it is the backbone for many other infrastructures. Therefore, protection of this infrastructure must be given the proper attention throughout government.*[5]

This information infrastructure, and the Internet in particular, is the connecting tissue for modern life and economy:

> *From education to recreation and from business to banking, the nation is dependent on telephones, cellular phones, personal digital assistants, computers, and the physical and virtual infrastructure that ties them all together. Almost all data and voice communications now touch the Internet—the global electronic network of computers (including the World Wide Web) that connects people, ideas, and information around the globe.*[6]

And the other critical infrastructures, such as electric power grid control systems, reactor control systems, emergency response systems, and so on, are increasingly carried over the Internet.

A Different Kind of Connectivity

It isn't electrical utility grids that are interconnecting the world as never before; they cover geographical regions, not the whole world. Airlines were instrumental in turning the world into a global village, yet far more people communicate with each other worldwide now than visit each other. It is communications systems, led by the Internet as it rapidly subsumes many other systems that are turning the world into a global neighborhood.[7] All the other infrastructures increasingly depend on the Internet.

The Internet's global reach, speed, and convenience produces both its great value via Metcalfe's Law (many users) and Reed's Law (many groups) and its potential for cascade failure that can occur on small or large scales, affecting a few businesses or entire industries.

A Different Scale Can Be a Different State

A world with fast global group-forming communications is different in kind. Sufficiently close connectivity can cause a state change, in the same manner as ice melting with heat,[8] or increasing population turning medieval towns into cities, or warmth and moisture causing a field to bloom with flowers.[9]

We've already seen this several times with the Internet. Around 1988 as the distributed and decentralized Domain Name System was implemented and several other factors came into play, the Internet entered a period of doubling in size every year, which continued until about 2000. In 1991, the first commercial ISPs appeared, producing a decisive shift into commercialization of the Internet infrastructure. In 1994, the web added a new level of convenience and started drawing new types of people and increasing commercialization. Around 2000, as a certain scale was reached and group-forming techniques became widely used, the web and the Internet became standard ways of doing business. Around 2003 Internet crime for pay expanded beyond spamming. In 2005, targets of such electronic crime and their customers started to get serious about doing something about it.

Each of these state changes occurred rather quickly, after a certain size or level of connectivity or technical change was achieved. As new kinds of interactions become possible among Internet neighbors, new patterns of activity emerge, which are then magnified by positive feedback loops or controlled by negative feedback.[10] Some of these emergent behaviors were predicted or even intended, and some of them weren't. Many of these behaviors have far-reaching effects that we are only just beginning to understand. Future growth or changes will produce still more emergent behaviors of which few have yet dreamed.

The Solution: Something Old, Something Borrowed, Something New

The Internet has significant potential for cascade failure because of its organization as a scale-free network with many hubs of various sizes. This scale-free organization is also what makes it so robust unless the hubs are directly targeted.

Old: Deploy Traditional Best Practices

One basic way to deal with risk is to increase the Internet's resilience by increasing redundancy and diversity. Then add encryption with good identity and access management. Patching bugs, firewalling unused ports, detecting and preventing intrusions, and Virtual Private Networks are all possible with existing Internet security solutions.

Borrowed: Import Tools from Other Industries

Yet because the Internet is beyond the control of any single organization, there is no way that any business can completely ameliorate its Internet risks, which have become too large for any business to ignore.

Fortunately, the tools we need to add to those we already had are mostly already available, because other industries have faced similar problems before. The solutions include financial risk transfer instruments such as self-insurance, insurance policies, reinsurance, retrocessional insurance using catastrophe bonds, and performance bonds.

Many types of solutions and even specific solutions are already known and simply need to be applied. The main thing is to admit there is a problem that causes pain and get on with applying the known solutions. To quote David Farber again:

> So, what CIOs should be doing is putting pressure on vendors to implement the best security measures. Essentially holding their noses to the grindstone, and not agreeing to any exemptions. It is not an easy problem.[11]

And this doesn't concern just CIOs, to quote findings from a U.S. House of Representatives subcommittee:

> Despite the growing threat, security and efforts to protect information often remain an afterthought frequently delegated to a Chief Information Officer or a Chief Technology Officer. Cybersecurity should be treated as a cost of doing business by the highest levels of an enterprise's leadership because the ability to conduct business and assure delivery of services to consumers—whether it is banking, electrical, or manufacturing—depends on ensuring the availability of information and related infrastructure.[12]

As Ross Anderson spelled out in 2001, this is not primarily a technical problem:

> . . . information insecurity is at least as much due to perverse incentives. Many of the problems can be explained more clearly and convincingly using the language of microeconomics: network externalities, asymmetric information, moral hazard, adverse selection, liability dumping and the tragedy of the commons.[13]

Technical solutions alone will not prevail, and technical executives alone cannot solve this problem.

The problem is big enough that all corporate strategists, from CFO, CTO, CIO, and marketing through the CEO to the board need to produce, implement, and enforce a risk management plan.

New: Feedback through Insurance and Reputation

As insurance companies get into the act, there will be feedback, as Farber notes:

> In the long term, a security standard is mostly going to be motivated by insurance companies. In most companies, even if they don't have direct cyber insurance, they have insurance that covers a lot of their operations. And

those insurance companies will start taking into account the risks that will be reflected in their premiums.[14]

Farber is far from the first to point this out; Dan Geer said it in 1998,[15] Hal Varian said it in the *New York Times* in 2000,[16] Bruce Schneier said it in 2001,[17] and I've been saying it since 2003. This state change will also come. Self-insurance methods such as Basel II require quantification and vigilance. SOX, GLBA, HIPAA, and FERPA also require various forms of quantification and ever-increasing vigilance, although mostly not about the Internet. Insurance and the other risk transfer methods require assessments and adjustments that require traditional security, just as fire insurance requires sprinkler systems. There may also be specialized feedback loops such as those involving performance bonds for ISPs.

Reputation systems can help encourage all businesses to improve their acts, by aiding consumers in deciding which vendors or service providers have the best risk management and are, thus, most likely to be robust in the face of perils and anomalies. This is the case both for traditional security vulnerabilities and for electronic crime such as phishing, pharming, and spyware. We also need reputation systems for the interaction of insurance with security, so as to avoid the kinds of problems currently occurring with medical insurance and health care provision. Customers want vendors and service suppliers that proactively manage such risks and that can be seen to be doing so. This is true regardless of whether the business is large or small, banking, financial, insurance, ISP, law enforcement, military, or government. Customers want products and organizations they can depend on, and in a scale-free world that means risk management.

Newer: Turn Externalities into Affordances

But why stop there? Why be concerned only with how the Internet brings risk? After all, aren't we all using it because of the opportunities it brings to do things more conveniently and efficiently, and to do new things? Why not turn unfortunate externalities into perceived affordances?[18, 19]

If an *externality* is a side effect of an economic transaction that affects somebody else, and an *affordance* is a property of an object or its environment that indicates how it can be used, how can an externality be perceived as an affordance? Miscreants do this all the time. They take advantage of software users' love of convenience and corporations' love of monoculture and vendors' bugs, all of which produce externalities in the form of vulnerabilities that can be perceived as affordances to exploit to build botnets and send spam, phishing, and blackmail messages. How can legitimate businesses turn their own or other peoples' externalities into affordances?

One answer is that they can decrease their negative externalities by improving security, thus improving the general state of the Internet and the economy and gaining a better reputation, which can help keep and attract customers and lessen the risk of big expenses when a vulnerability is exploited. In other words, proactively manage risk and leverage that risk management as a marketing advantage. Swiss Re has done that with environmental emissions control, not only reducing its emissions but also sponsoring a video program on the subject, thus spreading the word and advertising its own contributions.[20] Companies could do the same for Internet business risk management, including areas such as diversity and insurance that are not yet fashionable.

Successful companies have also been built on perception of the connections afforded by the web and the Internet, such as Google, eBay, and Amazon. Others include Technorati and Slashdot. Every company that uses the Internet perceives many of the obvious affordances of the Internet and the web. What others can your company perceive? Perhaps you can use ratings systems for its products and services, such as those that are so popular at all the just-mentioned companies. Maybe you can try not to hide vulnerabilities, exploits, or phishing and instead invite your customers to rate your company's success in managing such risks, while participating in reputation systems that compare such success with that of other companies.

There are many new solutions to be invented and applied that can be competitive advantages to businesses that produce and use them. Internet business risk management can be a new competitive core competence, or even a new line of business.

The discipline of writing a risk management plan and of organizing a company to implement it can help facilitate sufficient perception and flexibility not only to manage the emergent risk of a scale-free world but also to turn it to advantage.

Notes

1. Nicholas Weaver and Vern Paxson, "A Worst-Case Worm," *The Third Annual Workshop on Economics and Information Security (WEIS04)*, Digital Technology Center, University of Minnesota (May 13–14, 2004).

2. mi2g, "Silently preparing for the $100 billion cyber-catastrophe risk," *News Alert*, mi2g (February 16, 2004).

3. CNET News.com Staff, "The attack of the $2 million worm," *News.Com*, CNET (July 6, 2004). `http://news.com.com/The+attack+of+the+%242+million+worm/2100-7355_3-5258769.html?tag=cd.top`

4. Tissie Adhistia, "The big question: Will CIOs abandon the Internet?," *MIS Asia Magazine* (Singapore, August 7, 2005). `www.misweb.com/magarticle.asp?doc_id=24916&rgid=5&listed_months=0`

5. *Cybersecurity for the Homeland Report of the Activities and Findings by the Chairman and Ranking Member, Subcommittee on Cybersecurity, Science, and Research & Development of the U.S. House of Representatives Select Committee on Homeland Security* (Washington, DC, December 2004). `http://cryptome.org/cybersec-home.htm`

6. Ibid.

7. Thomas L. Friedman, *The World Is Flat: A Brief History of the Twenty-First Century* (New York: Farrar, Straus and Giroux, 2005).

8. Albert-Laszlo Barabasi, *Linked: How Everything Is Connected to Everything Else and What It Means* (Plume, April 2003).

9. Steven Johnson, *Emergence: The Connected Lives of Ants, Brains, Cities, and Software* (New York: Scribner, September 2002).

10. Ibid.

11. Op. cit. Adhistia, "The big question: Will CIOs abandon the Internet?"

12. Op. cit. *Cybersecurity for the Homeland Report.*

13. Ross Anderson, "Why Information Security is Hard—An Economic Perspective," *17th Annual Computer Security Applications Conference* (New Orleans, Louisiana, December 10–14, 2001). `www.acsac.org/2001/abstracts/thu-1530-b-anderson.html`

14. Op. cit. Adhistia, "The big question: Will CIOs abandon the Internet?"

15. Daniel E. Geer, Jr., "Risk Management Is Where the Money Is," *Digital Commerce Society of Boston* (November 3, 1998).

16. Hal R. Varian, "Managing Online Security Risks," *New York Times* (June 1, 2000).

17. Bruce Schneier, "Schneier on Security: The Insurance Takeover," *Information Security* (February 2001).

18. Donald A. Norman, *The Design of Everyday Things* (Basic Books, September 2002).

19. *O'Reilly Emerging Technology Conference—March 3–6, 2006—San Diego, California, Call for Participation.* O'Reilly. `http://conferences.oreillynet.com/cs/et2006/create/e_sess`

20. Alex Steffen, "The Great Warming and The Greening of the Reinsurance Industry," *Worldchanging.com* (December 25, 2004). `www.worldchanging.com/archives/001795.html`

Index

NUMERICS
$100 billion cybercatastrophe risk, 146

A
ACM (Association for Computing Machinery), 250
actuarial tables, 236
adjustments, 232
Advance Notice of Proposed Rule-making (ANPR), 96–97
Advanced Measurement Approach (AMA), 98–101
adverse selection, 246
advertising liability, 242–243
adware, 25, 203
affordances, 260–261
aggregation, 147, 231
aggregators, 173–174
AIG (American International Group), 68, 194
Akamai, 57
Alteon SSL-VPN (Nortel), 52
Alternative Standardized Approach (ASA), 98
AMA (Advanced Measurement Approach), 98–101

American Guaranty v. Ingram Micro, 108, 233–234
Anasazi, 223–225
anomalies
  causes of, 28
  defined, 22
  economic consequences, 127
  financial institutions, 115, 127
ANPR (Advance Notice of Proposed Rulemaking), 96–97
Anti-Phishing Working Group (APWG), 25, 64, 126, 196
antispam laws, 201
antispam measures, 195
AOL, 7
AOL v. St. Paul Mercury Insurance, 234
Apple iPod, 158
Application Performance Index (APDEX), 241
Application Software Provider (ASP), 142
applications and monoculture, 35
APWG (Anti-Phishing Working Group), 25, 64, 126, 196
Array Networks SPX3000, 52
Arthashastra (Vishnagupta Kautilya), 128–130

ASA (Alternative Standardized Approach), 98
ASP (Application Software Provider), 142
assessments, 78, 232, 247–248
Association for Computing Machinery (ACM), 250
attacks
  Man in the Middle (MITM), 155
  scob, 27
authentication, 56
authorization, 56
Aventail Netifice, 52

B

backups, 45–46, 148
Baltimore (HP), 53
bandwidth futures, 132
Bank of America, 46
Bank of Credit and Commerce International (BCCI), 96
banking
  Advance Notice of Proposed Rulemaking (ANPR), 96–97
  Basel Committee on Banking Supervision (BCBS), 95
  Basel I Capital Accord, 95–96
  Basel II New Capital Accord, 4, 79, 96–97
  collective action, 106, 110
  communication methods, 18
  congestion, 104–105
  dependence on the Internet, 22
  management summaries, 106–109
  nonredundant routes, 103–104
  obligation failure, 107
  operational risk approaches, 97–101
  physical damage, 108
  process failure, 109
  risk management, 79
  slow links, 101–103
  system failure, 108–109

Barabási, Albert-László (*Linked*), 82, 84
Basel Committee on Banking Supervision (BCBS), 95
Basel I Capital Accord, 95–96
Basel II New Capital Accord, 4, 79, 96–97
Basic Indicator Approach, 97
BitTorrent, 157
BJ's Wholesale Club, 249–250
blackmail, 26–27, 69
Black-Merton-Scholes option value, 6, 9
blogs, 10
BMC OpenNetwork, 53
bonds
  catastrophe bonds, 119–123, 188–189, 240
  government bonds, 195
  large enterprises, 152
  markets, 195
  performance bonds, 123–124, 192–194, 240
  pricing, 195
  strips, 188
  tranches, 188
bot herders, 11, 25–26
botnets, 26
bots, 25–26
bounties for vulnerabilities, 152–153
Bradner, Scott (professor), 18, 21
brand reputation, 16, 29
Brix, 57
broadband access, 214–215
broadcast networks, 9
business interruption insurance, 245
business risk insurance, 67
business transactions
  degradation of service, 236
  dependence on the Internet, 2, 22

C

CAIDA (Cooperative Association for Internet Data Analysis), 62

Canada
  ISP association, 214
  Personal Information Protection and
      Electronic Documents Act
      (PIPEDA), 1, 4
CAN-SPAM Act of 2003, 210
Capital Accord, 95–96
capital withholding, 241
Carnegie Mellon University (CMU), 26
Cartmell, Jennifer (former chief risk
    officer at Texaco), 141–142
case studies
  BJ's Wholesale Club, 249–250
  C-Class, 250–252
  Randal L. Schwartz, 250
catastrophe bonds, 119–123,
    188–189, 240
The Cathedral and the Bazaar (Eric Ray-
    mond), 180–181
causes of perils, 28
C-Class, 250–252
CDN (Content Delivery Services), 47
Center for Internet Epidemiology and
    Defenses (CIED), 60–61
centralized management, 58
CERT (Computer Emergency
    Response Team), 62
certificates, 56
chat rooms, 10
ChoicePoint, 147
Chubb, 194
CIED (Center for Internet Epidemiol-
    ogy and Defenses), 60–61
Cisco, 52, 54, 153–157
Citigroup, 46
Citrix Net6, 52
claims adjustment, 232
clearinghouses, 62–64
closed commercial networks, 7
closed standards, 59
CMU (Carnegie Mellon University), 26
CNA, 194

Collapse: How Societies Choose to Fail or
    Succeed (Jared Diamond), 88–90
collapse of the Internet, 18–20
collateral shredding, 132–133
collective action, 106, 110, 151, 238
commerce
  global competition, 31
  no-go areas, 130–131
  regulation, 31
communication method risk, 17–18
communications, 86–87
comparison indexes, 241
CompuServe, 7, 23
Computer Associates with eTrust +
    Netegrity, 53
Computer Emergency Response Team
    (CERT), 62
congestion, 104–105
consumer confidence, 150–151
content
  long tail of content, 173–174
  Media Risk, 242
  theft, 17
  third-party loss, 233
Content Delivery Services (CDN), 47
contingency plans, 76
contingent business interruption
    insurance, 245
contractual risk transfer, 74
Cooperative Association for Internet
    Data Analysis (CAIDA), 62
Counterpane, 53, 58
court cases
  American Guaranty v. Ingram Micro,
      108, 233–234
  AOL v. St. Paul Mercury Insur-
      ance, 234
crackers, 28–29
crisis management, 76
critical infrastructure, 217
Cyber Trust program (National Sci-
    ence Foundation), 60

cyber-insurance
  actuarial tables, 236
  adverse selection, 246
  advertising liability, 242–243
  aggregation, 231
  assessments, 232, 247–248
  business interruption insurance, 245
  business risk insurance, 67
  capital withholding, 241
  case studies, 248–252
  catastrophe bonds, 240
  claims adjustment, 232
  collective action, 238
  contingent business interruption
      insurance, 245
  current programs, 234–235
  current state of cyber-insurance,
      235–236
  Directors and Officers (D&O) insur-
      ance, 238
  eBusiness liability risk, 243–244
  Errors and Omissions (E&O) insur-
      ance, 238
  feedback, 260–261
  financial institutions, 117–118
  financial liability, 238–239
  first-party claims, 17
  first-party loss, 232, 244–245
  future of, 13
  general liability programs, 238
  Internet insurance companies,
      56, 67–68
  legal liability, 239
  Media Risk, 242
  moral hazard, 247
  performance bonds, 240
  physical damage, 233–234
  policy language, 237–238
  pricing, 245–247
  probabilistic models, 236
  professional liability programs, 238
  publishers liability policy, 242
  quality of service, 247
  quantification of Internet risks,
      236–237
  security, 239
  self-insurance, 151
  tailored policies, 248
  Technology Risk, 241–242
  third-party claims, 16–17
  third-party loss, 233
  traditional insurance, 151, 237–238
  Tropical Storm Risk (TSR), 130
  underwriting, 248
  vendor liability, 203–204
cybernatives, 169–171
CyberTrust's TruSecure certification
    product, 53

D

DARPA (Defense Advanced Research
    Projects Agency), 211–212, 221–222
Data Protection Directive (DPD), 1, 4
decentralized Internet model, 21, 58–60
deceptive practices
  adware, 25, 203
  pharming, 25, 202
  phishing
    criminal activity, 11, 23–24
    ISPs (Internet Service Providers), 202
    law enforcement, 202
    social engineering, 23–24
    spyware, 69
  spam
    antispam laws, 201
    CAN-SPAM Act of 2003, 201
    costs of, 23
    criminal activity, 11, 22–23
    history of, 22
    Internet Service Providers (ISPs), 22
    legal solutions, 68–69, 201
    pairwise connections, 10
    USENET newsgroups, 22
  spyware, 69, 202–203

Defense Advanced Research Projects Agency (DARPA), 211–212, 221–222

Defense Information Systems Agency (DISA), 211

degradation of service, 236

denial, 90–91

Department of Defense (DoD), 221

Department of Homeland Security, 18, 46, 48

DETER digital simulation testbed, 60

Diamond, Jared (*Collapse: How Societies Choose to Fail or Succeed*), 88–90

Directors and Officers (D&O) insurance, 238

DISA (Defense Information Systems Agency), 211

disaster accounting, 127, 246

diversity, 35, 47–49, 149–150

DNS (Domain Name System), 47, 258

DNS-OARC (Domain Name System Operations, Analysis, and Research Center), 61–62

D&O (Directors and Officers) insurance, 238

DoD (Department of Defense), 221

domain name squatters, 16

DPD (Data Protection Directive), 1, 4

dynamic reporting, 56

E

early warning and tracking of exploits, 128

eBay, 10, 184

EBO (Effects Based Operations) (U.S. military), 217–219

eBusiness liability risk, 243–244

economic damage
  anomalies, 127
  worms, 30

economic derivatives, 133–134

Economist Intelligence Unit (EIU), 113

economy
  economic policies and business judgment, 211
  funded research, 211–212
  innovation, 210
  productivity, 210–211

Effects Based Operations (EBO) (U.S. military), 217–219

eGap (Whale Communications), 52

EIU (Economist Intelligence Unit), 113

electric utilities, 189–190

Electronic Frontier Foundation (EFF), 18, 63, 158

e-mail
  phishing
    criminal activity, 11, 23–24
    ISPs (Internet Service Providers), 202
    law enforcement, 202
    social engineering, 23–24
    spyware, 69
  spam
    antispam laws, 201
    CAN-SPAM Act of 2003, 201
    costs of, 23
    criminal activity, 11, 22–23
    history of, 22
    Internet Service Providers (ISPs), 22
    legal solutions, 68–69, 201
    pairwise connections, 10
    USENET newsgroups, 22
  spoofs, 25

encryption
  backups, 46
  content theft, 17
  key escrow, 17
  large enterprises, 148–149
  limitations, 2
  spyware, 25
  subversion by people, 17
  uses, 51
  vendors, 56

enforcement of laws, 200–203

Enterprise-Wide Risk Management (EWRM), 141–142
EPN (NetSilica), 52
Ernst & Young, 58
Errors and Omissions (E&O) insurance, 238
ethics, 250
eTrust + Netegrity (Computer Associates), 53
Europe
  Data Protection Directive (DPD), 1, 4
  International Organization for Standardization's Open System Interconnection (ISO-OSI) protocols, 20
Everts, Steven (Senior Research Fellow at the Centre for European Reform in London), 85
EWRM (Enterprise-Wide Risk Management), 141–142
exploits
  defined, 22
  early warning and tracking, 128
  zero-day exploits, 128
externalities, 260–261

F
F5 FirePass, 52
Family Educational Rights and Privacy Act (FERPA), 4
Farber, David (professor), 256, 259–260
fear, 39–40, 91–92, 224–225
Federal Information Security Management Act (FISMA), 213
Federal Reserve, 96
Federal Trade Commission (FTC), 203
Federated Identity Management (FIM), 52–53
FedLine Advantage, 116–117
feedback, 259–260
FERPA (Family Educational Rights and Privacy Act), 4

fifth wave of computing, 172, 177–179
filters, 173–174
financial institutions
  anomalies, 115, 127
  bandwidth futures, 132
  catastrophe bonds, 119–123
  costs of breach of confidentiality, 128
  dependence on the Internet, 2, 22
  disaster accounting, 127
  early warning and tracking of exploits, 128
  economic derivatives, 133–134
  FedLine Advantage, 116–117
  innovation, 134–135
  insurance, 117–118
  losses, 114
  no-go areas, 130–131
  performance bonds, 123–124
  physical security systems, 114–115
  risk management, 79–80, 113–114
  shredding, 132–133
  smart connections, 133
financial liability, 238–239
financial risk-transfer instruments, 252
Financial Services Information Sharing and Analysis Center (FS/ISAC), 125
Financial Services Technology Consortium (FSTC), 79–80
Firefox, 180
FirePass (F5), 52
firewalls
  limitations, 2, 51
  uses, 51
first-party claims, 17
first-party loss, 232, 244–245
FISMA (Federal Information Security Management Act), 213
force majeure risks, 1, 11, 29
fortification, 49–52
fraud, 16
free software, 181

FS/ISAC (Financial Services Information Sharing and Analysis Center), 125
FSTC (Financial Services Technology Consortium), 79–80
FTC (Federal Trade Commission), 203

G

Garriott, Richard (computer game inventor), 28
Gates, Bill (founder of Microsoft), 28
Geer, Dan (Internet security expert), 13
general liability programs, 238
gigalapse (collapse of the Internet), 18
GLBA (Gramm-Leach-Bliley Financial Services Modernization Act), 4
Global Guerillas blog, 83
global products, 182–183
GOSIP, 212–213
governments
 agencies, 200
 ameliorative action, 199–200
 antispam laws, 201
 bonds, 195
 broadband access, 214–215
 coercive action, 199–200
 critical infrastructure, 217
 departments, 200
 Information Sharing and Analysis Centers (ISACs), 199
 insurers of last resort, 200
 law enforcement, 200–203
 levels of, 207
 limits of, 198
 lobbyists, 204–205
 mandating technical requirements, 212–213
 preventive advice, 198–199
 risk management, 81, 197–198, 225–227
 unfair practices, 203
 U.S. National Strategy to Secure Cyberspace, 198

Gramm-Leach-Bliley Financial Services Modernization Act (GLBA), 4
greed, 28
Grokster, 157–158
group-forming ability of the Internet, 10
group-forming networks, 10
growth laws, 4–6

H

hackers, 28
hardware vendors, 54
hierarchy of needs, 176–177
HIPAA (Health Insurance Portability and Accountability Act), 4
homeland security
 Department of Homeland Security, 18, 46, 48
 US-CERT (United States Computer Emergency Response Team), 62–63
HP Baltimore/Trulogica, 53
humint (human intelligence), 149
hypocrisy, 87

I

IBM, 53
ICANN (Internet Corporation for Assigned Names and Numbers), 20
iDefense, 152
Identity and Access Management (I&AM), 51–53
identity theft
 content theft, 17
 phishing, 23–24
 spyware, 24–25
IE (Internet Explorer), 27
IETF (Internet Engineering Task Force), 18
illicit bazaar, 82–83
IM (instant messaging), 23
incidence of risk, 126–127
incident reports, 146

inertia, 38–39

infection scanners, 56

Information Security & Negligence: Targeting the CClass (Carter Schoenberg), 250–252

information sharing, 179

Information Sharing and Analysis Centers (ISACs), 199

InfraGard, 63

Ingram Micro, 108, 233–234

innovation (in economy), 210

instant messaging (IM), 23

insurance
  actuarial tables, 236
  adverse selection, 246
  advertising liability, 242–243
  aggregation, 231
  assessments, 232, 247–248
  business interruption insurance, 245
  business risk insurance, 67
  capital withholding, 241
  case studies, 248–252
  catastrophe bonds, 240
  claims adjustment, 232
  collective action, 238
  contingent business interruption insurance, 245
  current programs, 234–235
  current state of cyber-insurance, 235–236
  Directors and Officers (D&O) insurance, 238
  eBusiness liability risk, 243–244
  Errors and Omissions (E&O) insurance, 238
  feedback, 260–261
  financial institutions, 117–118
  financial liability, 238–239
  first-party claims, 17
  first-party loss, 232, 244–245
  future of, 13
  general liability programs, 238
  Internet insurance companies, 56, 67–68
  legal liability, 239
  Media Risk, 242
  moral hazard, 247
  performance bonds, 240
  physical damage, 233–234
  policy language, 237–238
  pricing, 245–247
  probabilistic models, 236
  professional liability programs, 238
  publishers liability policy, 242
  quality of service, 247
  quantification of Internet risks, 236–237
  security, 239
  self-insurance, 151
  tailored policies, 248
  Technology Risk, 241–242
  third-party claims, 16–17
  third-party loss, 233
  traditional insurance, 151, 237–238
  Tropical Storm Risk (TSR), 130
  underwriting, 248
  vendor liability, 203–204

InsureTrust, 67

International Convergence of Capital Measurement and Capital Standards: A Revised Framework, 96

International Organization for Standardization's Open System Interconnection (ISO-OSI) protocols, 20

International Telecommunications Union (ITU), 20

Internet
  business transactions, 2
  centralized management, 58
  closed commercial networks, 7
  collapse predictions, 18–20
  decentralized model, 21, 58–60
  group-forming ability, 10
  growth laws, 4–6
  monoculture, 36–37
  option value, 6, 8–9
  scale-free network, 7–8
  state changes, 257–258

Internet commerce
  global competition, 31
  no-go areas, 130–131
  regulation, 31
Internet Corporation for Assigned
    Names and Numbers (ICANN), 20
Internet Engineering Task Force
    (IETF), 18
Internet Explorer (IE), 27
Internet peril detection, 56
Internet Protocol version 6 (IPv6), 36
Internet research
  Center for Internet Epidemiology
      and Defenses (CIED), 60–61
  clearinghouses, 62–64
  Cooperative Association for Internet
      Data Analysis (CAIDA), 62
  Cyber Trust program, 60
  DETER digital simulation testbed, 60
  DNS-OARC (Domain Name System
      Operations, Analysis, and
      Research Center), 61–62
  Security Through Interaction Model-
      ing (STIM) Center, 61
Internet Security Systems (ISS), 53, 64
InternetPerils, 53–55, 57, 64
intrusion detection, 56
intrusion prevention, 56
iPod, 158
IPv6 (Internet Protocol version 6), 36
ISACs (Information Sharing and
    Analysis Centers), 199
ISO 17799, 213–214
ISO-OSI (International Organization
    for Standardization's Open System
    Interconnection) protocols, 20
ISPs (Internet Service Providers)
  antispam measures, 195
  bonded and insured, 192–196
  Canadian ISP association, 214
  catastrophe bonds, 188–189
  goodwill payments, 187, 191–192
  performance bonds, 192–194
  phishing, 202

  redundancy, 33–34
  reporting practices, 64–65
  reputation, 196
  risk management, 80–81
  Service Level Agreements (SLAs),
      56–57, 80–81, 190–192
  spam, 22
  telephone companies, 20
  Texas Internet Service Provider Asso-
      ciation (TISPA), 214–215
  visibility, 36–37
ISS (Internet Security Systems), 53, 64
ITU (International Telecommunica-
    tions Union), 20

J
Jaynes, Jeremy (spammer), 68–69
Juniper
  Neoteris Netscreen, 52
  SSL-VPN, 54

K
Kautilya, Vishnagupta (*Arthashastra*),
    128–130
Kazaa, 157
key escrow, 17
Keynote, 57
KPMG, 58
Kushnir, Vardan (notorious Russian
    spammer), 68

L
large enterprises
  aggregation, 147
  agility, 143, 145
  backups, 148
  bonds, 152
  ChoicePoint, 147
  collective action, 151
  consumer confidence, 150–151
  diversity, 149–150
  encryption, 148–149
  Enterprise-Wide Risk Management
      (EWRM), 141–142

large enterprises *(continued)*
  focus, 144
  incident reports, 146
  management summaries, 146
  $100 billion cybercatastrophe risk, 146
  opportunities, 159–161
  outsourcers, 149
  passwords, 149
  pattern of communications, 144
  personal empowerment, 143–144
  research, 144
  risk management, 80, 141–143
  security, 147, 150
  self-insurance, 151
  social engineering, 149
latency, 101–103
law enforcement, 200–203
laws
  Basel II New Capital Accord, 4
  CAN-SPAM Act of 2003, 210
  Data Protection Directive (DPD), 1, 4
  Family Educational Rights and
    Privacy Act (FERPA), 4
  Federal Information Security Man-
    agement Act (FISMA), 213
  Gramm-Leach-Bliley Financial
    Services Modernization Act
    (GLBA), 4
  Health Insurance Portability and
    Accountability Act (HIPAA), 4
  PATRIOT Act, 209–210
  Personal Information Protection
    and Electronic Documents Act
    (PIPEDA), 1, 4
  Sarbanes-Oxley (SOX), 1, 3–4, 207–208
legal liability, 239
Levene, Lord (chairman of Lloyd's),
  145, 159
liabilities
  advertising liability, 242–243
  eBusiness liability risk, 243–244
  financial liability, 238–239
  general liability programs, 238
  legal liability, 239
  Media Risk, 242
  professional liability programs, 238
  publishers liability policy, 242
  software liability, 204–207
  spam liabilities, 201
  vendor liability, 203–204
Linked (Albert-László Barabási), 82
Lloyd's, 194
lobbyists, 204–205
long tail of content, 173–174

M
Man in the Middle (MITM)
  attacks, 155
Managed Security Monitoring (MSM),
  53–54
Marsh, 194
Marshall Plan, 85–86
Mazu Networks, 54
Media Risk, 242
Mercury Interactive, 57
Metcalfe, Bob (inventor of Ethernet
  and founder of 3COM), 5, 18–20
Metcalfe's Law, 4–5
Microsoft, 47, 53
military
  Defense Advanced Research Projects
    Agency (DARPA), 211–212,
    221–222
  Department of Defense (DoD), 221
  Effects Based Operations (EBO),
    217–219
  external detection systems for net-
    works, 221
  immune networks, 219–220
  self-healing networks, 219–221
Minitel, 7
MITM (Man in the Middle) attacks, 155
Mitnick, Kevin (cracker), 250
monoculture
  applications, 35
  diversity, 35

Internet, 36–37
network routers, 35
vulnerabilities, 3, 32–35
moral hazard, 247
Morris Worm, 28
Motion Picture Association of America (MPAA), 158
motivation, 87
MSN, 7
MSM (Managed Security Monitoring), 53–54
M-Tech, 53
mules, 26
multiplayer games, 10
Multipurpose Label Switching (MPLS), 36

N
named perils, 244–245
National Cyber-Forensics & Training Alliance (NCFTA), 63
National Institute for Standards and Technology (NIST), 211–212
National Science Foundation (NSF)
budget cuts, 212
Cyber Trust program, 60
DETER digital simulation testbed, 60
economic importance of, 211
Security Through Interaction Modeling (STIM) Center, 61
NCFTA (National Cyber-Forensics & Training Alliance), 63
Neoteris Netscreen (Juniper), 52
Net6 (Citrix), 52
NetAdvantage (AIG), 68
Netegrity (Trustgenix), 53
Netifice (Aventail), 52
Netilla, 52
NetScaler, 54
NetSilica EPN, 52
network routers, 35
New Capital Accord, 4, 79, 96–97
niche producers or suppliers, 173–174

NIST (National Institute for Standards and Technology), 211–212
no-go areas, 130–131
Nokia NSAS, 52
nonredundant routes, 103–104
Nortel (Alteon SSL-VPN), 52
Novell, 53
NSAS (Nokia), 52
NSF (National Science Foundation)
budget cuts, 212
Cyber Trust program, 60
DETER digital simulation testbed, 60
economic importance of, 211
Security Through Interaction Modeling (STIM) Center, 61

O
obligation failure (in banking), 107
Oblix (Oracle), 53
offline backups, 46
$100 billion cybercatastrophe risk, 146
online backups, 46
open software, 180–182
open standards, 59
OpenNetwork (BMC), 53
Opnix, 57
option value, 6, 8–9
Oracle Oblix, 53
outsourcers, 149

P
P2P (Point to Point), 157–158, 205
pairwise networks, 10
Passport (Microsoft), 53
passwords
humint (human intelligence), 149
large enterprises, 149
spyware, 24
PATRIOT Act, 209–210
People for Internet Responsibility (PFIR) conference on Preventing the Internet Meltdown, 18
performance bonds, 123–124, 192–194, 240

performance measurement, 56–57
PerilPoint, 104
perils
  causes of, 28
  defined, 21
  degradation of service, 236
  examples of, 21–22
  named perils, 244–245
Personal Information Protection and
  Electronic Documents Act
  (PIPEDA), 1, 4
PFIR (People for Internet Responsibility) conference on Preventing the
  Internet Meltdown, 18
pharming, 25, 202
phishing
  criminal activity, 11, 23–24
  ISPs (Internet Service Providers), 202
  law enforcement, 202
  social engineering, 23–24
  spyware, 69
physical damage
  banking, 108
  defined, 233–234
physical security systems, 114–115
PingIdentity, 53
PIPEDA (Personal Information Protection and Electronic Documents
  Act), 1, 4
piracy, 158–159
Point to Point (P2P), 157–158, 205
policy consultants, 56
policy language, 237–238
predictions of Internet collapse, 18–20
prevention, 69–70, 75–76
preventive advice, 198–199
PricewaterhouseCoopers, 113, 131
pricing
  bonds, 195
  insurance, 245–247
privacy, 16
privatization of research, 171–172
probabilistic models, 236

process failure, 109
Prodigy, 7, 23
productivity (in economy), 210–211
professional liability programs, 238
protocols
  International Organization for
    Standardization's Open System
    Interconnection (ISO-OSI) proto-
    cols, 20
  Internet Protocol version 6 (IPv6), 36
  Multipurpose Label Switching
    (MPLS), 36
  Simple Network Management Proto-
    col (SNMP), 36
publicly traded companies. *See* large
  enterprises
publishers liability policy, 242

Q

quality of service (for insurance), 247
quantification of Internet risks, 236–237

R

radical solution, 84–85
Raymond, Eric (*The Cathedral and the
  Bazaar*), 180–181
Recording Industry Association of
  America (RIAA), 158
redundancy, 33–34, 46–47
Reed, David (designer of the User
  Datagram Protocol), 5
Reed's Law, 4–6
regulation of Internet commerce, 31
reputation damage, 16, 29–30,
  77–78, 196
reputation systems, 74–75
research
  Center for Internet Epidemiology
    and Defenses (CIED), 60–61
  clearinghouses, 62–64
  Cooperative Association for Internet
    Data Analysis (CAIDA), 62
  Cyber Trust program, 60

DETER digital simulation testbed, 60
DNS-OARC (Domain Name System Operations, Analysis, and Research Center), 61–62
Security Through Interaction Modeling (STIM) Center, 61
restraining orders on vulnerability disclosures, 153–154
retrocessional SCOR, 188
RIAA (Recording Industry Association of America), 158
risk management
  assessment of risks, 78
  banks, 79
  consultants, 56, 58
  current state of, 11–12
  denial, 90–91
  fear, 39–40, 91–92
  financial institutions, 79–80, 113–114
  governments, 81, 197–198, 225–227
  incidence of risk, 126–127
  inertia, 38–39
  insurance, 13
  insurers, 81
  Internet Service Providers (ISPs), 80–81
  large enterprises, 80, 141–143
  prevention, 69–70
  small enterprises, 80, 167–169
  strategies
    crisis management, 76
    financial instruments, 74
    motivation, 87
    prevention, 75–76
    reputation systems, 74–75
    risk transfer, 74, 76–77
  what's at risk, 77–78
  who needs it, 12
risk transfer, 74, 76–77
risks
  brand reputation, 16, 29
  communication method risk, 17
  content theft, 17

first-party claims, 17
force majeure, 1, 11, 29
  fraud, 16
  privacy, 16
  theft, 15
  third-party claims, 16–17
  traditional risk transfer, 15–17
Ritchie, Dennis (inventor of Unix), 28
Robb, John (*Global Guerillas* blog), 83
routers, 35
RouteScience, 57
RSA, 53

S
SafeOnline, 68
SafeWeb (Symantec), 52
SAIC (Science Applications International Corporation), 53, 125
San Diego State University, 17
SANS (SysAdmin, Audit, Network, Security), 63
Sarbanes-Oxley (SOX), 1, 3–4, 207–208
Sarnoff, David (radio and TV pioneer), 5
Sarnoff's Law, 4–6
SCADA systems, 216
scale-free networks, 7–8
Schneier, Bruce (Internet security expert), 13
Schoenberg, Carter (*Information Security & Negligence: Targeting the CClass*), 250–252
Schwartz, Randal L. (computer expert), 250
Science Applications International Corporation (SAIC), 53, 125
scob, 27
SCOR, 188–189
script kiddies, 28
Secure Socket Layer VPN (SSL-VPN), 52
SecureWorks, 53

security
  fear, 224–225
  Federal Information Security Management Act (FISMA), 213
  insurance, 239
  large enterprises, 147, 150
  outsourcers, 149
Security Through Interaction Modeling (STIM) Center, 61
security vulnerabilities, 204
self-healing networks, 219–221
self-insurance, 151
Sendmail, Inc., 182
September 11, 2001, 33
Service Level Agreements (SLAs), 56–57, 80–81, 190–192
Shibboleth open source FIM project, 53
Shirky, Clay (inventor of Technorati blog), 174–175
shredding, 132–133
sigint (signal intelligence), 149
Simple Network Management Protocol (SNMP), 36
Slammer worm, 30
SLAs (Service Level Agreements), 56–57, 80–81, 190–192
slow links, 101–103
small enterprises
  competitiveness, 183–184
  cybernatives, 169–171
  fifth wave of computing, 172, 177–179
  flexibility, 169
  global products, 182–183
  information sharing, 179
  long tail of content, 173–174
  open software, 180–182
  privatization of research, 171–172
  risk management, 80, 167–169
smart connections, 133
smartmobs, 8, 133
SNMP (Simple Network Management Protocol), 36
social engineering, 23–24, 149
Sockeye, 57

software
  bounties for vulnerabilities, 152–153
  free software, 181
  monoculture software, 3, 32–33
  open software, 180–182
  P2P, 205
  security vulnerabilities, 204
  unfair practices, 27–28
  vulnerability disclosure, 152–155
software liability, 204–207
solutions
  backups, 45–46
  diversity, 35, 47–49
  fortification, 49–52
  redundancy, 46–47
SOX (Sarbanes-Oxley), 1, 3–4, 207–208
spam
  antispam laws, 201
  CAN-SPAM Act of 2003, 201
  costs of, 23
  criminal activity, 11, 22–23
  history of, 22
  Internet Service Providers (ISPs), 22
  legal solutions, 68–69, 201
  pairwise connections, 10
  USENET newsgroups, 22
spoofs, 25
SPX3000 (Array Networks), 52
spyware, 24–25, 69, 202–203
SSL-VPN (Secure Socket Layer VPN), 52
St. Paul Mercury Insurance, 234
Stallman, Richard (inventor of GNU Emacs and founder the Free Software Foundation), 28
Standardized Approach, 97–98
state changes of the Internet, 257–258
state laws, 4
STIM (Security Through Interaction Modeling) Center, 61
strategies for risk management
  contractual risk transfer, 75
  crisis management, 76
  financial instruments, 74

motivation, 87
prevention, 75–76
reputation systems, 74–75
risk transfer, 76–77
strips (bonds), 188
Sun (Waveset), 53–54
Surkov, Vladislav (deputy head of Russia's presidential administration), 142–143
Symantec SafeWeb, 52
SysAdmin, Audit, Network, Security (SANS), 63
system failure, 108–109

T

tailored policies, 248
technical subterfuge, 24
Technology Risk, 241–242
Technorati blog, 174–175
Telecommunications Infrastructure Fund (TIF), 214–215
telemarketing, 10
telephone companies, 20
terrorism, 209–210, 215–219
Texas Internet Service Provider Association (TISPA), 214–215
theft
  content theft, 17
  phishing, 23–24
  spyware, 24–25
  traditional theft, 15
third-party claims, 16–17
third-party loss, 233
Thompson, Ken (inventor of Unix), 28
Tiananmen Square demonstrations, 8
TIF (Telecommunications Infrastructure Fund), 214–215
Time Warner, 46
TippingPoint, 152–153
TISPA (Texas Internet Service Provider Association), 214–215
Tomlinson, Ray (inventor of networked e-mail), 28
Torvalds, Linus (inventor of Linux), 28

traditional insurance, 151, 237–238
traditional risk transfer, 15–17
tranches (bonds), 188
transactions. See business transactions
Tropical Storm Risk (TSR), 130
Trulogica (HP), 53
TruSecure (CyberTrust), 53
Trustgenix Netegrity, 53

U

underwriting, 248
unfair practices, 27–28, 203
United Nations (UN), 20
United States Computer Emergency Response Team (US-CERT), 62–63
University of California at Berkeley, 17
University of California at San Diego, 17
University of Texas at Austin, 17
unsolicited bulk electronic mail. See spam
U.S. Army, 48
U.S. Department of Defense (DoD), 221
U.S. Department of Homeland Security, 18, 46, 48
U.S. laws
  CAN-SPAM Act of 2003, 210
  Family Educational Rights and Privacy Act (FERPA), 4
  Gramm-Leach-Bliley Financial Services Modernization Act (GLBA), 4
  Health Insurance Portability and Accountability Act (HIPAA), 4
  PATRIOT Act, 209–210
  Sarbanes-Oxley (SOX), 1, 3–4, 207–208
U.S. military
  Defense Advanced Research Projects Agency (DARPA), 211–212, 221–222
  Department of Defense (DoD), 221
  Effects Based Operations (EBO), 217–219

U.S. military *(continued)*
external detection systems for networks, 221
immune networks, 219–220
self-healing networks, 219–221
U.S. National Strategy to Secure Cyberspace, 64, 198
US-CERT (United States Computer Emergency Response Team), 62–63
USENET, 8, 82
utilities, 189–190

V
Varian, Hal (Internet security expert), 13, 204
vendor liability, 203–204
Virginia Computer Crimes Act, 68
visibility, 36–37
VPNs (Virtual Private Networks), 52
vulnerabilities
bounties, 152–153
defined, 22
monoculture, 3, 32–35
restraining orders on disclosures, 153–154
security vulnerabilities, 204
wireless networks, 29
vulnerability disclosure, 152–155

W
Waveset (Sun), 53
wealth (as a solution to Internet crime), 83–84
Web logs (blogs), 10
Weinberger, David, 59
Weinstein, Lauren, 18–20
Whale Communications (eGap), 52
Williams, Roberta (computer game inventor), 28
wireless networks, 29
worms
economic damage, 30
Morris Worm, 28
Slammer, 30
Wozniak, Steve (inventor of Apple Computer), 28

Y
Yahoo! groups, 10

Z
zero-day exploits, 128
zombies, 25–26